Citizen convicts

Manchester University Press

Citizen convicts

Prisoners, politics and the vote

Cormac Behan

Manchester University Press

Copyright © Cormac Behan 2014

The right of Cormac Behan to be identified as the author of this work has been asserted by him in accordance with the Copyright, Designs and Patents Act 1988.

Published by Manchester University Press
Altrincham Street, Manchester M1 7JA, UK
www.manchesteruniversitypress.co.uk

British Library Cataloguing-in-Publication Data is available

ISBN 978 1 5261 1697 0 *paperback*
ISBN 978 0 7190 8838 4 *hardback*

First published by Manchester University Press in hardback 2014

This edition first published 2017

The publisher has no responsibility for the persistence or accuracy of URLs for any external or third-party internet websites referred to in this book, and does not guarantee that any content on such websites is, or will remain, accurate or appropriate.

Printed by Lightning Source

For my mother and father

Contents

List of figures and tables	viii
Table of legislation	ix
Table of cases	xi
Foreword by Christopher Uggen	xiii
Acknowledgements	xvi
Introduction	1
1 Citizenship by civic virtue?	7
2 Prisoners and the politics of enfranchisement	26
3 Political change, penal continuity and prisoner enfranchisement	61
4 Voting and political engagement	91
5 Enfranchisement – the prisoner as citizen	124
6 Civic engagement and community participation	144
7 Imprisonment and citizenship	175
Bibliography	202
Index	219

List of figures and tables

Figures

4.1	General election 2007: registration and voting patterns	99
4.2	General election 2007: party preference	102
4.3	Are you political?	104
4.4	Political awareness among prisoners	105
4.5	Political issues	109
4.6	Levels of trust	112
4.7	Voting in Irish prisons: 2007–11	122
5.1	Abstentionism among prisoners	130
6.1	Civic participation prior to prison	148
6.2	Civic participation inside prison	152

Tables

1.1	Arguments for and against disenfranchisement of prisoners	23
4.1	General election 2007: voting in Irish prisons	97
4.2	General election 2007: regression analysis of voters in prison	116
4.3	Lisbon Treaty referendum 2008: voting in Irish prisons	116
4.4	Lisbon Treaty referendum 2008: voting by prison	117
4.5	Local, European and by-elections 2009: voting in Irish prisons	119
4.6	Local, European and by-elections 2009: voting by prison	119
4.7	General election 2011: voting in Irish prisons	120
4.8	General election 2011: voting by prison	121

Table of legislation

Australia
Commonwealth and Franchise Act 1902
Electoral and Referendum Amendment (Electoral Integrity and Other Measures) Act 2006

Canada
Canada Elections Act 2000

Ireland
Electoral Act 1923
Prevention of Electoral Abuses Act 1923
Prisons (Visiting Committee) Act 1925
Rules for the Government of Prisons 1947
Juries Act 1976
Electoral (Amendment) (No. 2) Act 1986
Electoral Act 1992
Electoral (Amendment) Act 2006
Prisons Act 2007

Norway
Enforcement of Sentences Act 2002

South Africa
Electoral Law Amendment Act 2003

United Kingdom

Forfeiture Act 1870
Representation of the People Act 1918
Representation of the People Act 1981
Representation of the People Act 1983
Human Rights Act 1998
Representation of the People Act 2000
Criminal Justice Act 2003

Table of cases

Australia

Roach v. *Electoral Commission* [2007] HCA 43, 26 September 2007

Canada

Sauvé v. *Canada (Chief Electoral Officer)* [2002] 3 SCR 519

European Commission of Human Rights

Holland v. *Ireland*, Application no. 24827/94 (judgment of 14 April 1998)

European Court of Human Rights

Hirst v. *United Kingdom (No. 1)*, Application no. 74025/01 (judgment of 30 March 2004)
Hirst v. *United Kingdom (No. 2)* [GC], Application no. 74025/01 (judgment of 6 October 2005)
Frodl v. *Austria*, Application no. 20201/04 (judgment of 8 April 2010)
Greens and M.T. v. *United Kingdom*, Application no. 600041/08 and no. 60054/08 (judgment of 23 November 2010)
Scoppola v. *Italy (No. 3)*, Application no. 126/05 (judgment of 22 May 2012)

Hong Kong

Chan Kin Sum Simon v. *Secretary for Justice and Electoral Affairs Commission*, High Court AL 79/2008
Leung Kwok Hung v. *Secretary for Justice and Electoral Affairs Commission*, High Court AL 82/2008

Choi Chuen Sun v. *Secretary for Justice and Electoral Affairs Commission*, High Court AL 83/2008

Ireland

Breathnach v. *Ireland and the Attorney General* [2000] IEHC 53
Breathnach v. *Ireland and the Attorney General* [2001] IESC 59
Draper v. *Attorney General* [1984] ILRM 643

South Africa

August and Another v. *Electoral Commission and Others*, CCT 8/99 [1999]
Minster of Home Affairs v. *National Institute for Crime Prevention and Re-Integration* (NICRO), CCT 03/04 [2004]

United Kingdom

W. Smith v. *Electoral Registration Officer* [2007] CSIH 9 XA33/04
Pearson and Martinez v. *Secretary of State for the Home Department EWHC* [2001] Admin 239 (4 April 2001)
Pearson and Martinez v. *Secretary of State for the Home Department EWCA* [2001] EWCA Civ 927 (18 June 2001)
Pearson and Others v. *Home Office* [2001] CO/31/01 and CO/448101, 2001
Raymond v. *Honey* [1983] 1 AC 1
R. v. *Secretary of State, ex parte Toner and Walsh* [2007] NIQB 18

United States

Washington v. *State*, 75 *Alabama* 582 [1884]
Green v. *Board of Elections of City of New York J S* [1967] USCA2 375; 380 F.2d 445 (13 June 1967)
Richardson v. *Ramirez*, 418 U.S. 24 [1974]

Foreword

When I first arrived with my audio recorder to ask prisoners about disenfranchisement, the officials were incredulous. 'You want to ask about *politics*? These guys don't care about *voting*. Your interviews won't last 5 minutes'. Ah, but people do care about voting – especially people who have been told they cannot vote. To be sure, many had never voted and many would never have the opportunity to do so. Nevertheless, they had wide-ranging political opinions and experiences, so those hasty interviews turned into much longer conversations.

But prison officials were not the only sceptics. The initial response from academics was downright discouraging. Criminologists could not imagine how political rights would be salient to US prisoners, when they had so many other pressing material needs. To be fair, law professors viewed the topic as 'interesting', but only insofar as it engaged some rather esoteric and narrowly framed philosophical and legal questions. And, to my great surprise, political scientists and sociologists seemed completely uninterested in disenfranchisement. Many dismissed voting as a 'thin' form of political participation – something hardly worth mentioning these days. *Real* political engagement, for these scholars, meant activism and movement participation.

Cormac Behan knows better than that. Long before scholars like Jeff Manza and I took up felon disenfranchisement in *Locked Out*, Cormac had been teaching political education in Irish prisons. I cannot overemphasise the importance of this experience – and the depth that it brings to *Citizen Convicts*. Frankly, too much of the scholarly work on disenfranchisement has a lamentable 'armchair' quality. That is, it seems to have been written at great remove from those affected by the practice.

Just as certain themes seem to inspire more than their share of bad poetry – take moonflowers, for example – so too, the topic of felon disenfranchisement seems to inspire a lot of untethered bloviating: untethered because the work is not grounded in concrete empirical referents; bloviating because the platitudes are too easy, the metaphors too obvious.

One might see little harm in trotting out naïve platitudes about disenfranchisement, without ever engaging the people who have lost or regained that right. Yet such authors tend to make equally untethered assumptions about the actual human beings subject to disenfranchisement, treating them as some sort of strange and exotic species. Depending on the political sensibilities of the writer, they might be demonised as brutes, sentimentalised as harmless victims or romanticised as revolutionaries.

Citizen Convicts, in contrast, offers a sharp and cogent presentation of the actual political behaviour of real people in prisons. But it does more than that. After a balanced discussion of the rationale for and against felon disenfranchisement, Doctor Behan presents a textured analysis of case studies in South Africa, Israel, Australia and Canada, as well as the United States and the United Kingdom. This offers an excellent framing for the detailed and authoritative analysis of the fascinating case of the Republic of Ireland. In both the Republic and in Northern Ireland, prisoners and former prisoners have long played an exceptionally visible and pivotal part in political life.

Two eye-opening empirical chapters come next: results of the first comprehensive survey about prisoners' political life, and a qualitative presentation of in-depth interviews with 50 prisoners. We learn that about 10 per cent of eligible prisoners cast ballots in 2007 and that they tended to favour Fianna Fáil, Sinn Féin and the Green Party. Rates of voting and volunteering *within* prison are significantly higher, however, both exceeding 50 per cent among interview participants. The next chapter broadens the scope of analysis to include other forms of civic engagement and participation, inside and outside prison walls. Finally, the book concludes by making a strong case for viewing prisoners as citizens and creating the space needed for their more active participation.

Although prisoners may have a more complicated relationship with the state than other groups, their political views and experiences are not all that dissimilar from those of your friends and neighbours. Which issues are most important to them? Certainly not crime and punishment. *Citizen Convicts* reveals that they were far more likely to list the health service, the economy and political corruption as the most important political issue. Here and throughout, we learn precisely how prisoners remain citizens while incarcerated – and how we cannot assume the roles they play as prisoners trump or even dominate their political identities and behaviours.

Some prison walls are real, but others are illusory. I invite you to engage with Cormac Behan's work and to reflect on its implications for the conceptual wall dividing 'prisoner' and 'citizen' in public consciousness.

Christopher Uggen
Distinguished McKnight Professor of Sociology
University of Minnesota

Acknowledgements

It is a great pleasure to thank the many people who have provided assistance during the writing of this book. Firstly, I would like to express my gratitude to all those who participated in the surveys and interviews that form the basis of this study. They contributed to the development of my ideas and enriched my understanding of political participation among prisoners. The Governors and staff of the prisons where the research was undertaken made me welcome. The co-operation of Governor Liam Dowling of Arbour Hill Prison, Governor John O'Brien of the Training Unit and Governor Hector MacLennan of Shelton Abbey Prison was much appreciated. Frank Daly, Aisling Kerr and Ian Stuart Mills of the Department of the Environment, Heritage and Local Government and John McDermott of the Irish Prison Service readily provided data on registration and voting among prisoners. Dick Roche, former Minister for the Environment, Heritage and Local Government kindly agreed to be interviewed for this study.

This book began as a PhD thesis. I would especially like to thank my supervisor Ian O'Donnell for all his guidance and support over the course of my research. Mairead Seymour encouraged me to undertake this study at an early stage. A number of people helped along the way, including Chris Bennett, Donal Coffey, Richard Collins, Anne Costello, Suzanne Egan, Angela Ennis, Ted Fleming, Deirdre Healy, Ben Hunter, Richard Kirkham, Nicola Hughes, Bill Muth, Aogán Mulcahy, Mary Rogan, Brandon Rottinghaus, Mick Ryan, Zacahry Sex, Richard Sinnott and Kevin Warner. I am grateful for the support from the Center for the Study of Correctional Education at California State University, San Bernardino, especially Thom Gehring, Carolyn Eggleston, Randall Wright and Scott Rennie. Christopher Uggen very kindly agreed to write the foreword. I am particularly indebted to Paula Egan, Stephen Farrall, Bernie Hanlon, Gwen Robinson and Jim Wallington who read full drafts of the manuscript. I appreciate their honesty. Any errors and opinions remain my own.

Acknowledgements

I would not have been in a position to undertake this research without an *Ad Astra* scholarship from University College Dublin and I am very happy to acknowledge this financial support. I am grateful to the publishers of the *British Journal of Criminology*, the *Prison Journal* and the *Howard Journal* for allowing me to use some of the material in this book that was initially published in these journals.

I was fortunate to begin this study at the UCD Institute of Criminology which provided a warm and rich learning environment. I completed this book in my new home at the Centre for Criminological Research at the University of Sheffield. I am grateful for the assistance from both academic and administrative staff in Dublin and Sheffield.

I spent 14 years teaching history and politics in Irish prisons. I am indebted to the students I had the opportunity to teach and the staff and teachers of the City of Dublin Vocational Education Committee for their co-operation, support and especially good humour over the years. I stand in awe at the endeavours of teachers and students as they engage in pedagogy in the hope of a better future.

Trisha Murphy deserves special recognition. As my constant companion during my PhD studies, her patience, encouragement, love and partnership made the experience far more enjoyable than it might have been.

I am so lucky to be surrounded by such a kind, caring and warm family. My five wonderful sisters, Úna, Ciara, Fiona, Catriona and Áine, in different ways, inspired me to continue with my research. It is above all my parents who merit special acknowledgement. They have provided the greatest support and encouragement for all my work and I hope they will accept this book as a token of my appreciation. Therefore, it is with my deepest gratitude that I dedicate this book to my Mother and Father.

Sheffield
June 2013

Introduction

> Voting allows the prisoner to feel part of a wider community, something incarceration takes away. It also allows the prisoner to vote for and against changes which may affect his/her time in custody and upon release. I do hope that our vote is not a wasted one – if we are valued enough to be asked to vote, then I hope our wants, needs and requests are listened to. Being in custody takes away a large part of a person's feeling of self-worth, being allowed to vote gives back some of that lost feeling. This in turn will make better citizens.
>
> Gavin, Irish prisoner, serving life

> There was nothing similar in other jurisdictions ... It was one of those occasions when Ireland was shown to be progressive and doing something that nobody else in Europe was doing. We could defend our position because we hadn't taken the vote. We weren't fearful of going to the Court of Human Rights. It just struck me that we had an opportunity to give prisoners the vote. And the sky didn't fall down.
>
> Dick Roche, Minister for the Environment, Heritage and Local Government (2004–7), Republic of Ireland

On 24 May 2007, voters in the Republic of Ireland went to the polls. It was a historic general election for a number of reasons. The Taoiseach (prime minister), Bertie Ahern, repeated the achievement of the towering political figure of twentieth-century Ireland, Eamon de Valera, by being returned for a third term. The Green Party entered government for the first time, taking two cabinet positions. As a consequence of their disastrous result in the election, the Progressive Democrats, the party that had promised to 'break the mould in Irish politics', eventually dissolved. The only representative of the Socialist Party, Joe Higgins, almost universally considered to be one of the best orators of the previous Dáil (Lower House of Parliament), lost his seat. Amid the fog of election coverage, probably the most significant feature was virtually overlooked. It was the first time in Irish history that every eligible citizen had the opportunity to vote. In the 2007 general election, Irish prisoners, like their fellow citizens, went to the polls.

Prisoners could now exercise their franchise due to legislation introduced less than a year previously. The Irish government changed the law to allow all prisoners to vote, even after the Supreme Court had decided that such action was not required and despite a sometimes stifling concern on the part of politicians to avoid being seen as soft on crime or compassionate towards prisoners, for fear of losing electoral support. Significantly, the legislation was passed quietly, without the controversy that has accompanied similar initiatives in other jurisdictions.

The fact that prisoners could now vote was, with the exception of a few newspaper articles, neglected in both popular and academic analysis. This is perhaps unsurprising. As apart from penal reform and human rights groups, the fact that previously, a group of citizens – prisoners – could not vote, received little or no attention. In 2005, an independent think-tank, the Democracy Commission (Harris, 2005: 6) in its examination of the state of democracy in Ireland, recommended extending 'the postal voting option to all registered voters, including prisoners'. Few other studies on Irish elections or politics mentioned, or considered the reasons behind, prisoners' exclusion from the franchise.

Prisoner enfranchisement remains one of the few contested electoral issues in twenty-first-century democracies. It is at the intersection of punishment and representative government. In a democratic polity, the deliberate denial of the right to vote to any section of the population has very serious implications, both symbolic, in terms of devaluing citizenship, and practical, in terms of affecting electoral outcomes. Conversely, the extension of the franchise is similarly emblematic of a political system's priorities and emphases. The debate about prisoner enfranchisement is significant because it gives us some insights into the objectives of imprisonment, society's conflicted attitude towards prisoners, the nature of democracy and the concept of citizenship.

This book is about prisoners and voting. It is the first comprehensive study of prisoners and the franchise in any jurisdiction. Using the Republic of Ireland as a case study, it analyses the experience of prisoner enfranchisement and locates it in an international context. While the empirical focus is on one jurisdiction, the issues raised have wider bearing, as many countries face dilemmas as to whether, or how, to include prisoners in civil society. Considering the extraordinary rise in imprisonment in many countries, especially in the United States, in the late twentieth and early twenty first centuries, the demand for enfranchisement continues to grow, especially from prisoners and activists, creating a more pressing need to learn from jurisdictions that allow prisoners to vote. As prisoner enfranchisement increasingly becomes a subject of controversy, the debates, legislation, turnout and voting patterns in the Republic of Ireland can provide an example to other jurisdictions.

The Republic of Ireland is in the 'unusual position of being influenced by European human rights norms as well as by the Anglo-American drive towards increased punitiveness' (Griffin and O'Donnell, 2012: 611). In the case of prisoners and the franchise, it was the influence of European rather than Anglo-American standards that prevailed. The Republic of Ireland enfranchised prisoners, at a time when legislators in the United States and the United Kingdom have shown a marked reluctance to do so. In the same month that the Oireachtas (Irish parliament) enfranchised prisoners, the United Kingdom's Department for Constitutional Affairs (2006: Foreword) launched a consultation process with the statement that '[t]he government is firm in its belief that individuals who have committed an offence serious enough to warrant a term of imprisonment, should not be able to vote while in prison'. Four years later, during a debate in the UK parliament, the new Prime Minister, David Cameron was unequivocal. It would make him 'physically ill even to contemplate' giving votes to prisoners (*Hansard*, HC Debates, 3 November 2010, vol. 517, col. 921). In the United States, the leader of the Republicans in the Massachusetts Senate, Francis Marini, argued that the practice of allowing prisoners to vote 'makes no sense ... We incarcerate people and we take away their right to run their own lives and leave them with the ability to influence how we run our lives' (cited in the *Wall Street Journal*, 1999: A26).

Ewald and Rottinghaus (2009: 18–19), in the first book on international developments in prisoner enfranchisement, argued that despite a number of publications and advocacy reports, the 'study of disenfranchisement law in the international context remains far short' of the goal of a comprehensive comparative analysis. There is a lack of data on basic topics such as how many prisoners vote. They concluded that, 'in almost all cases, we still do not have even rudimentary histories of prisoner voting policies, despite the fact that close study of almost any country reveals that the rules have changed, sometimes quite profoundly'. In 2006, the rules changed profoundly in the Republic of Ireland, creating for the first time a fully inclusive electorate. This book contributes to the scholarship on comparative prisoner enfranchisement and our understanding of civic and political engagement among prisoners in Ireland and internationally.

In the course of their examination of active citizenship in Ireland, a government-appointed taskforce concluded that there was a 'need for ongoing analysis and research on civic engagement' (Taskforce on Active Citizenship, 2007c: 26). This book will enrich that analysis, especially as it examines a section of the population that has hitherto been neglected in studies on politics and civil society. However, the issues raised in this book will have resonance in the debates about enfranchisement outside the Republic of Ireland. While the book analyses the level of political participation among prisoners and explores opportunities for civic engagement, the study locates prisoners' right to vote in wider historical, social, political and civil rights contexts. It concludes that enfranchisement is one element, albeit an important one, within a wider mosaic of prisoners' rights and opportunities for participative citizenship. The Irish experience indicates that, even when prisoners are enfranchised, obstacles remain, both real and symbolic, to prisoners embracing citizenship fully.

The book begins with an analysis of the theoretical and legal arguments for and against the enfranchisement of citizens behind bars. The standpoints taken by different sides in the debate usually indicate their perspectives on democracy, punishment and the social construction of criminality. Chapter 1 outlines the historical development of 'civic death' statutes which underpin much of the legislation and arguments behind disenfranchisement. It reviews the reasoning of those in favour of disenfranchisement who make the case that prisoners (and sometimes ex-prisoners) have broken the social contract, put themselves outside the law voluntarily, and should be denied the opportunity to decide who will make the law. Opponents of disenfranchisement point to its arbitrary nature, criticise its lack of proportionality and emphasise the rehabilitative function of encouraging prisoners to engage in civil society through the electoral process. While considering both sides, this chapter concludes that allowing prisoners to maintain access to the franchise, along with other rights, conveys a real and symbolic message of inclusion. Enfranchisement encourages prisoners to preserve their connection with society by participating in citizenship activities inside prison and envisages a time post-imprisonment, when they can contribute more fully as citizens to society outside.

Chapter 2 reviews the debates on enfranchisement in a number of countries that allow prisoners to vote, including Australia, Israel, Canada and South Africa. As the debates are ongoing and because they have been particularly vigorous in the US and the UK, special attention is given to these jurisdictions. In the United Kingdom, politicians from both major parties have resisted enfranchising prisoners, despite a ruling from the European Court of Human Rights (ECtHR) allowing for the enfranchisement of some prisoners. One politician from within the ruling Conservative Party urged the government to reject the judgment as it 'gave rise to an ostensible conflict between the requirements of international law and British democracy' (Rabb, 2011: 24). The matter was so serious and so central to British democratic traditions that the solution was simple. The UK should repudiate its obligations under international treaties (Rabb, 2011: xii), and therefore risk suspension from the Council of Europe. Disenfranchisement of both prisoners and ex-prisoners in the United States has engaged politicians, legal theorists, philosophers and penal reformers for decades. By 2012, over 5.8 million citizens were disqualified from voting due to a current or past felony conviction, one in every 40 adults (Uggen *et al.*, 2012: 1). Due to the disproportionate incarceration of minorities, more African-American men were disenfranchised in 2010 than in 1870, the year the 15th amendment was ratified, which prohibited the enactment of laws that deny the right to vote on the basis of race (Alexander, 2010: 175). Felon and ex-felon disenfranchisement laws have removed millions from the voting register, tearing at the fabric of minority communities and casting doubt on the US desire to be seen as a beacon of liberal democracy.

Chapter 3 examines the Irish experience of prisoner enfranchisement. It begins by considering the involvement of prisoners in politics prior to and post-independence. It explores why, despite the prominence of prisoners and ex-prisoners in the development of the Irish State, the enhancement of prisoners' rights and penal reform have rarely been considered policy priorities. It concludes that, although politicians were keen to promote their prison past, they were less eager to allow their experience to inform their penal policy. Rather, they were happy to leave prison behind and wished to distinguish their activities from, and tended to ignore the plight of, those who remained incarcerated. The chapter concludes by examining the debates leading to the legislation that allowed prisoners to vote and finds that while enabling prisoners to vote was very significant, the quiet passing of the legislation made enfranchisement of prisoners in Ireland just as remarkable.

In 2007, Irish prisoners voted for the first time. Chapter 4 presents the results of a study on voting and political engagement among Irish prisoners. Research was undertaken in three prisons, and the first comprehensive survey of prisoners' views on voting and political engagement internationally found that the party that achieved the highest vote among the general population also polled highest among prisoners. Using quantitative data, it elaborates on key findings, and some deeper meanings behind the results are unravelled. The 2007 vote and subsequent polls confirmed general trends in voter turnout in different prisons. Voting patterns among prisoners generally followed the characteristics in wider society: older, better educated, more trusting citizens with a tradition of voting were more likely to cast their vote.

Chapter 5 considers prisoners views on political participation and civic engagement. Using data from interviews with 50 prisoners, it is designed to give a voice to those who felt silenced by their imprisonment and, as emerged in the interviews, believed they were neglected, even by those politicians who embraced enfranchisement. Topics include prisoners and the franchise, motivation behind political participation, the election campaign (or lack of) within prison, and some suggestions from prisoners about the desirability of deeper civic engagement. Enfranchisement of prisoners did not have the outcome desired by legislators and more transformative measures are needed than a change in legislation if the goals of inclusion, participation and civic engagement are to be achieved.

Chapter 6 moves from political participation to examine wider aspects of civic engagement, both inside and outside prison. Prisons are generally controlled institutions with a regime, routine and order designed to facilitate the secure confinement of their populations. This chapter explores the opportunities for active citizenship behind bars and considers if incarceration transforms prisoners into compliant citizens, so disconnected from the outside that it diminishes rights, limits opportunities and undermines their citizenship.

Chapter 7 concludes the book by arguing that if the objective of enfranchisement is not just to enable prisoner voting, but to promote active citizenship and support rehabilitation, the introduction of legislation, however welcome, is not sufficient. Other aspects of citizenship need to be considered. Voting is one part of the mosaic of citizenship. It is central to the modern concept, but at its core is participation. The chapter gives examples of institutions where prisoners were civically engaged more often than just at election time, and found that these were more successful in promoting lived and participative citizenship. It concludes that for enfranchisement to be meaningful and convicts to be encouraged to participate as citizens involves re-imagining imprisonment. It also necessitates re-conceptualising enfranchisement, viewing it as more than just a change in the law enabling convicts to vote, but also as part of a deeper and wider process of engaging and empowering citizens.

1
Citizenship by civic virtue?

Introduction

The cases for and against voting rights for prisoners have been widely examined in academic literature and political discourse (see, for example, Abramsky, 2006; Campbell, 2007; Clegg *et al.*, 2006; Easton, 2011; Ewald and Rottinghaus, 2009; Itzkowitz and Oldak, 1973; Kleinig and Murtagh, 2005; Manfredi, 1998; Manza and Uggen, 2006; Mauer, 2011; Plannic, 1987; Ramsay, 2013; Reiman, 2005). It is widely accepted that even in the most advanced liberal democracies there are limitations on the right to vote, depending on citizenship, age, mental competency and residency (Blais *et al.*, 2001). What should these limitations be and who should decide on them? In the case of prisoners, should the withdrawal of the franchise be determined by a judge, decided by the executive with legislative approval or settled by the people? Should the denial of the vote be a collateral consequence of imprisonment or part of the penalty for breaking the law? Should prisoners be denied the right to vote at all? The arguments for and against the enfranchisement of prisoners yield a number of insights into the objectives of imprisonment, the desire for penal reform, the complexities of citizenship and what restrictions, if any, there should be on participation in a democratic polity.

This chapter will consider the cases for and against prisoner enfranchisement. It begins by examining the justification for denying prisoners the vote. It then considers the arguments in favour of allowing prisoners access to the franchise and concludes by making the case in favour of prisoner enfranchisement, arguing that it has both individual and community benefits.

The case for prisoner disenfranchisement

There are historical, philosophical, legal and political arguments for denying prisoners the right to vote. This section outlines the arguments for prisoner disenfranchisement. Based on the ancient concept of 'civic death', proponents argue that prisoners (and in some cases ex-prisoners) should be stripped of their rights of citizenship, especially voting. They suggest that those who have committed a crime have broken the social contract, put themselves outside the law voluntarily, and therefore should be denied the opportunity to decide who will make the law. Disenfranchisement should be used to remind prisoners that citizenship is a privilege and must be earned by civic virtue. Removing the right to vote from prisoners will deter others from committing a crime. Disenfranchisement, those in favour argue, expresses society's symbolic denunciation of criminal activity with moral condemnation to accompany the denial of liberty.

Civil death

Disenfranchisement has its roots in the ancient concept of 'civil death' based in Greek, Roman, Germanic and Anglo-Saxon legal traditions. In ancient Greece, 'civil death' meant that certain offenders forfeited all their civil rights, including the right to property and possession, the right to inherit and bequeath, the right to bring suit, the right to vote and the right to appear in court (*Harvard Law Review* (HLR), 1989: 1302; Itzkowitz and Oldak, 1973: 721). In Roman law, an individual pronounced 'infamous' was prohibited from serving in the army, appearing in court, making speeches, attending assemblies and voting (HLR, 1989: 1302). Being declared infamous could be for a criminal or immoral act. In later times, Germanic tribes used 'outlawry' to punish those who committed serious crimes. The outlaw was expelled from the community, their property confiscated and they were denied all rights. During the Middle Ages, the outlaw was deprived of legal existence. Ultimately, in extreme cases, the outlaw, being outside society and therefore beyond protection from the realm, could be killed with impunity (Itzkowitz and Oldak, 1973: 722–3).

English law created its own punishment of *attainder*. In feudal England, the Crown seized the property of felons as part of their punishment. The attained, for a felony or crime of treason, was liable to three penalties: forfeiture – the confiscation of chattels and goods; 'corruption of the blood' – they were unfit to inherit, possess or leave their estate to heirs, and the land was forfeited to the local lord; and finally, the attained was 'dead in law' – they could not bring suit or appear as a witness in court (Itzkowitz and Oldak, 1973: 724). The convicted could not perform any legal function, including voting (Ewald, 2002: 1060). Some aspects of civil death disappeared over time but others were embraced by many former British colonies and common law jurisdictions (Easton, 2006; Ewald, 2002). While most civil death statutes have been abolished in modern democracies, one of the few which remains as a direct result of conviction and sentence to imprisonment is loss of the right to vote.

Social contract

Those who argue for disenfranchisement of prisoners and ex-prisoners use a social contractarian model with reference to Hobbes, Locke, Rousseau and Kant. In social contract theory, the stripping of any citizen of political rights is problematic. But for those who break the social contract there must be a sanction. Hobbes argued that whoever 'breaketh his Covenant ... cannot be received into any Society' (cited in Plannic, 1987: 155). Locke believed that a murderer has 'declared War against all Mankind, and therefore may be destroyed as a Lyon or Tyger' (cited in Plannic, 1987: 156). Rousseau believed that 'since no man has a natural authority over his fellow, and force creates no right, we must conclude that conventions form the basis of all legitimate authority over men' (Rousseau, [1762] 1973: 185). However, there were exceptions, as 'every malefactor by attacking social rights, becomes on forfeit a rebel and a traitor to his country; by violating its laws he ceases to be a member of it; he even makes war upon it' (Rousseau, [1762] 1973: 209). For Kant, those who transgress the criminal law are unfit to be citizens. They have lost their citizenship by their 'own criminal act, in which case, although he is allowed to stay alive, he is made into a mere tool of the will of someone else, either of the state or of another citizen' (cited in Plannic, 1987: 157).

One modern proponent of felon and ex-felon disenfranchisement summed up the social contract argument: 'To participate in self-government, you must be willing to obey the rule of law', suggested Roger Clegg, president and general counsel of the Center for Equal Opportunity and former deputy assistant attorney general in the Reagan and Bush (senior) administrations. 'Voting requires certain minimum, objective standards of trustworthiness, loyalty and responsibility, and those who have committed serious crimes against their fellow citizens don't meet those standards' (Clegg, 1999). Society, therefore, has a right to decide who should be allowed to exercise the franchise. In the European Court of Human Rights (ECtHR), the United Kingdom government argued along these lines. In the case of *Hirst* v. *UK* (see Chapter 2), it made the case that disenfranchisement deprived:

> those who had breached the basic rules of society of the right to have a say in the way such rules were made for the duration of their sentence. Convicted prisoners had breached the social contract and so could be

regarded as (temporarily) forfeiting the right to take part in the government of the country. (*Hirst* v. *UK (No. 2)*, 2005)

Another modern advocate of disenfranchisement, Peter Ramsay (2013: 11), argues that prisoners have 'themselves repudiated their democratic citizenship rights by the implicit denial of citizenship entailed in their offence'. Disenfranchisement is proportionate because it is for the period of time an individual is in prison, presumably for an offence serious enough to warrant incarceration. He argues that allowing prisoners to vote is 'faking democracy' because while incarcerated they are not part of the process of 'collective self-rule' (2013: 11). Prisoners cannot exercise self-government because during their confinement they are entirely dependent on the executive. The democratic process is undermined by allowing to vote those who cannot contribute to collective self-government and would be 'a contribution to counterfeiting democracy, extending the outward form of democratic government as a cover for the absence of the political substance of democracy – the self-government of the people' (Ramsay, 2013: 11). Finally, he states that: 'Prisoner disenfranchisement, by ensuring that the political playing field is formally equal and free of executive control, is one of the institutional forms of political equality' (Ramsay, 2013: 14).

Purity of the ballot box

Those in favour of disenfranchisement regularly quote an 1884 case in the Alabama Supreme Court. This ruled that the 'manifest purpose' of disenfranchisement is:

> to preserve the purity of the ballot box, which is the only sure foundation of republican liberty, and which needs protection against the invasion of corruption, just as much as that of ignorance, incapacity or tyranny ... The presumption is, that one rendered infamous by conviction of felony, or other base offense indicative of great moral turpitude, is unfit for the privilege of suffrage, or to hold office, upon terms of equality with freemen who are clothed by the State with the toga of political citizenship. It is proper, therefore, that this class should be denied a right, the exercise of which might sometimes hazard the welfare of communities, if not that of the State itself. (*Washington* v. *State*, 1884)

The ballot box must remain 'pure' and should not be polluted by voters who have 'waived their right to participate in those decisions' argues Todd Gaziano (1999), director of the Center for Legal and Judicial Studies at the conservative think-tank, the Heritage Foundation. Allowing the vote to anyone who has shown such disregard for their fellow citizens and disrespect for the democratic process undermines the democratic polity for all. Citizens must remember that 'voting is a right, but it is also a privilege' (Clegg, 1999).

Proponents of disenfranchisement argue that those who have abided by the law are worthy to be given the right to decide who should become lawmakers because they are the only ones who value that privilege. One modern argument is 'not that criminals should be disenfranchised because they fail to show the appropriate respect to the outcomes of democratic processes' but rather that 'the citizens of a legitimate democratic state have a broad collective right to order their affairs as they so choose' (Altman, 2005: 264 and 266). The citizenry are entitled to disenfranchise convicts while imprisoned. 'Such a decision may fall short of some ideal of political virtue, but it is a morally permissible choice for a democratic state to make' (Altman, 2005: 271).

Allowing prisoners and in some cases ex-prisoners to vote contaminates elections by corrupting the entire democratic process. A democratic polity that excludes prisoners will be much healthier and robust for all citizens, even wayward ones, because if prisoners:

> were exercising civic rights, they would not have become criminals in the first place; and if they had acquired democratic political virtue as a result of their punishment, they would themselves insist that criminals not be allowed to exercise any civic rights until their release. Democratic regimes should recognise that the more criminals desire to exercise the rights of citizens, the more it benefits both the democracy and the criminals to deny them; and that this is true whether or not criminals desire civic rights for virtuous reasons. (Plannic, 1987: 163)

Convicts and ex-convicts, advocates of disenfranchisement argue, have proved that they cannot be trusted and are more likely to engage in voter fraud because they have shown little respect for the law. Prisoners should be treated differently to other citizens because they have acted in a way that indicates they are deficient in civic character. To participate as an equal in society, according to Manfredi (2009: 274) 'requires, in other words, self-control over impulsive behaviour'. He continued:

> The nexus between prisoner disenfranchisement and the preservation and promotion of liberal democratic values is thus found in the exclusion from political participation of individuals who manifestly demonstrated that their character is self-regarding, present orientated, and impulsive. In short, disenfranchisement is reasonable because criminal offenders are, in general, less empathetic and more impulsive than other citizens. (Manfredi, 2009: 274)

The right to vote is a very special right and should be treated as such. For proponents of enfranchisement, to deny the vote to untrustworthy citizens will inspire respect for the law, and may even deter some who are considering engaging in criminal activity. Judge Madala of the South African Constitutional Court reminded prisoners that they had put themselves outside the body politic voluntarily by engaging in criminal activity: 'If the prisoner loses the chance to vote, that will cause him or her to remember the day he or she could not exercise their right to vote because of being on the wrong side of the law' (*Minister of Home Affairs v. Nicro*, 2004).

Punishment as character forming

Those who argue for disenfranchisement believe individuals sentenced to prison lose not only their liberty, but by virtue of being incarcerated, other rights. It is sometimes an intended outcome of imprisonment and at times one of the unintended consequences. In most countries, among the modern 'pains of imprisonment' (Sykes, 1958) are the loss of the effective enjoyment of the right to privacy, to communicate freely with the outside world, to intimate relationships, and many other aspects of daily life taken for granted in a democratic society. And those in favour of disenfranchisement believe that losing the right to vote should be a direct, rather than merely a collateral, consequence of imprisonment. Christopher Manfredi (1998: 297), in his review of criminal disenfranchisement, argued that:

> [C]riminal disenfranchisement does not require that individuals prove in any positive sense that they possess liberal democratic civic virtue. Instead it merely uses serious criminal conduct to indicate the absence of civic virtue. Moreover where criminal disenfranchisement is not permanent, it recognises the presumptive capacity of all citizens to acquire civic virtue by restoring full political rights to individuals on release from custodial supervision.

Only citizens have the right to vote and 'it would not be reasonable to consider criminals as citizens' (Plannic, 1987: 154). Abiding by the law is as important a part of good citizenship as voting. To disobey the law, communally created, undermines the right to the benefits of that mutuality. Citizens should only be allowed to vote if the rest of society is 'reasonably sure that they will exercise that right in good faith – that they share a common commitment to our nation, our government and our laws' (Clegg, 2001: 162). Indeed, disenfranchisement can communicate to prisoners that 'the rights of liberal citizenship entail a responsibility to avoid conduct harmful to other citizens', according to Manfredi (2009: 277). Further, it 'promotes the use of punishment to form character by supporting the moral norm-setting of criminal law' (Manfredi,

2009: 277). Participation in civil society on an equal basis should be only open to citizens. The person who commits a crime:

> disqualifies himself from participating in the formation of new laws. Society does not bar criminals when it imprisons them; criminals excluded themselves from society. A criminal act places the criminal at society's discretion. He remains subject to the laws that he had previously accepted, just as he remains protected by them, but he no longer has the right of political participation. During the time of his imprisonment a criminal is a subject not a citizen. (Plannic, 1987: 154)

Voting bloc

Advocates of disenfranchisement believe that if prisoners are allowed access to the franchise they will become a voting bloc. They will vote for candidates who are soft on crime because convicts are 'in the aggregate less likely to be trustworthy, good citizens' (Clegg, 2001: 172). Prisoners will elect candidates who will change laws in favour of the 'criminal community'. This consideration is especially acute in the US where local law enforcement administrators and civic leaders are directly elected. Their case is that sex offenders could then influence the election of school boards and organised crime gangs could decide the outcome of elections for district attorneys. It even opens up the possibility of prisoners voting for judges and parole boards. Prisoners, they argue would form anti-law enforcement voting blocs. Legal justification was given to this argument in the 1967 New York case of *Green* v. *Board of Elections*. Gilbert Green had been convicted in the 1950s of conspiring to 'organise the Communist Party and advocating the overthrow of the government by force and violence'. On release, he sought to assert his right to vote. Judge Friendly explained the rationale behind disenfranchisement.

> It can scarcely be deemed unreasonable for a state to decide that perpetrators of certain serious crimes shall not take part in electing the legislators who make the laws, the executives who enforce these, the prosecutors who must try them for further violations, or the judges who are to consider their cases ... A contention that the equal protection clause requires [a state] to allow convicted Mafiosi to vote for district attorneys or judges would not only be without merit but as obviously so as anything can be. (*Green* v. *Board of Elections*, 1967)

Let the people decide

Those who argue against allowing prisoners to vote contend that their fellow citizens object to them voting. This argument was used by the UK and South African governments in court cases to try to prevent prisoners' access to the franchise (see Chapter 2). The UK government argued that allowing prisoners to vote was 'offensive to many people' and the South African government believed that this would 'send an incorrect message to the public that the government is soft on crime'. In a US poll, only 10 per cent of respondents were in favour of allowing felons serving a sentence to vote, 32 per cent believed that incarcerated felons should lose their right to vote, and 35 per cent believed that felons while they are in prison, on parole or probation should lose the vote. A further 16 per cent would ban all convicted felons permanently (data cited in Dhami, 2005: 240–1). Manza *et al.* (2004), in their US study, found only 31 per cent of those surveyed believed incarcerated felons should have the right to vote; however, 80 per cent believed the right to vote should be restored to ex-felons. In October 2005, in the wake of the *Hirst* judgment (see Chapter 2), a poll conducted by the *Manchester Evening News* found that 74 per cent of respondents were against giving prisoners the right to vote (data cited in Easton, 2011: 220). Five years later, as a new UK government considered how to deal with prisoner enfranchisement, a poll found that 76 per cent of respondents thought that prisoners should not be allowed to vote. Only 17 per cent believed that they should retain the right to exercise their franchise (YouGov/*The Sun*, 2010).

Proponents of disenfranchisement argue that even if most prisoners come from socially deprived areas and this may skew electoral contests in favour of higher social classes, the victims of crime are predominately from poorer socio-economic categories and more marginalised areas. So instead of empowering the poor by allowing lawbreakers to vote, enfranchisement will take rights from poorer law-abiding citizens and give them to lawbreakers (Clegg *et al.*, 2006: 24). While there may be competing rights in this philosophical debate, the victims of crime and those who obey the law must win out over prisoners who have disobeyed the law, hurt their fellow citizens and breached the social contract.

Regaining the right to vote
Writing from a US perspective, where many states do not allow ex-prisoners to vote (see Chapter 2), Roger Clegg has argued that the right to vote should be removed automatically while an individual is in prison, but further, it should not be restored immediately on release. This part of the punishment should act as a deterrent because '[s]ociety is simply not required, nor should it be required, to ignore someone's criminal record once he gets out of prison' (Clegg, 2001: 174). He goes on to suggest that those who consider undertaking criminal activity

should be aware that they will forfeit the right to vote when they commit a crime. It is part of the punishment. However, reformed convicts need not worry. There are exceptions. Re-enfranchisement of ex-prisoners will be on a case-by-case basis as not all crimes or former convicts are the same and the process of rehabilitation, which necessitates respecting the obligations and responsibilities of citizenship, is varied (Clegg *et al.*, 2006).

In short, the proponents of disenfranchisement believe it is the most powerful message, both real and symbolic, to both law-abiding and non-law-abiding citizens of the importance society places on obeying the rules created by representatives of the people. A belief in the democratic process means that those who are not willing to accept the outcome of that process – the passing of laws – debar themselves from the right to participate in it. 'The disenfranchisement of criminals', according to Plannic (1987: 162), 'is one of the surest signs of the political virtues of democracy'. Those who argue that allowing prisoners to vote is more egalitarian, 'would be betraying its own principle and corrupting its political virtue with the "spirit of extreme equality"' (Plannic, 1987: 162). The polity must be kept pure, even for those who are currently denied the right to vote. Those who argue for prisoner disenfranchisement are convinced that the rights of citizenship are inextricably linked with responsibilities and obligations. Failure to appreciate these responsibilities takes away some rights of citizenship, central to which is the right to vote.

The case for prisoner enfranchisement

Those who argue in favour of allowing prisoners to vote usually make the case around a number of themes: democratic legitimacy, the nature of citizenship, inclusion and rehabilitation. They believe that without consent being given by all the members of society, the whole polity is undermined. Allowing prisoners to vote communicates to the wider population that they are still part of the community, encourages prisoners to maintain their connection with society inside and prepares them better for life on the outside. It may go some way to creating a penal system built on inclusion, normalisation and the potential for transformation. Proponents of prisoner enfranchisement usually adhere to the reform or rehabilitation model. Allowing prisoners to engage in the electoral process will encourage them towards a sense of community spirit and support them in becoming law-abiding citizens. Others argue from an egalitarian perspective – prisoners are in greater proportion from poorer socio-economic areas and therefore their communities are under-represented and become more marginalised. They argue that removing prisoners' rights, in this case voting, becomes another of the 'collateral consequences' of punishment, 'that is accomplished through the diminution of the rights and privileges of citizenship' (Travis, 2002: 15).

Citizen or subject
Those who would enfranchise prisoners argue that depriving any person of the right to vote negates the social contract as power is wielded without the authority to do so. The stripping of the right to vote undermines the social contract that should always be mutual. Taken one step further, should individuals be obliged to obey laws created by people who were not given authority to rule over them? This raises an important philosophical question on the moral authority of rule without consent. Those who are incarcerated are removed from society and, if disenfranchised, are stripped of the right to vote. Subsequently, this 'reduces people from citizens to subjects' (Reiman, 2005: 13).

Johnson-Parris (2003: 112) believes that while it could be argued that felons have broken the social contract, they are 'unequal parties to a contract that is fundamentally unfair in its formulation and substance'. In certain cases, 'social contracts should be invalidated on the grounds that they are unconscionable'. This point is especially pertinent for prisoners who, in the majority, come from communities with lower levels of civic engagement and little identification with the nuances of the social contract. This leaves poor or minority communities at greater risk of under-representation.

Advocates of enfranchisement believe that individuals bring citizenship rights with them to prison. These are set out in various policy documents and international agreements, including the UN Standard Minimum Rules for the Treatment of Prisoners (United Nations, 1955), the European Convention on Human Rights (1950), European Prison Rules (Council of Europe, 2006) and various national prison rules. These include the right to legal representation, a free and fair trial, a safe living environment, etc. In *Raymond* v. *Honey* ([1983] 1 AC 1), Lord Wilberforce stated that: 'under English law, a convicted prisoner, in spite of his imprisonment, retains all civil rights which are not taken away expressly or by necessary implication'. The European Court of Human Rights in the *Hirst* case ruled that prisoners 'in general continue to enjoy all the fundamental rights and freedoms guaranteed under the Convention save for the right to liberty' (*Hirst* v. *United Kingdom (No. 2)*, 2005).

Elected choosing the electorate

Disenfranchising a section of the population based on their actions, even if they are illegal, tests the limits of liberty in a democracy. It leads to those who have the vote making a judgment on deciding who has the right to the franchise and who will subsequently be legislators and executive. According to the European Court of Human Rights, to deny the right to vote to prisoners is 'tantamount to the elected choosing the electorate' (*Hirst* v. *United Kingdom (No. 2)*, 2005). It tilts the outcome of elections in favour of those who are allowed to vote. Cheney (2008: 144) concluded that 'the issue of votes for prisoners goes to the heart of those who are given the power to participate in the political process and those who are dis-empowered'. Those arguing in favour of stripping prisoners of voting rights have historically drawn on similar arguments that have been used to restrict voting rights of women, the working class, people of no property and minority communities.

Who is sent to prison is politically decided by those who make laws, juries who sit in judgment and judges who pass sentence. Some advocates of prisoner enfranchisement argue that as prisons are important public institutions, it is essential to encourage those who are housed in penal institutions to contribute to the debate on the role and function of prison and wider penal policy. As stakeholders in the penal system and as citizens, prisoners should have a voice in the debates about criminal justice policies. Prisoners are rarely asked for their opinion and are usually spoken for, or more often about. Healy (2009: 180) has pointed out that the 'voices' of prisoners 'are rarely heard' in public policy, especially criminal justice, debates. Marc Mauer of the US advocacy group, the Sentencing Project (Mauer, 2011: 558) asks, 'why would we not want to have the perspectives of the people who have experienced those conditions more directly incorporated into the electoral discussion?' Those with direct experience of the criminal justice system have insights that could inform the public and enrich policy debates about the strengths and weaknesses of the penal system. There is a widespread belief among advocates of prisoner enfranchisement that allowing prisoners to vote will stimulate an informed public debate on penal reform and lead to a more humane prison environment and a progressive penal system (Cheney, 2008; Easton, 2011; Richards and Jones, 2004).

Social construction of criminality

A legalistic examination of disenfranchisement is too narrow. Advocates of prisoner enfranchisement locate the law and lawbreakers in a wider context. The debate on enfranchisement is intertwined with the social construction of criminality. Those who make laws, prosecute wrongdoers, judge the accused and sentence the guilty, all have an impact on whether an individual will be sent to prison. Coyle (2005: 11) points out that internationally, 'the marginalised groups in any society are invariably over represented in prisons'. Some lawbreakers are more likely to be imprisoned than others. The bias evident in prison populations internationally indicates that a disproportionate number of people from poorer and minority communities are arrested for wrong-doing, prosecuted, end up before the courts and are imprisoned. As we shall see in Chapter 2, this point had been raised in the political and legal debates in Australia, Canada and especially the US.

Those who would allow prisoners to vote believe that the debate must move from an analysis of the social contract to an understanding of the social compact that binds community together. The ways in 'which the members of the upper-classes harm others are generally treated as regulatory matters, or if as crimes, not as grave ones' (Reiman, 2005: 4). Corporate lawbreakers who undermine the social compact are more likely to remain free and, therefore, retain their rights as citizens. Tax evaders break the bonds of community, undermine the social contract and weaken the social compact by stealing from their fellow citizens. However, they are less likely to be imprisoned than individuals who steal from private institutions. Consequently, some types of wrong-doers end up losing the vote in higher numbers, due to the bias in the criminal justice and wider political system.

The prisoner as 'other'
Proponents of enfranchisement suggest the issue goes beyond the right to vote. It says something about a society's attitude towards those who break the law. 'Disenfranchisement is driven not by pragmatic realities or theoretical principles but rather by the atavistic and deep-rooted social need to define the boundaries of the community by stigmatising some persons as outsiders' (HLR, 1989: 1301). Those who argue that prisoners and ex-prisoners contaminate the 'purity of the ballot box' tend to label prisoners as other, separate; deviants who act out of the ordinary, with distinct values and who would vote differently than the rest of society. As the judge in *Washington* v. *State* put it: 'this *class* should be denied a right' (emphasis added). They are somehow impure and, if allowed, will contaminate the rest of the law-abiding electorate. If prisoners are liable to infect the process, they can be placed outside it. Once they are so positioned, it becomes easier to exclude. Prisoners then become 'othered' (see Garland, 2001: 184–6). As Mauer (2011: 554) notes, disenfranchisement 'generally is premised on assumptions

about people in prison that portray them as qualitatively distinct from citizens in the outside world'. Imprisonment defines the person, sometimes while they are incarcerated and in many countries, even on their release. The label can be attached to them for the rest of their lives. 'If prisoners are without a vote, without a citizen status', argues Easton (2011: 230), 'they are effectively non-persons, which legitimates the view the prisoners should be forgotten and marginalises them in the minds of governments and the public'.

Reintegration
Reintegration is a prominent theme for those who argue in favour of prisoner enfranchisement. Permanent disenfranchisement (as happens in some US states) suggests that an individual will never change and indeed is incapable of so doing (see Dhami, 2005: 243). Engaging in the political process might create more respect for laws and lawmakers. The vast majority of those incarcerated will return to society and exclusion from the political process may be counter-productive for the purposes of reintegration (Uggen *et al.*, 2004). It provides a practical impediment to the objective of promoting respect for the law. This is essential for a more pro-social outlook, encouraging prisoners to lead law-abiding lives. Crutchfield (2007: 711) acknowledged that while 'no solid evidence exists to show that disenfranchisement causes re-offending' there is little to suggest that it benefits the objectives of the criminal justice system, in particular the desire to reduce recidivism. There is evidence to imply that it may be counter-productive as part of a crime-control mechanism as it alienates ex-prisoners even further from law-abiding conformity (Crutchfield, 2007: 708). While Uggen and Manza (2004: 213) noted that while there was no longitudinal study of released prisoners and their community involvement:

> statistical data suggest that a relationship between voting and subsequent crime and arrest is not only plausible, but also supported by empirical evidence ... While the single behavioural act of casting a ballot is unlikely to be the sole factor to turn felons' lives around, the act of voting manifests the desire to participate as a law-abiding stakeholder in a larger society.

If the goal of imprisonment is deterrence, there is little evidence that removing the franchise will achieve this goal. Prison populations tend to be young, at a time in their lives when the voting habit is weaker. Therefore, losing the right to vote at a young age does not necessarily deter, but if it is removed for life as happens in some US states, it punishes the individual at a time when they are no longer in prison, may have reformed, matured and are more likely to vote. 'The effects of felon disfranchisement are not only limited only to the disfranchised themselves, but also extend to eligible and future voters who are discouraged from voting', according to the National Association for the Advancement of Colored People (NAACP) (2011: 26). It continued: 'These laws marginalize the voices of community members who are deprived of the collective power of voting alongside relatives and neighbors, and engender a culture of non-participation that erodes mainstream civic engagement'. Denying prisoners the franchise is not a risk-based strategy. When one is considering whether or not to commit a crime, 'the additional threat of losing the vote is unlikely to deter her, unless she especially treasures voting' (LaFollette, 2005: 250). In those countries that disenfranchise prisoners and ex-prisoners, there is no evidence to suggest that it has been a catalyst for reduced levels of crime or imprisonment.

Election outcomes
If prisoners are denied the franchise, election results are further distorted, argue those in favour of prisoner enfranchisement. Prisoners can be included in data for the purpose of census returns and in deciding the number of representatives in electoral districts. Therefore, constituencies with a large number of prisoners may be allowed greater representation. But prisoners are denied the opportunity to cast their vote in this electoral district. In the US, ex-felons are counted in census returns that determine congressional districts. As many ex-felons are not allowed to vote, this skews the electoral outcome by disallowing those who have completed their sentence from voting in the community in which they now live (Crutchfield, 2007: 712). According to Alexander (2010: 188), there is also a racial element to these laws. New prison construction in the US occurs in predominately white, rural communities, housed overwhelmingly with prisoners from minority communities. 'Black political power has been suppressed' and this 'echoes not so much Jim Crow as slavery'.

The denial of the vote to a prisoner is also related to the timing of an election, the date of which is not set out in law in many jurisdictions. If an individual is serving a sentence on election day for a minor offence they may be denied the opportunity to exercise their franchise. Some may not even have been convicted of a crime. An individual could be in prison awaiting trial, as a civil debtor, a fine defaulter or for contempt of court. An individual could serve a number of years in prison for a more serious offence and still have the opportunity to vote, if they were no longer incarcerated on election day. If voting is 'the most tangible manifestation of the social contract' (Easton, 2006: 451), these considerations make it somewhat arbitrary in relation to that contract. It is a very capricious way of dealing with a citizen, especially in countries where few sentencing guidelines exist.

It is imprisonment that will decide if a prisoner keeps or loses the right to vote rather than their receiving a conviction. In the *Hirst* case, examined in Chapter 2, two judges of the European Court of Human Rights observed that 'the reasons for handing down a custodial sentence may vary. A defendant's age, health or family situation may result in his or her receiving a suspended sentence. Thus the same criminal offence and the same criminal character can lead to a prison sentence or to a suspended sentence' (*Hirst* v. *United Kingdom (No. 2)*, 2005). They concluded that the reason the right to vote is denied 'is the fact that the person is in prison'. In federal jurisdictions, two individuals may be convicted of the same crime in two different states, and one may be sentenced to a term of imprisonment and not allowed to vote while the other receives a non-custodial sentence and exercises their franchise. This has particular impact in US elections with such large numbers imprisoned and wide variations between states on voting rights for prisoners and ex-prisoners.

Punishment to fit the crime
Even some of those who oppose disenfranchisement concede there may be exceptions. Kleinig and Murtagh (2005: 228) argue that there is 'a plausible case' to disenfranchise those on death row or serving life sentences. 'Although they remain citizens, we have deemed their acts to disqualify them permanently from the ongoing life of the community'. In many criminal justice systems, punishment is directly related to the crime. For example, somebody convicted of driving while over the legal alcohol limit may be banned from driving as part of their penalty. Conviction for fraud may include a prohibition on becoming a company director as part of the punishment. For certain types of crime, an electoral punishment may be fitting; perhaps those who commit electoral fraud should receive an electoral penalty (Kleinig and Murtagh, 2005). The European Court of Human Rights, which ruled in favour of prisoner enfranchisement in the *Hirst* and *Frodl* cases, examined in Chapter 2, accepted that there may be circumstances which justify limiting voting rights. In *Hirst*, the court ruled that a gross abuse of political office could justify depriving an individual from running for political office in the future. In *Frodl*, the court found that there needed to be a connection between the offence and punishment for the denial of the right to vote to be justified. However, some opponents of disenfranchisement reject this scenario. They argue that:

even if a correlation between past offences and future election crimes could be proven, our criminal justice system is based on the premise that once a criminal has completed his sentence, society has the burden of proving guilt of a new crime beyond a reasonable doubt and does not have the right to punish the ex-criminal in advance on the basis of probability. (Itzkowitz and Oldak, 1973: 739)

In short, those who would allow prisoners to vote believe that allowing prisoners and ex-prisoners to participate in civic activities will encourage them to embrace a citizen role. Removing the right to vote is part of a process of 'othering' prisoners, reducing them from citizen to subject. Enfranchisement is inclusionary and sends out a powerful moral message that all are acceptable, even those who have broken the social contract. Allowing prisoners to vote will, proponents of enfranchisement argue, encourage respect for laws. It affirms prisoners' membership of the wider social order, strengthens community and social bonds, and is part of the rehabilitative process of re-connecting with society.

Table 1.1 sets out the arguments in favour of and against prisoner enfranchisement.

Conclusion

In *Richardson* v. *Ramirez* (1974), the US Supreme Court by a margin of six to three upheld a law banning those convicted of an 'infamous crime' from voting. In summing up (see Campbell, 2007, for an analysis of this case), the majority rejected the argument that disenfranchisement was 'outmoded' because 'it is not for us to choose one set of values over the other'. They concluded: 'If respondents are correct, and the view which they advocate is indeed the more enlightened and sensible one, presumably the people of the State of California will ultimately come around to that view. And if they do not do so, their failure is some evidence, at least, of the fact that there are two sides to the argument' (*Richardson* v. *Ramirez*, 1974). This chapter has outlined the two sides of the argument. It will conclude by constructing the case in favour of enfranchisement.

Civic death is an antiquated and outdated concept and anathema to the ideals of universal representative government. The denial of the right to vote by the judiciary, executive or legislature undermines the consent on which modern democratic authority is built. Society cannot go back to a time when an elite decided who should be the electorate. Voting is a fundamental right of every citizen, not a privilege to be dispensed by the powerful. Denying the right to vote 'is a symbolically serious matter, as marking one's temporary and permanent exclusion from the rank of

Citizenship by civic virtue?

Table 1.1: Arguments for and against disenfranchisement of prisoners

For disenfranchisement	Against disenfranchisement
Civil death should be part of punishment	Civil death is out-dated
Prisoners have broken the social contract and have voluntarily put themselves outside the social order	Social contract cannot be negotiated away
Preserve the purity of the ballot box	Undermines the democratic polity by denying the vote to a section of the population
Ex/prisoners will vote in bloc to change laws in their favour	Citizens should not be debarred from the electoral process because of their voting preferences
Majority of people are against allowing prisoners to vote	Elected should not be allowed to decide the electorate
Government has an obligation to those who obey laws to punish those who break laws	Allowing convicts to vote will encourage respect for laws
To disallow those who have broken laws to engage in the political process shows how much respect society has for laws	Convicts will be less inclined to obey laws that they have had no role in deciding upon
Powerful moral symbol from society that the convict's behaviour is unacceptable	Symbolic statement to the convict that they are acceptable
Punishment can be used to form character	Allowing prisoners to vote will be a lesson in civic education
It will act as a deterrent	It is rehabilitative
Expressive punishment and moral condemnation	Retribution should have no place in modern penality
Disenfranchisement is exclusionary	Enfranchisement is inclusionary

full citizen, and thus from full membership of society' (Duff, 2005: 213). To remove the right to vote undermines citizenship, which affects not just prisoners, but all citizens. The social contract, universally agreed, is central to modern democracy and without universality, the social contract is diminished.

For those who would argue that imprisonment should comprise more than the denial of liberty, including the removal of the franchise as a direct or 'collateral consequence' of imprisonment, this changes the nature of that punishment. Prison is about loss of liberty, not the loss of citizenship. If imprisonment, rather than conviction, is the deciding feature, this is a very arbitrary way of denying citizenship rights as, in many jurisdictions, many (in some cases, the majority) of those who receive a conviction are not given a custodial sentence (although, as outlined in Chapter 2, in some US states those on parole and probation lose the vote). Unless there are substantive reasons otherwise, imprisonment should not remove the most significant manifestation of citizenship in a modern democracy, the right to vote.

To disenfranchise because of presumed voting preference – the voting bloc argument – undermines the concept of democracy. Diversity is the oxygen of democracy. In a modern democracy, laws are open to change and modification through decisions of the people, determined by voting. Individuals come together as aggregates to engage in the political process. They co-operate in the formation of political parties that lie at the heart of democratic society. There are many examples of voting blocs. Political parties get elected with new policies, promising that laws will be altered and society transformed. Concerned citizens come together for municipal elections to vote for candidates on single issues that may affect just their community. Private individuals and corporations attempt to influence the political process with contributions to campaign spending, to ensure that laws are changed or to preserve the status quo. Private companies spend millions each year on lobbying and campaign donations. On persuading those in power to amend laws, there is no mention of such loaded terms as a voting bloc. For good or ill, voting blocs, whether or not they are phrased as such, are part of the democratic process. And as the findings in this book (see Chapters 4–6) demonstrate, there is no evidence to suggest that prisoners vote as a bloc, that they agree collectively on political preferences or that they all hold similar views. Nevertheless, even if evidence suggested a voting bloc, in a modern democracy, exclusion because of political preference is unacceptable.

Removing the right to vote not only undermines the social contract but damages the social compact on which community and citizenship is constructed. While prisoners may have broken the social contract and therefore, argue proponents of disenfranchisement, voluntarily put themselves outside the social order, others who have damaged the social compact are less likely to appear before the courts and subsequently end up in prison and therefore be denied the franchise. While it is argued that governments have an obligation to those who obey the law to punish those who break the law, this fails to locate the law in a wider social and political context.

There are strong arguments and evidence that prisoners' maintaining a link with society outside, and in particular with their local community, can act as spur towards reintegration. To remove the right to vote – one of the most important aspects of citizenship – adds to the dislocation from, and disconnection with, the world outside prison walls. It creates another layer of punishment beyond the denial of liberty, becomes an instrument of social exclusion, and can have significant longitudinal consequences in terms of voting among ex-prisoners. To deny the right to vote not only undermines an individual's citizenship, it can weaken the fabric of communities that have greater proportions of their citizens incarcerated.

Denial of the vote also says something about society's treatment of prisoners. It encourages the prisoner to be treated as 'other', part of an 'untouchable class'; a 'second-class citizen', or a 'conditional citizen'. These phrases imply the status of citizenship has changed for the incarcerated. However, citizenship cannot be limited. Imprisonment cannot deny or reduce citizenship. One cannot be a half citizen, a conditional citizen, a second-class citizen. Each one is a contradiction, the adjective rendering the noun meaningless.

If citizenship, as some of the proponents of disenfranchisement believe, has to be earned by civic virtue, this challenges the legitimacy on which modern democracy is built. It moves from a social contract model to a civically virtuous paradigm. But who will determine the civically virtuous – the executive, legislature, judiciary or fellow citizens? This reconstitutes the modern democratic framework from a broadly inclusive citizenry, with equality of access and participation, to a polity where the powerful – even if they are the majority – dispense rights of participation as privileges to those they deem to be civically virtuous.

As was pointed out in *Richardson v. Ramirez* (1974), there are two sides to the argument about the enfranchisement of prisoners. This chapter examined both sides of the debate. To enfranchise or disenfranchise the imprisoned indicates more than just whether one believes in the denial of the vote to a section of the population. It usually derives from differing notions of citizenship, contrasting interpretations of democracy and a range of perspectives on the use(s) of punishment. However, as we shall see in the next chapter, frequently, when prisoner enfranchisement enters political and popular discourse, more mundane matters, rather than philosophical questions, tend to dominate the discussion on whether prisoners should have access to the franchise. It is to some of those debates that we now turn.

2

Prisoners and the politics of enfranchisement

Introduction

Prisoner enfranchisement remains one of the few contested electoral issues in twenty-first-century democracies. This chapter examines the politics of, and international jurisprudence on, prisoner enfranchisement. It considers jurisdictions where it has become a matter of legal quarrel and political debate. As outlined in the last chapter, the debate on prisoner enfranchisement is at the intersection of punishment and representative government, encompassing issues such as the purpose(s) of imprisonment, the nature of the social contract and the meaning of citizenship. In the political debates, the language used and the arguments put forward in favour of, or against, enfranchisement go beyond whether or not prisoners should have the right to vote. It usually gives an indication of the proponent's perspective on the objectives of imprisonment. The first part of this chapter sets out international policy and practice on prisoners and enfranchisement. It then examines countries which have generally come down in favour of allowing some or all prisoners to vote and concludes by looking at jurisdictions that have attracted most attention – the United States and the United Kingdom – in political and judicial attempts to prevent prisoners' access to the ballot box.

International policy and practice

Globally, policy and practice differ widely in prisoners' access to the franchise. International human rights conventions do not mention prisoners' right to vote; nevertheless, international practices are important because these may become '*de facto* laws, requiring adherence by virtue of treaty obligations' (Rottinghaus and Baldwin, 2007: 697). Even if an international treaty does not necessarily form part of a nation's laws, it can influence domestic jurisprudence and become a point of reference by which legislation is judged.

Under Article 2 of the United Nations Declaration of Human Rights (1948), every human being is entitled to all the rights and freedoms set forth in the Declaration, 'without distinction of any kind, such as race, colour, sex, language, religion, political or other opinion, national or social origin, property, birth or other status'. Article 21 continues, that everyone 'has the right to take part in the government of his country, directly or through freely chosen representatives'. Article 25 of the International Covenant on Civil and Political Rights (ICCPR) states: 'Every citizen shall have the right and opportunity ... without unreasonable restrictions to vote and be elected at genuine periodic elections ... guaranteeing the free expression of the will of the electors' (United Nations, 1966).

Electoral law
Electoral law is complex. In some countries it varies from state to state or province to province. For prisoners, it is rarely straightforward and therefore 'documenting the official voting rights of prisoners and ex-prisoners is difficult' according to Rottinghaus and Baldwin (2007: 692, footnote 13), 'because many constitutions and electoral laws are not explicit on the rights of these individuals'. A 2003 study found that of the 54 countries examined which either totally barred or had restrictions on prisoner voting, 4.3 million were not allowed to exercise their franchise because of their incarceration – three quarters of these were in the US and the Russian Federation (Rottinghaus, 2005: 25–6).

Blais *et al.* (2001: 44–5 and 53) found that of the 63 countries they examined, 23 disenfranchised prisoners including Brazil, India, the United Kingdom and Venezuela. Sixteen allowed prisoners to vote including Germany, Namibia and Sweden. In others such as Japan and Sao Tome and Principe, only some prisoners lost their vote. Of the 108 countries where they could clarify the position, Rottinghaus and Baldwin (2007: 693) found that of the proportion of nations that 'specifically expressed a law governing prison voting', 58 per cent do not allow prisoners to vote. They concluded that it 'seems that a country's internal political and civil freedoms are as important in predicting prison enfranchisement as the classification of a country as a democracy' (Rottinghaus and Baldwin, 2007: 694). While prisoner enfranchisement may be influenced by the state of a country's democracy, it can also be shaped by its penal policy. However, as we will see in many of the jurisdictions in the next section, judicial rulings, rather than penal policy, democratic representation or popular will can have a more decisive impact on whether prisoners can access the ballot box.

Asserting prisoners' right to vote

This section will examine a number of jurisdictions where enfranchisement has culminated in legal dispute and resulted in some or all prisoners being allowed to vote. In Israel, prisoner enfranchisement challenged the essence of democracy, when the courts had to decide if the killer of the representative of the people should be allowed to decide on his successor. In Palestine, prisoners' access to the ballot box was argued as part of their struggle for liberation. In Canada, South Africa and Australia, governments introduced legislation to restrict prisoners' access to the franchise, only to have it rejected by the courts. In Hong Kong, within a year of a court ruling, the administration decided to enfranchise all prisoners. In these jurisdictions, by and large, it has been left to the judiciary to rule in favour of upholding prisoners' right to vote, reflecting on many of the issues examined in Chapter 1. When executives and legislatures have considered prisoners' access to the franchise, more often than not, they have generally been against enhancing prisoners' rights. We begin by examining one of the most extraordinary cases in the debate over whether prisoners should have the right to vote.

Israel: 'the infrastructure of democracy'

In 1995, Yitzhak Rabin, Prime Minister of Israel, was shot dead by Yigal Amir as he left a peace rally in Jerusalem. Soon after, an election was called and under Israeli law all prisoners were allowed to vote. In the case of *Alrai* v. *Minister of the Interior*, the Israeli courts refused to revoke Amir's citizenship, which would have prevented him voting in the election to replace Rabin. The court declared that disenfranchisement would hurt not just Amir, but Israeli democracy (Ewald, 2004: 134). Imprisonment was his punishment, the Supreme Court ruled, and 'without the right to vote, the infrastructure of all other fundamental rights would be damaged . . . [I]n a democratic system, the right to vote will be restricted only in extreme circumstances enacted clearly in law'. The court found that the right to vote and be elected 'are the infrastructure of democracy' (original in Hebrew; translation cited in Wilson, 2009: 110–11 and 129).

Shimon Peres, who took over as Prime Minister on Rabin's death, doubtless spoke for many when he asked, 'how can you murder and also be entitled to vote?' (*Washington Post*, 29 May 1996). Appalled by Amir's participation in the election to replace her husband, Rabin's widow, Leah, believed that it 'was an unprecedented scandal . . . this man does not deserve to vote' (*Jerusalem Post*, 1996). In the election to choose the successor to the man he had killed, Amir was the first to vote in his prison; his attorney declaring, 'he's concerned about Israel and the future' (*Jerusalem Post*, 1996).

On the Knesset website, there is information in English about prisons and places of detention where electors are allowed to vote (www.knesset.gov.il). During the 2001 election, 42 polling stations were set up in prisons and detention centres. In the 2006 general election, more than 9,000 prisoners were eligible to vote, one of whom – British electrician, Daniel Pinner – stood for election (Grayeff, 2006a).

Palestine: 'the rights of prisoners, as part of society to participate'
In 2005, elections were held to choose a successor to Palestinian President, Yasser Arafat. In contrast to its earlier decision in the Yigal Amir case, the Israeli Supreme Court refused an application to allow over 11,000 Palestinian prisoners held in Israeli jails to vote. The court rejected the petition by Palestinian Prisoner Affairs Minister, Hisham Abdul Razeq, and two prisoner representatives on the grounds that it was not administratively feasible to organise voting in time for the election. However, according to the Palestinian Central Elections Commission (CEC) (2005: 269–70), 'this left open the possibility of Palestinian prisoners and detainees voting in future elections'. The case was taken when the Israeli government refused to allow prisoners to vote; the Defence Minister Shaul Mofaz saying that they had 'already made enough concessions to the PNA [Palestinian National Authority] by allowing East Jerusalem residents to vote' (Palestine Media Centre, 2005). The CEC 'conducted a meeting with the minister of prisoners and ex-prisoners to discuss this issue and has affirmed the rights of prisoners, as part of Palestinian society, to participate in the elections' (CEC, 2005).

For the presidential election, the CEC decided that as an exception, those incarcerated in Israeli jails could register by proxy and one of their relatives could cast their ballot 'in order to guarantee prisoners' rights to stand as candidates, vote, and participate in political life like any other Palestinian citizen' (CEC, 2005: 33). Political prisoners were also allowed to register, to permit them to stand in future elections. Those incarcerated in Palestinian prisons, 'who had not yet received the verdict of the court were registered, since Palestinian Elections Law permits them to register and participate in the elections' (CEC, 2005: 33). On his victory as President of the Palestine National Authority, Mahmoud Abbas dedicated his victory to 'the 11,000 prisoners behind bars' and pledged not to rest until all were set free (Palestine Media Centre, 2005).

In the 2006 elections to the Palestinian Legislative Council (PLC), the Israeli authorities refused to make any arrangements which might 'allow for the participation of prisoners in the polling process' (CEC, 2006: 35). Nevertheless, denial of access to the ballot box did not prevent prisoners from engaging in political activity. A total of 31 prisoners in Israeli jails stood for election to the PLC, of whom 14 were successful. These included Marwan Barghouti, who headed the Fatah List, and the West Bank Hamas leader, Sheikh Hassan Yousef. Another prisoner was elected from a Palestinian prison. Prisoners, therefore, made up over 11 per cent of the 132 seat PLC (Grayeff, 2006b).

South Africa: 'it says that everybody counts'
The South African debate on prisoner enfranchisement was politically, socially and historically charged. Many of those who became lawmakers in the 1990s were ex-prisoners or part of a movement, the African National Congress (ANC), that was led by Nelson Mandela, one of the most famous prisoners of the twentieth century. The new South African constitution, agreed in 1996, guaranteed every adult citizen the right to 'vote in elections for any legislative body established in terms of the Constitution, and to do so in secret; and to stand for public office and, if elected to hold office' (Section 19, 3(a) and (b)).

In the election to decide the successor to Nelson Mandela in 1999, there were no provisions in place to allow prisoners to vote. In a case taken by two prisoners wishing to exercise their franchise, the country's Constitutional Court rejected the government's argument that there would be immense financial, logistical and administrative difficulties if prisoners were allowed to vote. The government's argument was that as parliament had not passed any law restricting their right to vote, prisoners still maintained that entitlement. However, the court went further and instructed the government and the Electoral Commission to make 'all reasonable arrangements' to enable prisoners to vote in the forthcoming election because the right to vote imposes 'positive obligations on the legislature and the executive' (*August v. Electoral Commission*, 1999).

Mindful of the recent ending of apartheid and the denial of democratic rights to the majority, Justice O'Regan ruled: 'To build the resilient democracy envisaged by our constitution we need to establish a culture of participation in the political process'. The court went on to declare that:

> The vote of each and every citizen is a badge of dignity and of personhood. Quite literally, it says that everybody counts. In a country of great disparities of wealth and power it declares that whoever we are, whether rich or

poor, exalted or disgraced, we all belong to the same democratic South African nation; that our destinies are intertwined in a single interactive polity. (*August v. Electoral Commission*, 1999)

There was another matter observed by the court concerning the disenfranchisement of prisoners, namely the distinction between those convicted and those in prison who were not in a position to pay bail or fines. The court noted that in December 1998, 54,121 of 146,278 prisoners were awaiting trial. On 15 February 1999, more than 20,000 prisoners granted bail had been unable to pay it. There were also nearly 200 prisoners in prison because they were unable to pay fines imposed on them (*August v. Electoral Commission*, 1999). How to deal with prisoners on remand has been an issue for legislators and courts internationally. Remands (with the exception of those who have been convicted, awaiting sentence) are still innocent and the argument cannot be used that they are not entitled to vote because they have broken the law. One observer suggested that the decision was, 'strongly influenced by policy considerations regarding the numbers of unconvicted prisoners then currently incarcerated' (Mbodla, 2002: 92).

With the Electoral Law Amendment Act 2003, the government attempted to roll back the Constitutional Court's decision. The legislation sought to exclude prisoners serving a sentence without the option of a fine from registering and participating in elections (Muntingh, 2004: 76). The legislation ended up back in court with the government arguing that it would be costly and logistically too difficult to register all prisoners and it would be unfair to make special provisions for prisoners if similar arrangements were not made for law-abiding citizens. 'Making provision for convicted prisoners to vote would in these circumstances', submitted the government, 'send an incorrect message to the public that the government is soft on crime' (*Minister of Home Affairs v. Nicro*, 2004). The Chief Justice rejected the government's argument in unambiguous terms.

> It could hardly be suggested that the government is entitled to disenfranchise prisoners in order to enhance its image; nor could it reasonably be argued that the government is entitled to deprive convicted prisoners of valuable rights that they retain in order to correct a public misconception as to its true attitude to crime and criminals. (*Minister of Home Affairs v. Nicro*, 2004)

The court reiterated its earlier ruling guaranteeing prisoners the right to vote. In a majority verdict, it ordered the government to put in place mechanisms to allow all prisoners to vote in the forthcoming elections. The Chief Justice, Arthur Chaskalson, who had appeared as defence counsel in several major political trials (including the Rivonia Treason Trial, which led to the conviction and imprisonment of Nelson Mandela and other leaders of the ANC) reminded the ANC government of the country's recent past: 'In light of our history where denial of the right to vote was used to entrench white supremacy and to marginalise the great majority of the people of our country, it is for us a precious right which must be respected and protected' (*Minister for Home Affairs* v. *Nicro*, 2004). The court rejected the government's blanket ban as disproportionate on the basis that it did not discriminate between those who had longer or shorter sentences. The legislation targeted 'every prisoner sentenced to imprisonment without the option of a fine' (*Minister for Home Affairs* v. *Nicro*, 2004).

However, since part of the ruling was that the government failed to make a convincing case for disenfranchisement, some commentators believed that this decision may be revisited if the government put forward a more convincing argument (Muntingh, 2004: 79). One of those who took the case on behalf of prisoners conceded that if the intense public and media debates surrounding the decision were any indication of the mood of the general public, 'the Constitutional Court did not make a very popular decision' (Muntingh, 2004: 78).

Canada: 'teaching democratic values and social responsibility'
In 2002, the Canadian Supreme Court by a margin of five to four found a 1993 electoral law to be unconstitutional. In a case taken by Richard Sauvé against the federal government, the court ruled that the law denying the vote in federal elections to prisoners serving sentences over two years was repugnant to Section 3 of the Canadian Charter of Rights and Freedoms. This guarantees that: '[e]very citizen of Canada has the right to vote in an election of members of the House of Commons or of a legislative assembly and to be qualified for membership therein'. However, this was qualified somewhat by Section 1 of the Charter which 'guarantees the rights and freedoms set out in it subject only to such reasonable limits prescribed by law as can be demonstrably justified in a free and democratic society'.

In *Sauvé* v. *Canada ((No. 2)*, 2002), the majority found that the 'right to vote is fundamental to our democracy and rule of law and cannot be lightly set aside'. The denial of the right to vote would not promote civic responsibility as the government had argued but it was 'more likely to send messages that undermine the respect for the law and democracy than messages that enhance those values'. The court rejected the government's argument that denying prisoners the right to vote because of some 'vague and symbolic objectives' of enhancing civic responsibility and respect for the rule of law. It refused to accept the position that certain categories of prisoner should receive additional punishment by denying them the right to vote. It also rejected the lack of proportionality in the exclusion of all prisoners sentenced to over two years to vote in federal elections. Denying 'prisoners the right to vote imposes negative costs on prisoners and on the penal system. It removes a route to social development and undermines correctional law and policy towards rehabilitation and integration' (*Sauvé* v. *Canada (No. 2)*, 2002). The Supreme Court ruled that the government had 'failed to identify particular problems that require denying the right to vote, making it hard to conclude that the denial is directed at a pressing and substantial purpose'. Therefore, it declared that they could not 'permit elected representatives to disenfranchise a segment of the population'. The court concluded that to 'deny prisoners the right to vote is to lose an important means of teaching them democratic values and social responsibility' (*Sauvé* v. *Canada (No. 2)*, 2002). (For an analysis of the majority and minority judgments in this case, see Manfredi, 2009.)

The majority held there was another point to be considered in denying the vote to prisoners; its effect on minority populations. 'In light of the disproportionate number of Aboriginal people in penitentiaries' the court ruled that the law had a 'disproportionate impact on Canada's already disadvantaged Aboriginal population' (*Sauvé* v. *Canada (No. 2)*, 2002). Aboriginal offenders are 'disproportionately represented at all levels of the criminal justice system, including in the federal correctional system'. In 2008, Aboriginal people represented approximately 17 per cent of all admissions to federal institutions, compared to 1.7 per cent of the Canadian adult population (Correctional Service of Canada, 2008).

Judge Gonthier delivered a dissenting judgment. After surveying international jurisprudence on disenfranchisement, he argued that this was an issue for parliament to decide. There was, he suggested, a flaw in an analysis 'which suggests that because one social or political philosophy can be justified, it necessarily means that another social or political philosophy is not'. He believed that different philosophical interpretations of rights 'are perhaps inevitable in a pluralist society'. He then quoted the Canadian Judge Linden in a previous case who had ruled that he:

> would leave to philosophers the determination of the 'true nature' of the disenfranchisement. It may be argued that this legislation does different things – it imposes a civil consequence, it fixes a civil disability, it imposes a criminal penalty, it furthers a civic goal, it promotes an electoral goal, or it is part of the sentencing process. I believe that these arguments, made

alone, are of limited assistance. There are elements of all these ideas and ideals at work here. (*Sauvé* v. *Canada (No. 2)*, 2002)

Much public debate followed the ruling that allowed nearly 13,500 federal prisoners the opportunity to vote in future elections (Ispahani, 2009: 48). Some scathing attacks were launched against what were portrayed as activist judges straying into the realms of politics and penal policy. One commentator was excoriating in his criticism and cast the net wide. He argued that support for the Supreme Court's views 'could no doubt be found in the ethereal nether regions of Canadian criminology departments (where no one is ever deemed responsible for what they do)' (Morton, 2002: A23). He suggested that the judgment went against the wishes of the Canadian people and that a better option would have been to offer prisoners courses on liberal democracy.

Australia: 'exercise of the franchise reflects notions of citizenship'

Considering its past as a penal colony and treatment of Aboriginal people, it is perhaps understandable that the debate on prisoner enfranchisement in Australia was historically, culturally and racially charged. The Australian Constitution was passed by referendums in various states between 1898 and 1900. Section 7 reads: 'The Senate shall be composed of senators for each State, directly chosen by the people of the State, voting, until the Parliament otherwise provides, as one electorate'. Section 24 reads: 'The House of Representatives shall be composed of members directly chosen by the people of the Commonwealth'.

Section 4 of the Commonwealth Franchise Act 1902, disqualified from voting those who were convicted of an offence punishable by imprisonment for over a year. In 1983, the issue was revisited and disenfranchisement would now include those convicted 'under sentence for an offence punishable ... by imprisonment for five years or longer'. In 1995, due to administrative difficulties determining who was eligible to vote, as it was based on potential rather than actual sentence, the law was changed. The new law disqualified from voting those actually serving a sentence of five years or longer. This change in the law resulted in more prisoners being allowed to vote. At the time, the number disenfranchised was estimated at between 6,000 and 11,000. In 2004, this law was amended to disenfranchise those serving three years or more. In 2006, all prisoners were disenfranchised under the Electoral and Referendum (Electoral Integrity and Other Measures) Act. Therefore, any prisoner serving a sentence of imprisonment was no longer entitled to vote (Redman *et al.*, 2009: 170–5).

In August 2007, in time for the upcoming general election, the Australian High Court struck down the new legislation. Four of the six judges believed that the 2006 Act did not sufficiently differentiate between the gravity of crimes. The court found that there were circumstances in which limitations could be placed on the right to vote but there was not enough evidence in the case of Vicki Roach, an Aboriginal prisoner, who took the case. It should only be for a 'substantial' reason. The court emphasised the centrality of the franchise to the concept of representative government and 'the existence and exercise of the franchise reflects notions of citizenship and membership of the Australian federal body politic' (*Roach* v. *Electoral Commission*, 2007). They rejected the argument that the mere fact of criminal conduct sufficiently serious to warrant imprisonment necessitates this exclusion. There was no distinction in treatment between those who were serving a few days and those serving much longer sentences. The court continued: 'the franchise is critical to representative government, and lies at the centre of our concept of participation in the life of the community, and of citizenship' (*Roach* v. *Electoral Commission*, 2007).

Even though this new restriction did not affect her personally as she was serving a sentence of six years' imprisonment, Vickie Roach argued that the High Court judgment in favour of prisoners vindicated their human rights. Her solicitor argued that, 'with Aboriginal Australians incarcerated at a rate of almost 13 times that of their fellow Australians, it is also a vindication of Aboriginal rights' (cited in Kissane, 2007).

Writing about the case soon after the judgment, High Court Judge Kirby declared: 'As for those serving shorter sentences, they remain entitled to choose their rulers'. In a similar statement to the South African Chief Justice, he drew on the uniqueness of Australian history and identity.

> That is why the decision of the High Court is such an important one. It is part of the mosaic of law that defines the identity of the Australian community. Unlike the United States, Australia would never tolerate excluding millions – or thousands of citizens from the vote because of past convictions. It is vigilant against alteration of voting rights for partisan political advantage. It celebrates democracy and representative government as a core feature of what it means to be Australian. (Kirby, 2007)

Hong Kong: 'incentive to citizen-like conduct'

In December 2008, the Hong Kong High Court ruled on three cases of judicial review dealing with the enfranchisement of prisoners (HCAL 79/2008; HCAL 82/2008; HCAL 83/2008). The court found that:

> When the legitimate aims of restricting voting rights are to prevent crime by sanctioning the conduct of convicted prisoners, to give an incentive to citizen-like conduct, to enhance civic responsibility and respect for the rule of law, and to impose an additional punishment for breaching the social contract, the nature and gravity of the offence and sentence in question as well as the culpability and individual circumstances of the prisoner must be relevant considerations. A blanket and total disenfranchisement simply does not take into account those matters. (Section 116)

The court concluded that they had 'come to the view that the general, automatic and indiscriminate restrictions on the right to vote and the right to register as an elector cannot be justified under the proportionality test' (Section 164). However, the judgment emphasised that:

> the Court is not suggesting that some form of restrictions on voting (or even registration) cannot be imposed by the legislature against those in jail (and others) ... The Court is not otherwise concerned with where the cut-off line should be drawn and how it should be drawn. That is a matter for the legislature. (Section 165)

In a swift response to the High Court ruling, the government of the Hong Kong Special Administrative Region (HKSAR) undertook a consultative process. After a little over a month of consultations, the SAR government put forward three options: remove restrictions on all prisoners' right to vote; disallow some prisoners from voting based on the length of a sentence of over ten years; and a third option, to allow those serving over ten years to vote as they neared the end of their sentence. A majority of the submissions received during the consultation supported prisoners' right to vote and in an opinion poll, approximately 57 per cent believed prisoners should have the right to vote regardless of sentence, with 34 per cent believing prisoners should be denied the franchise (HKSAR, 2009b: 10).

The consultation examined not just enfranchisement, but also registration, canvassing, access to election literature and the location of ballot boxes in prisons. The government of the HKSAR (2009b: 16) announced within a month of the conclusion of the consultation that due to public support, they would enfranchise prisoners. Legislation was quickly enacted and the Voting by Imprisoned Persons Ordinance came into effect in October 2009. By the end of the year, the Commissioner of Correctional Services reported that they had 'provided for the practical arrangement' for prisoners to register as 'electors in custody' (Hong Kong Correctional Services, 2009).

These jurisdictions that allow prisoners to vote have little in common in terms of their history, political culture, civic institutions and penal policies (See Cavadino and Dignan, 2006). The decision to allow prisoners to vote usually reflects rulings by the judiciary more often than decisions by governments and/or legislatures, with the latter tending to come down against enhancing prisoners' rights. When confronted with the choice of whether or not to enfranchise prisoners, there is a sometimes stifling concern on the part of politicians to avoid being seen as soft on crime or prisoners for fear of losing electoral support. It is two countries where politicians have been somewhat more successful in their attempts to prevent prisoners (and in some cases ex-prisoners) from voting that we will now consider.

Resisting enfranchisement

The next section examines how the debates and judicial decisions on prisoner enfranchisement have played out in the United States and the United Kingdom, where the issue has engaged widespread political and popular debate. In contrast to many of the countries studied in the previous section, the judiciary in the US and UK have usually, either refused to get involved in what they deem as the prerogative of parliament and/or the executive, or have come down explicitly against allowing prisoners to vote. We will begin by examining the United States of America.

United States of America: 'an outlier in the world scene'

In no other country in the world has prisoner and ex-prisoner enfranchisement been debated so widely, analysed philosophically in such depth and fought through the courts so continuously than in the United States of America. There are wide variations in both penal policy and electoral laws in different US states; however, much of the debate has focused on the disenfranchisement of ex-felons. In the US, a felony conviction is imposed for more serious crimes and felons typically spend their time in prisons run by the state and/or federal government. Those convicted of less serious misdemeanours usually spend their time in jails run by the city or county. In the debates on enfranchisement, the term felon is usually used for anybody who has ever received a felony conviction, even if they are released from prison and have served their sentence. In the following section, the term felon will be used for anybody who is still in prison. Those who have finished their sentence, which may include a period of parole or probation, will be termed ex-felon. While some people in jail are eligible to vote, it differs from state to state. In California, for example, those in state prison and on parole are not allowed to vote, while county jail inmates retain that right – unless they have been convicted of a felony and are awaiting transfer to a state prison (see www.sentencingproject.org).

The United States has attracted most attention for its ex-felon disenfranchisement laws in both academic literature and media debate (see, for example, Abramsky, 2006; Campbell, 2007; Clegg *et al.*, 2006; Crutchfield, 2007; Ewald, 2002 and 2004; Manza and Uggen, 2006; Rottinghaus, 2005; Uggen *et al.*, 2012). This is, perhaps, understandable considering the numbers in prison and the potential impact on electoral contests. By 2011, the US had the highest imprisonment rate in the world, at over 716 per 100,000 (International Centre for Prison Studies, 2012) and 7.1 million people were under correctional supervision, in the nation's prisons or jails, on probation or parole (Sentencing Project, 2013). In 2007, one in every 100 adults was behind bars. For white men 18 years or over, one in every 106 was incarcerated; one in every 36 Hispanic men 18 years or over and one in every 15 black men 18 years or over was behind bars (Pew Center, 2008: 6). This 'grim milestone' of imprisonment has 'fiscal and moral costs', editorialised the *New York Times* (2008: A20). One of those costs is the level of disenfranchisement of felons and ex-felons, particularly among minority populations.

The US stands out as 'an outlier in the world scene, the only nation that currently disenfranchises large numbers of non-incarcerated felons (including a large group of *ex-felons* who have completed their sentences)' (Manza *et al.*, 2004: 276). Ex-felon disenfranchisement laws remain 'the last major restriction on the voting rights of adult citizens' (Ewald, 2004: 109) in the US and they are the largest single group of American citizens who are 'barred by law from participating in elections' (Keyssar, 2000: 308). By 2005, 5.3 million citizens, nearly 2.5 per cent of the voting population, were disenfranchised because of a current or previous felony conviction (Manza and Uggen, 2006: 250).

Ex-felon disenfranchisement has a long history in the US dating back to the Revolution (1776) and particularly since Reconstruction (1865–77). The 14th amendment to the Constitution, passed in 1868 in the aftermath of the Civil War, allows for the vote to be removed from those who engage 'in rebellion, or other crime'. The 15th amendment, passed two years later, stated that the right of US citizens 'to vote shall not be denied or abridged by the United States or by any State on account of race, color, or previous condition of servitude'. Despite these constitutional guarantees, Ewald (2002: 1054) suggested that '[c]riminal disenfranchisement policy in the United States is located squarely at the intersection of voting rights and criminal justice – and it is tainted by the racial history of both policy areas'.

The debate over the right to vote is also entangled with the separation of powers between state and federal government (Clegg *et al.*, 2006; Gaziano, 1999; Itzkowitz and Oldak, 1973). Each state controls its electoral law and has the authority to decide whether felons or ex-felons have the right to vote in state and federal elections (Dhami, 2005: 237). In 2010, 48 states and the District of Columbia forbade felons from voting while in prison. Thirty-five states prohibited persons on parole and/or felony probation from voting and in twelve states a felony conviction can lead to a lifetime ban. In four states – Iowa, Kentucky, Florida and Virginia – all those who have a felony conviction permanently lose their voting rights, even if they never spend a day in prison. Voting rights can only be restored through a pardon from the governor; however, it is rarely applied for, or granted (Mauer, 2011: 551). With such large numbers incarcerated, both felon and ex-felon disenfranchisement laws are bound to have a very real impact.

Similar to Canada and Australia, critics point out that while 'disenfranchisement policies are theoretically race-neutral in their intent, in practice they produce a severely disproportionate racial effect' (Mauer, 2011: 560). The disproportionate disenfranchisement of African Americans, for a number of reasons, including felony convictions, led the National Association for the Advancement of Colored People (NAACP) to bring the issue before the United Nations Human Rights Commission. They pointed out that of the 5.3 million disenfranchised, over 4 million 'have completed their sentences, and live, work, pay taxes, and raise families in their communities. Nearly two million, or 38 per cent of the disfranchised are African American, and more than 10 per cent are Latino' (NAACP, 2011: 25). In some states, to get the vote restored after incarceration, all outstanding debts have to be paid including fines and court costs. 'This additional impediment to restoration of voting rights', according to the NAACP (2011: 28), 'is dangerously similar to the insidious practice of poll taxes – requiring a fee in order to vote'.

Since the 1990s, and due to, among other reasons, the sheer numbers with felony convictions and the persuasive arguments of organisations such as the Sentencing Project and Human Rights Watch, there have been moves towards relaxing the restrictions on ex-felons voting. In November 2006, Rhode Island electors passed a measure that removed the ban on voting for people under felony probation and parole supervision. This restored the vote to an estimated 15,000 citizens. Due to changes in the law in 2007 in Maryland, the right to vote was restored to over 50,000 citizens. The new law automatically restored the right to vote for all persons upon completion of sentence. Before this change, voter eligibility was on a sliding scale of offence type and criminal history, which created confusion for those convicted of felonies and for state agencies in compiling accurate data on voter eligibility (Porter, 2010: 2 and 16). Prior to Maryland's reforms, its disenfranchisement laws were among the most complex in the United States (King, 2006: 10). From 1997 to 2010, through legislative reforms, it is estimated that more than 800,000 voters nationwide had been re-enfranchised (Mauer, 2011: 553).

In Florida 'still reeling from the controversy of the 2000 election' (King, 2006: 7) and by 2005 home to 957,000 disenfranchised ex-felons (Manza and Uggen, 2006: 90), there was some progress towards re-enfranchisement. On coming to office in 2007, Governor Charlie Crist unveiled proposals to speed up the process of allowing ex-felons to regain their right to vote. The Clemency Board adopted new rules that automatically restored the rights of ex-felons who had committed non-violent crimes, completed their sentences and probation, and paid victim compensation. Previously, it could take years to restore voting rights (Fineout, 2007). Clemency is essentially the state's restoration of civil rights, including the right to vote, the right to serve on a jury and the right to hold public office. In addition, restoration of civil rights may allow ex-felons to be considered for certain types of employment (for further details see www.restoremyvote.org). Before the law was changed, the Florida chapter of the American Civil Liberties Union estimated that a third of the state's black men were barred from voting (Thompson, 2008).

These gains have not been without setbacks. In response to the establishment of a Political Action Committee by prisoners, Paul Cerutti, the acting Governor of Massachusetts, decided to crack down on political activity among the state's prisoners. Until this time, felons in Massachusetts, along with Vermont and Maine, had been allowed to vote in federal elections. It was, according to one commentator, 'the first time in the state's history [that] the legislature moved to take away a group's right to vote'. However, she was not surprised, 'this being an election year and the group being prisoners' (cited in Cassidy, 1998). The leader of the Republicans in the Massachusetts Senate, Francis Marini, believed the practice of allowing prisoners to vote turned the social contract on its head. 'It makes no sense', he argued, '[w]e incarcerate people and we take away their right to run their own lives and leave them with the ability to influence how we run our lives' (cited in *Wall Street Journal*, 1999). In a constitutional referendum, 60 per cent of the Massachusetts electorate voted in favour of removing the right to vote from felons (Clegg *et al.*, 2006: 3). In 1998, Utah passed a referendum with 82 per cent in favour of eliminating voting rights for felons (Clegg *et al.*, 2006: 4). By 2011, Florida rolled back many of the laws enacted four years previously. It now had, according to the NAACP (2011: 26), 'the most restrictive felon disenfranchisement approach in the country'.

Olivares *et al.* (1996: 16) found that one of the reasons for the increase in the restrictions on prisoners was that there was 'little opposition by convicted offenders in the presence of legislative action limiting rights and interests of convicted offenders. Stated simply, convicted felons have no uniform voice to argue against legal restrictions on civil rights'. It seemed that when prisoners' voices entered public discourse, it led to a backlash and calls for their rights to be reduced. According to Keyssar (2000: 331), the result in Massachusetts was 'testimony both to the unpopularity of convicted felons and to the emphatically nonlinear evolution of the franchise'.

However, the disenfranchisement 'by law of millions of American citizens is only half the story' (Wood and Bloom, 2008: 1). Many states' laws are so complicated and cumbersome that relatively few ex-felons undertake the process of re-registering to vote. Ex-felons who are no longer disenfranchised find the process of registration complex and off-putting, keeping a higher number of eligible citizens off the electoral rolls, even though they are legally entitled to vote (Cardinale, 2004: 16). Because of the complexity of electoral laws, some prisoners avoid registration as they are unsure of their status, and fear they might be committing a crime, by engaging in voter fraud if they register without being eligible. A report by the American Civil Liberties Union and the Brennan Center for Justice concluded that:

> there is persistent confusion among election officials about their state's felony disenfranchisement policies. Election officials receive little or no training on these laws, and there is little or no co-ordination or communication between election offices and the criminal justice system. These factors, coupled with complex laws and complicated registration procedures, result in the mass dissemination of inaccurate and misleading information, which in turn leads to the de facto disenfranchisement of untold hundreds of thousands of eligible would-be voters throughout the country.
> (Wood and Bloom, 2008: 1)

With so many ex-felons disenfranchised, this not only excludes millions from voting but has a real impact on election results. Uggen and Manza's (2002: 786–7) study of US election contests and felon disenfranchisement, concluded that '[b]y removing those with Democratic preferences from the pool of eligible voters, felon disenfranchisement has provided a small but clear advantage to Republican candidates in every presidential and senatorial race from 1972 to 2000'. During the 2000 presidential election, 537 votes separated George W. Bush and Al Gore in Florida when the US Supreme Court decided the outcome. Over 600,000 Floridians were disenfranchised because of a prior felony conviction. Analysis of voting patterns and political preferences found that, even with a conservative estimate of the numbers of ex-felons voting, Al Gore would have won the state by over 30,000 votes, thus changing the outcome in the Electoral College (Uggen and Manza, 2002: 792 and 797). It is not an exaggeration to say that the dis-enfranchisement of ex-felons in all likelihood gave the state and election to George W. Bush and changed the course of American (Manza and Uggen, 2006: 8) and, it could be argued, world history.

Similarly, the large number of ex-felons who could not vote potentially affected the 2004 presidential race in the key battleground state of Ohio (Crutchfield, 2007: 707). During the 2008 presidential election, the NAACP canvassed presidential candidates on their views on felon disenfranchisement. Barack Obama supported voting rights for ex-felons with the Count Every Vote Act. No reply was received from John McCain. Felon disenfranchisement was debated in the press and some states introduced legislation to allow ex-felons to vote. Despite the changes in state laws and concerted registration efforts by NGOs and lobby groups, the *Washington Post* reported that by August 2008, 'the presidential campaigns of Sens. John McCain and Barack Obama have not designated anyone to go after this group' (Thompson, 2008). This was despite the emphasis on voter turnout within both campaigns. In the same month, David Plouffe, Obama's campaign manager suggested that voter registration and turnout was the key to victory. 'We spend a lot of time on this', he claimed. 'It's not sexy ... but it's how elections are won' (cited in Staunton, 2008).

Due to the sheer number of prisoners and ex-prisoners denied the vote and the depth of disenfranchisement the issue is a source of regular debate. In the 2008 legislative year, 75 bills relating to felon disenfranchisement in 22 states were introduced. Some were to liberalise and others to restrict enfranchisement. However, as Easton (2011: 233) notes: 'Very few bills promoting enfranchisement succeeded as politicians are wary of being associated with measures that they think will be unpopular with the public'. By 2010, the Obama administration stated: 'The President's position is that, for felons, once you've served your sentence ... you should have your voting rights restored' (White House, 2010). Despite this assertion, the numbers disenfranchised continued to increase. Data prepared for the 2012 presidential election estimated that disenfranchisement of felons and ex-felons had increased to some 5.85 million citizens, one in every 40 adults (Uggen *et al.*, 2012: 9).

Alexander Keyssar (2000: preface) has argued that 'these debates and contests' about the right to vote indicate 'much about the meaning of democracy in American political life and culture'. America has 'debated, and fought over, limitations on the right to vote from the revolution to the late twentieth century'. Because of the racial disparities in imprisonment rates, the disenfranchisement of ex-felons has the same outcome at the beginning of the twenty-first century as it did in the late nineteenth century, namely 'the decrease in African-American voter participation' (Crutchfield, 2007: 712–13). Disenfranchisement laws 'have been more effective in eliminating black voters in the age of mass incarceration than they were during Jim Crow' (Alexander, 2010: 188–9). The large numbers incarcerated tears at the fabric of minority communities in particular, with not only disproportionate numbers of adult males absent, while incarcerated, but politically excluded long afterwards, sometimes for life.

Europe: 'the free expression of the opinion of the people'

By 2002, the countries of the Council of Europe held nearly 2 million of the world's 8.7 million prisoners (Stern, 2002: 131). There are wide variations, some countries allowing all prisoners to vote; others limit this right and some have blanket disenfranchisement. The situation was reviewed by the European Court of Human Rights (ECtHR) in the *Hirst* (*No. 2*, 2005) case. Eighteen countries in Europe allowed prisoners to vote without restrictions. They included Albania, Azerbaijan, Croatia, the Czech Republic, Denmark, Finland, the Former Yugoslav Republic of Macedonia, Germany, Iceland, Lithuania, Moldova, Montenegro, the Netherlands, Portugal, Slovenia, Sweden, Switzerland and the Ukraine. In the 2000 elections in Kosovo, registered prisoners who had not been convicted of a felony were permitted to vote (Rottinghaus, 2005: 32).

Twelve states limited voting for prisoners. These included Austria, where the right to vote was removed from prisoners sentenced to terms exceeding one year 'if they committed the crime with intent'. Reflecting the history and politics of Bosnia and Herzegovina, restrictions applied to those accused of serious violations of international law or who had been indicted before the International Tribunal. In France, prisoners were allowed to vote if given this right by the court. In Italy, serious offenders and bankrupts who were sentenced to more than five years lost the right to vote. Minor offenders debarred from holding public office lost the right at the discretion of the judge. In Luxembourg, prisoners retained the vote unless the court removed it as part of sentencing. In Norway, the right was rarely revoked by a court, and was usually restricted to treason and national security issues. In Poland, prisoners sentenced to three or more years could lose the vote. In Romania, prisoners could be debarred from voting if the principal sentence exceeded two years (see *Hirst* v. *United Kingdom (No. 2)*, 2005).

In 13 states throughout Europe all prisoners were barred from, or unable to vote. These were Armenia, Belgium, Bulgaria, Cyprus, Estonia, Georgia, Hungary, Ireland, Russia, Serbia, Slovakia, Turkey and the United Kingdom (*Hirst* v. *United Kingdom (No. 2)*, 2005). According to Section 32 of the Russian constitution, adopted in 1993, 'Deprived of the right to elect and be elected shall be citizens recognised by court as legally unfit, as well as citizens kept in places of confinement by a court sentence'. In Belgium, the period of disqualification may extend beyond the prison term.

United Kingdom: 'parliament to decide, not a foreign court'
The history of voting in the United Kingdom, like many other countries of the world, has been one based on privilege (Brown, 2007; Foot, 2005; Keyssar, 2000). The Representation of the People Act 1918 led to a three-fold increase in the number of people allowed to vote, from 7.7 to 21.4 million. All men over 21 and women over 30 were for the first time allowed to vote (Foot, 2005). With this mass suffrage came dilemmas about what restrictions, if any, there should be on the right to vote.

The 1870 Forfeiture Act provided that any person convicted of treason or a felony lost the right to vote in parliamentary and municipal elections. Under Section 2, anyone convicted of such offences was barred from 'civil office under the Crown or other public employment ... or of being elected, or sitting, or voting as a member of either House of Parliament, or of exercising any right of suffrage or other parliamentary or municipal franchise whatever within England, Wales, or Ireland'. Murray (2013: 515–16) contended that although the Forfeiture Act did not cover those convicted of a misdemeanour or sentenced to less than 12 months for committing a felony, effectively all prisoners were disenfranchised because they were unable to register and also were prevented from attending the polling station to vote. For a brief period in the late 1960s, with the passing of the Criminal Law Act 1967, prisoners in the UK could participate in elections. However, this was revoked in 1969 and a blanket ban on prisoners was imposed (for prisoner voting rights in the UK in the post-war period, see Murray, 2013: 518–21). After the election to the Westminster parliament of Irish Republican Army (IRA) hunger striker, Bobby Sands, in 1981 (see Chapter 3), the UK government rushed through parliament the Representation of the People Act which stated that a 'person found guilty ... and sentenced or ordered to be imprisoned or detained indefinitely or for more than one year, shall be disqualified for membership of the House of Commons' (Representation of the People Act 1981, Section 1).

Section 3 of the Representation of the People Act 1983 stated that a 'convicted person during the time that he is detained in a penal institution in pursuance of his sentence is legally incapable of voting at any parliamentary or local government election'. As there was no facility to allow them to vote, all prisoners (whatever their status) were in effect excluded from the franchise. This was amended to allow remand prisoners to vote with the Representation of the People Act 2000. During the debate, George Howarth MP, for the government, stated that while they were amending the legislation to allow remand prisoners to vote, 'it should be part of a convicted prisoner's punishment that he loses rights and one of them is the right to vote' (*Hansard*, HC Debates, 15 December 1999, vol. 341, col. 300).

In 1998, the Human Rights Act incorporated the European Convention on Human Rights (ECHR) into United Kingdom law. Three years later, the High Court rejected an application from three prisoners under Articles 3, 10 and 14 of the ECHR that the denial of the vote contravened the Convention. Article 3 of Protocol No.1 of the ECHR binds countries to 'hold free elections at reasonable intervals by secret ballot, under conditions which will ensure the free expression of the opinion of the people in the choice of the legislature'. The Court refused to interfere with the powers of the legislature. Drawing on the social contract argument, Lord Justice Kennedy believed that 'there would seem to be no reason why Parliament should not, if so minded, in its dual role as legislator in relation to sentencing and as guardian of its institutions, order that certain consequences shall follow upon conviction or incarceration' (*Pearson and Martinez* v. *Secretary of State for the Home Department EWHC* [2001] *Admin 239*, 4 April).

In rejecting their right to appeal this judgment, Lord Justice Brown agreed with Lord Justice Kennedy that 'whatever may be regarded as the true rationale underlying prisoners' disenfranchisement', it does not offend the Convention. He believed that 'it is for Parliament alone either to abolish it or narrow it if it can be persuaded that it would be right to do so. It is not properly open to the courts in the circumstances of this case to judge it disproportionate or otherwise inappropriate, having regard to the considerations in play'. He admitted, '[p]olitically I am not unsympathetic to the applicants' cause. Jurisprudentially, however,

I regard it as doomed' (*Pearson and Martinez* v. *Secretary of State for the Home Department EWCA* [2001] *Civ* 927, 18 June).

One of those involved in the case, John Hirst, appealed the case to the European Court of Human Right (ECtHR). Before this court delivered its ruling, prisoner enfranchisement became a matter of public debate. In 2003, a question was raised in the House of Lords asking whether denying the right to vote to prisoners was compatible with the International Covenant on Civil and Political Rights. The Home Office Minister, Baroness Scotland of Asthal, replied that 'prisoners convicted of a crime serious enough to warrant imprisonment have lost the moral authority to vote'. Furthermore, '[p]risoners have a variety of ways in which they can express their views about conditions in prison, including writing to their Member of Parliament and many do' (*Hansard*, HL Debates, 20 October 2003, vol. 653, col. 143). This statement was rejected by one of the patrons of Unlock, the National Association of Reformed Offenders, as 'quite simply, a disingenuous remark presuming that the only thing likely to motivate prisoners to vote would be potential improvement of prison conditions'. It 'suggests they have a callous indifference to any government policies which might actually affect their families outside of prison walls' (Cheney, 2008: 137). The Prison Reform Trust and Unlock among others launched a campaign in an effort to keep the pressure on the government. To deny sentenced prisoners the franchise 'fails to deter offenders, makes no contribution to their rehabilitation and does nothing to protect the public'. They continued: 'Instead, it excludes still further those already on the margins of society. It also ensures that prison reform stays low on the political agenda' (Bottomley, 2004: 4).

In March 2004, the ECtHR ruled that there had been a breach of Article 3 of Protocol No. 1 of the European Convention on Human Rights. The 'exclusion from voting imposed on convicted prisoners in detention was disproportionate'. The court conceded that although the right to vote and participate in elections are 'central to democracy and the rule of law, they are not absolute and may be subject to limitations' (*Hirst* v. *United Kingdom (No. 1)*, 2004). However, it rejected as 'arbitrary' and 'disproportionate' a ban on all convicted prisoners. It accepted that while this is 'an area in which a wide margin of appreciation should be granted to the national legislature ... It cannot accept however that an absolute ban on voting by any serving prisoner in any circumstances falls within an acceptable margin of appreciation' (*Hirst* v. *United Kingdom (No. 1)*, 2004). In effect, the court decided that some prisoners in the United Kingdom had their human rights contravened by being denied the vote.

The UK government appealed this judgment to the Grand Chamber of the ECtHR on the basis that under the ECHR the right to vote was not absolute and furthermore, 'the finding of a violation was a surprising result, and offensive to many people'. Convicted prisoners, argued the government, forfeited the right to take part in deciding who should govern as they had 'breached the social contract'. The government claimed that disqualification would achieve the aims of preventing crime, punishing offenders, enhancing civic responsibility and respect for the rule of law by 'depriving those who had breached the basic rules of society of the right to have a say in the way such rules were made' (*Hirst* v. *United Kingdom (No. 2)*, 2005). Disenfranchisement only affected those who had been given a custodial sentence. The duration was 'accordingly fixed by the court at the time of sentencing' (*Hirst* v. *United Kingdom (No. 2)*, 2005). The government seemed to be arguing that it was the judiciary, rather than the legislature, who were denying citizens the right to vote by sentencing them to imprisonment. This is in spite of the earlier refusal of the judiciary in the UK to stray into the political domain.

There were a number of interventions from third parties, including the Prison Reform Trust, arguing that the denial of the right to vote dated back to 1870 and was rooted in the concept of civil death. The government of Latvia also intervened because they feared that the Grand Chamber's judgment would have a 'horizontal effect on other countries which imposed a blanket ban on convicted prisoners voting'. They argued that imprisonment was used as a last resort and therefore although the voting ban was automatic 'it still related to the assessment of the crime itself and the convict's personality' (*Hirst* v. *United Kingdom (No. 2)*, 2005).

Before the Grand Chamber delivered judgment, prisoner enfranchisement again entered the political arena. In the course of the 2005 general election, the Liberal Democrat leader, Charles Kennedy, raised the issue. 'We believe that citizens are citizens. Full stop'. Expanding on this, he stated: 'If you take the view as we do in principle that an individual citizen is an individual, that means that you have the full entitlement that goes with it in terms of voting' (cited in Chapman, 2005). Labour's general election co-ordinator, Alan Milburn, replied that people would be 'disgusted' with Charles Kennedy's plans and this would 'add insult to injury'. The Liberal Democrats were more interested in 'criminals and yobs' than 'hardworking families who play by the rules' (cited in Chapman, 2005). Reflecting the zero sum argument between the rights of prisoners and the rights of victims that can be a feature of political debate, the Conservatives also opposed the Liberal Democrat policy.

The 'criminal justice system is already weighted too far in favour of the criminal, not the victim. It is very important that the Liberal Democrats are never allowed to implement this policy which would unbalance it even further' (cited in White, 2008: 5).

In October 2005, the Grand Chamber of the ECtHR delivered its verdict. By a margin of 12 votes to 5, it found against the British government. While the Grand Chamber accepted that each signatory to the ECHR must be allowed a margin of appreciation in this sphere, 'the right to vote is not a privilege'. The automatic blanket ban lacked proportionality and encompassed those who served from one day to life in prison, from those who were convicted of minor to the most serious offences. Rejecting the UK government's argument that parliamentary approval had been given for this measure, the Grand Chamber also offered some advice to European parliamentarians: 'It cannot be said that there were any substantive debates by members of the legislature on the continued justification in light of modern-day penal policy and human rights standards for maintaining such a general restriction on the right of prisoners to vote' (*Hirst v. United Kingdom (No. 2)*, 2005).

The court rejected the UK's defence that to allow prisoners to vote would cause offence to the public. In a similar plea from the UK government to that of its South African counterpart's concern about public opinion, a comparable rebuke was forthcoming from the court. Judge Calfisch remarked that 'decisions taken by the court are not made to please ... members of the public but to uphold human rights principles' (*Hirst v. United Kingdom (No. 2)*, 2005). Furthermore, participation in the democratic process may begin the reintegration of prisoners into society. He reminded the court: 'It cannot simply be assumed that whoever serves a sentence has breached the social contract'.

In the immediate aftermath of the judgment, the Lord Chancellor, Lord Falconer, replied for the government: 'I can make it absolutely clear', he affirmed, 'that in relation to convicted prisoners, the result of this is not that every convicted prisoner is in the future going to get the right to vote' (cited on BBC News, 6 October 2005). Some media comment focused on the possibility of a voting bloc among prisoners influencing the outcome of the elections. For example, on the Isle of Sheppey there were three institutions, with 2,224 prisoners. It was pointed out that the Labour MP, Derek Wyatt, had a majority of just 79. The three jails on the Isle of Wight had 1,618 prisoners and the MP's majority was 2,826 (cited in Ford, 2005). The Prison Reform Trust estimated that the ban on prisoner voting rights may have affected the outcome in at least some marginal constituencies in the 1997 election. Examples were given, such as Dorset South, which had three prisons with nearly 1,500 prisoners, and a Conservative candidate won by 77 votes (Dhami, 2005: 244).

In December 2006, in response to the court's judgment and the criticism of lack of substantive debate on prisoner enfranchisement, the UK government began a two-stage consultative process; the first to determine if enfranchisement should be taken forward and the second to examine the practicalities of any change in the law. It issued a consultation paper setting out the legal situation and put forward its response (Department for Constitutional Affairs (DCA), 2006). Lord Falconer continued to maintain the position that '[t]he government is firm in its belief that individuals who have committed an offence serious enough to warrant a term of imprisonment, should not be able to vote while in prison'. He argued that successive governments considered that the 'right to vote forms part of the social contract between individuals and the state'. The loss of that right, 'reflected in the current law, is a proper and proportionate punishment for breaches of the social contract that resulted in imprisonment' (DCA, 2006: Foreword). The consultation document laid out a number of options: retain the current ban on voting rights for convicted prisoners; enfranchise prisoners sentenced to less than a specified term; allow sentencers to decide on withdrawal of the franchise; or enfranchise all tariff-expired life sentence prisoners (DCA, 2006: 23–5).

The Prison Reform Trust (PRT) accused the government of 'procrastination' in appealing the original decision and then initiating a consultation process that was 'flawed' because it did not allow for the enfranchisement of all prisoners (PRT, 2007). It was also pointed out that prisoners sentenced for contempt of court, fine defaulters and remand prisoners retained the right to vote. British citizens convicted and imprisoned abroad had the right to vote in UK elections (Cheney 2008: 138). They noted that even prisoners held in British and American jails in Iraq were allowed to maintain their voting rights, which the occupying forces argued was to aid the democratic process (PRT, 2007). Critics suggested the position of the government was contradictory and located the debate in the wider context of citizenship.

> Thus the government revels in the use of the rhetoric of citizenship when speaking with pride of the part it plays in the rehabilitation and resettlement of prisoners . . . yet that same government denies them full citizenship in practice. It seems something of a contradiction (if not a cruel game) to virtually 'thrust' active citizenship forward during a prisoners' sentence as a crucial element to be practised for resettlement, while alienating them from, arguably, the most important role of being an active citizen. (Cheney, 2008: 139)

In March 2007, while the consultative process was ongoing, an election was due to be held in Northern Ireland. Six days before elections to the devolved Assembly, a challenge was heard in the High Court to allow prisoners to vote in the forthcoming election. If prisoners could not be accommodated in their European Convention right, according to the affidavit, then the court should order postponement of the elections until such time as the applicants were allowed to vote. However, the government was adamant that as the consultation process into the outcome of the ECtHR judgment was ongoing, prisoners should not be allowed to vote. They argued that if the elections were postponed, 'the historic progress towards devolution would come to nothing' (*Toner and Walsh v. Secretary of State*, 2007).

The court dismissed the prisoners' application because it was 'a matter of profound importance to the people of Northern Ireland that no impediment be placed in the path of that progress'. The lack of prisoners' access to the ballot box would not be allowed to delay the election or obstruct that progress. While accepting that the government was undertaking a consultative process, it did not escape criticism as the court ruled that it found 'little evidence of a determination to prioritise appropriately the task that was defined by the *Hirst* decision' (*R. v. Secretary of State, ex parte Toner and Walsh*, 2007).

Elections were due to be held for the Scottish parliament in May 2007 and a former prisoner, William Smith, took the Scottish Secretary of State to court claiming that denying prisoners the right to vote contravened the ECHR. The court accepted that there would be no amending legislation to allow Scotland's 7,000 sentenced prisoners to vote in the May 2007 elections. However, the judges declared that the blanket ban on prisoners voting was incompatible with their human rights (*Smith v. Electoral Registration Officer*, 2007).

In the run-up to the election to the Scottish parliament, prisoner enfranchisement again entered the political domain, with the Liberal Democrats arguing that the right to vote was fundamental in a democracy, but conceding that those guilty of the worst crimes should not be allowed to vote. The Scottish Conservatives came out against votes for prisoners, as did the Labour Party. Kenny MacAskill, of the Scottish National Party, later Cabinet Secretary for Justice in the Scottish government, argued that the *Hirst* decision was 'utter nonsense'. He believed that the European Convention on Human Rights should be about protecting victims and 'ensuring equality for law abiding citizens, not giving the franchise to those who do not respect the law and commit serious offences' (MacAskill, cited on BBC News, 24 January 2007).

The government had completed what they later termed the 'first phase' of the consultation process by March 2007 and in April 2009 they launched the 'second stage' after giving 'careful consideration' on how to respond to the ECtHR judgment. By this stage, the government had reached 'the preliminary conclusion that to meet the terms of the judgment a limited enfranchisement of convicted prisoners in custody should take place' (Ministry of Justice, 2009: 21). Postal voting was the most likely mechanism with prisoners declaring a 'local connection', and eligibility would be based on sentence length.

The consultation paper put forward four options – those sentenced to less than one, two or four years would retain the right vote. The final option was that those sentenced to two years or under would automatically retain the right to vote and prisoners who received a sentence of between two and four years could apply to vote but only where a judge allowed it in a specific case. 'The Government', claimed the consultation document, 'remains inclined towards the lower end of the spectrum of these options' (Ministry of Justice, 2009: 24). The seriousness of the offence should determine eligibility to vote and 'the Government does not intend to permit the enfranchisement of prisoners sentenced to 4 years' imprisonment or more in any circumstances' (Ministry of Justice, 2009: 25). The government did not deem it appropriate for those convicted with an offence connected with the electoral process to vote and prisoners who were in the post-tariff part of their life sentence would also not be allowed to vote. The consultation document noted that if all prisoners serving less than one year were allowed to vote this would enfranchise 6,700 electors; less than two years, 13,900; and less than four years, 28,800 (Ministry of Justice, 2009: 27).

During this period of consultation, other issues emerged in the debate. Opponents of enfranchisement began to use the *Hirst* judgment to denounce European 'interference'. In reporting the launch of the second consultation process the *Daily Express* in an outraged front page article suggested: 'Europe Says: Give Votes to Convicts' (Milland, 2009). It reported that: 'Thousands of rapists, killers and paedophiles will get the right to vote after ministers caved in to pressure from Europe'. In the course of a debate in the House of Lords, the Conservative peer, Lord Tebbit, asked: 'Is it not clear that despite the judicial imperialism, to which we are becoming accustomed, the British people have not been asked to give their view on the matter, and that the Parliament of this Kingdom has not yet been invited to give its view on this matter?' (*Hansard*, HL Debates, 20 April 2009, vol. 709, col. 1248).

In December 2009, the Council of Europe's Committee of Ministers adopted another resolution calling on the UK government to lift the blanket ban on prisoners' voting and expressed 'serious concern' that the 'substantial delay in implementing the judgment' risked the next general election (due to take place by June 2010) failing 'to comply with the Convention'. It urged the government 'to rapidly adopt the measures necessary to implement the judgment of the Court'. Four months later, this Committee issued another warning to the UK government and 'strongly urged the authorities rapidly to adopt measures, of even an interim nature, to ensure the execution of the court's judgment before the forthcoming general election' (cited in *Greens and M.T. v. United Kingdom*).

During the debate on the Constitutional Reform and Governance Bill 2010, which took place prior to the general election, an amendment to enfranchise prisoners was proposed by Lord Ramsbotham, the former Chief Inspector of Prisons. He criticised the Labour government for delaying the implementation of the *Hirst* judgment and was scathing in his criticism of the government's procrastination.

> [Y]ou would expect that a Government who pride themselves on acting within the law ... would abide by the decision of the highest court to which they could appeal ... But no, frightened of offending reactionary public opinion by appearing not to be tough on criminals ... the Government determined to prevaricate for as long as possible, going to absurd lengths, such as suggesting that prisoners had lost the moral authority to vote. (*Hansard*, HL Debates, 7 April 2010, vol. 718, col. 1643)

However, the election took place in May 2010 without any measures to include prisoners in the franchise. The Committee of Ministers revisited the issue in June and December 2010, reiterated their criticism of the UK government and expressed the hope that the scheduled elections in Scotland and Wales in 2011 would be carried out in a way that complied with the ECHR.

In November 2010, after an election which led to a new coalition government of Conservative and Liberal Democrats, Mark Harper, the Cabinet Office Parliamentary Undersecretary, reported that more than 1,000 cases were pending by prisoners seeking compensation for their being denied the right to vote (*Hansard*, HC Debates, 2 November 2010, vol. 517, col. 772). Despite the Liberal Democrats previously voicing support for prisoner voting, their coalition partner and Conservative Prime Minister, David Cameron, set the tone for the new government's position: 'It makes me physically ill even to contemplate having to give the vote to anyone who is in prison. Frankly, when people commit a crime and go to prison, they should lose their rights, including the right to vote'. However, he conceded that some prisoners would have to be enfranchised. 'We are in a situation that I am afraid we have to deal with. This is potentially costing us £160 million, so we have to come forward with proposals . . . painful as it is' (*Hansard*, HC Debates, 3 November 2010, vol. 517, col. 921).

In January 2011, the UK government conceded that while it would have to comply with the ECHR ruling, it was going to enfranchise just for Westminster and European elections. They had to take into consideration a new case in the ECtHR, *Greens and M.T.*, which found in November 2010 that the UK had violated the *Hirst* judgment for its refusal to enact legislation. It stated that the government must abide by the timeline set out by the Committee of Ministers of the Council of Europe. In February 2011, Robert Greens had applied for his case to be heard in the Grand Chamber of the ECtHR in an attempt to get the government to introduce legislation in time for the local and devolved elections in England in May 2011. The next month the government referred the *Greens and M.T.* judgment to the Grand Chamber.

In February 2011, after a report by the House of Commons Political and Constitutional Reform Committee heard evidence that the situation in the United Kingdom was illegal under international law and the UK's treaty obligations, a backbench debate was scheduled on prisoner enfranchisement. The initiators of the debate hoped this would satisfy one of the ECtHR's rulings, that the lack of political discussion undermined the legitimacy of disenfranchisement. The UK parliament would engage in wide-ranging discussion and would give their response to the court.

The debate was proposed by high ranking members of both the Conservative and Labour parties. David Davis, the Conservative MP, suggested there were two different issues at stake in the debate. First, the right of the ECtHR or the UK parliament to decide on the matter and second, voting rights for prisoners. Taking up the latter subject, he supported the concept: 'if you break the law, you cannot make the law'. If a crime is serious enough for a perpetrator to be sent to prison, 'a person has broken their contract with society to such a serious extent that they have lost all these rights: their liberty, their freedom of association and their right to vote'. However, he conceded that, 'if there were an argument that giving prisoners the vote would cut recidivism, cut re-offending rates and help the public in that way, I would consider the matter, but giving prisoners the vote would not stop one crime in this country, and that is after all the point of the justice system in the first place' (*Hansard*, HC Debates, 10 February 2011, vol. 523, col. 494). Bernard Jenkin, Conservative MP, suggested that votes for prisoners 'was never an issue in the British prison system until the lawyers got hold of it through the European Convention on Human Rights, and to that extent it is completely irrelevant to the real issues that face our prison system and the prisoners in it' (*Hansard*, HC Debates, 10 February 2011, vol. 523, col. 494).

Former Home Secretary, Labour MP Jack Straw, in supporting the motion, asked whether, 'through the decision in the *Hirst* case and some similar decisions, the Strasbourg Court is setting itself up as a supreme court for Europe with an ever-widening remit' (*Hansard*, HC Debates, 10 February 2011, vol. 523, col. 502). After much discussion, the House of Commons passed, by a majority of 234 to 22, the following motion:

> That this House notes the ruling of the European Court of Human Rights in the *Hirst* v. *United Kingdom* in which it held that there had been no substantive debate by members of the legislature on the continued justification for maintaining a general restriction on the right of prisoners to vote; acknowledges the treaty obligations of the UK; is of the opinion that legislative decisions of this nature should be a matter for democratically-elected lawmakers; and supports the current situation in which no sentenced prisoner is able to vote except those imprisoned for contempt, default or on remand. (*Hansard*, HC Debates, 10 February 2011, vol. 523, col. 586)

The elected representatives of the British people had finally given their response to the European Court of Human Rights. Over a year later in response to the *Scoppola* judgment (see below) Prime Minister David Cameron voiced his approval for the parliamentary vote: 'I have always believed that when someone is sent to prison they lose certain rights, and one of those rights is the right to vote. Crucially, I believe that it should be a matter for Parliament to decide, not a foreign court. Parliament has made its decision, and I completely agree with it' (*Hansard*, HC Debates, 23 May 2012, vol. 545, col. 1127). Continuing the cross-party rejection of *Hirst*, one of the leaders of the opposition Labour Party, Ed Balls, supported the Prime Minister: 'This is one of those times in politics where there is cross-party consensus. The court first said this in 2004 that prisoners should be able to vote, and Labour then said we disagree ... If David Cameron is going to go out there and fight this one, we will be supporting him on that' (cited in Whitehead, 2012). However, it was still up to the government to take action in response to the *Hirst* judgment.

ECtHR response to Hirst: 'the margin in this area is wide'
After the *Hirst* judgment, a number of European countries introduced legislation to enfranchise prisoners. As will be seen in Chapter 3, the

Irish government decided to enfranchise all prisoners. In 2006, Cyprus, which had previously banned prisoners from voting, enfranchised all prisoners, with polling stations set up inside prisons. In Belgium new legislation was passed in 2009 removing the automatic link between conviction and disenfranchisement. The sentencing judge was now required to rule explicitly on whether persons convicted of a crime or a misdemeanour should be deprived of their voting rights as an additional punishment. In Moldova, prisoners were able to vote following legislation in 2010. In Austria, following *the Frodl* v. *Austria* judgment in the ECtHR (see below), discussions took place to respond to the judgment. In Slovakia, after a Constitutional Court ruling in February 2009 annulled enactments banning prisoners from voting as unconstitutional, a measure was introduced to ban prisoners serving a custodial sentence for a serious offence from voting. All other prisoners are allowed to vote (White, 2013: 45–57).

In April 2010, the European Court of Human Rights heard another case similar to *Hirst*. It concerned an Austrian law that barred from voting prisoners serving a term of imprisonment over one year. The applicant, Helmut Frodl, was jailed for life in 1993 and was refused access to the franchise. He argued that his rights had been contravened under the National Assembly Elections Act. The court recognised that the Austrian law differed from the UK because it did not provide for the blanket ban of all convicted prisoners, regardless of the seriousness of their offence or their individual circumstances. Prisoners lost the right to vote in Austria if the final sentence was more than one year. It also accepted that Section 44 (2) of the National Assembly Election Act allowed the judge to conditionally suspend the legal consequences of the conviction, including disenfranchisement. Therefore the Austrian legal system made legal provision for consideration to be given to individual circumstances. However, the court (Section 25) reiterated a point made in the *Hirst* judgment that:

> prisoners in general continue to enjoy all the fundamental rights and freedoms guaranteed under the Convention save for the right to liberty ... It is inconceivable, therefore, that a prisoner should forfeit his Convention rights merely because of his status as a person detained following conviction. Nor is there any place under the Convention system, where tolerance and broadmindedness are the acknowledged hallmarks of democratic society, for automatic disenfranchisement based purely on what might offend public opinion.

However, the court conceded that rights under Article 3 of Protocol No. 1:

are not absolute. There is room for implied limitations and Contracting States must be allowed a wide margin of appreciation in this sphere since there are numerous ways of organising and running electoral systems and a wealth of differences, *inter alia*, in historical development, cultural diversity and political thought within Europe which it is for each Contracting State to mould into their own democratic vision.

The court accepted that Article 3 of Protocol No.1 of the ECHR 'does not therefore exclude the possibility of restrictions on electoral rights being imposed on an individual who has, for example, seriously abused a public position or whose conduct has threatened to undermine the rule of law or democratic foundations'. However, it continued: 'The severe measure of disenfranchisement must not, however, be resorted to lightly and the principle of proportionality requires a discernible and sufficient link between the sanction and the conduct and circumstances of the individual concerned'. It ruled that:

> Disenfranchisement may only be envisaged for a rather narrowly defined group of offenders serving a lengthy term of imprisonment; there should be a direct link between the facts on which a conviction is based and the sanction of disenfranchisement; and such a measure should preferably be imposed not by operation of a law but by the decision of a judge following judicial proceedings.

Consequently, the ECtHR found by six votes to one that there had been a breach by the Austrian government of the Convention.

The UK government had received an extension to the deadline to introduce legislation by the ECtHR because of a pending judgment, *Scoppola v. Italy*. The UK government sought representation in this case as 'third party intervener', arguing that each signatory to the ECHR should be free to adopt its own legal system, based on its own social policy, and be free to choose which arm of the state (legislature, executive or judiciary) should have the powers to decide on prisoners' voting rights. They drew the court's attention to the vote in the House of Commons which overwhelmingly rejected allowing prisoners' access to the franchise.

In *Scoppola*, the court noted that there 'is room for implied limitations and the Contracting States must be afforded a margin of appreciation in this sphere'. It continued that 'the Court has repeatedly affirmed that the margin in this area is wide'. It found that the decision to disenfranchise Scoppola, who had previously been sentenced to life imprisonment, reduced on appeal to 30 years, was within that margin of appreciation because the ban on prisoners' voting in Italy was not absolute, but related to the length of sentence and seriousness of crime. They ruled by 16 votes to one that there had not been a violation in this case of Article 3 of Protocol No. 1 of the ECHR (*Scoppola* v. *Italy (No. 3)*). However, in the dissenting opinion, Judge Thor Bjorgvinnson argued that UK legislation was a 'blunt instrument' removing the right to vote 'in an indiscriminate manner'. He opined that while there were differences between *Scoppola* and *Hirst*, 'these differences are not sufficient to reach a different conclusion'. He differed from the majority because he found:

> the distinction made in this judgment between these two cases as a ground for justifying different conclusions to be unsatisfactory. The present judgment offers a very narrow interpretation of the *Hirst* judgment and in fact a retreat from the main arguments advanced therein. Regrettably the judgment in the present case has now stripped the *Hirst* judgment of all its bite as a landmark precedent for the protection of prisoners' voting rights in Europe. (Thor Bjorgvinnson, *Scoppola* v. *Italy (No. 3)*)

The UK government was given six months from the date of the *Scoppola* judgment to respond with legislation.

On 22 November 2012, just over 24 hours before the deadline, and more than seven years since the *Hirst* judgment, the UK government gave its response to the European Court of Human Rights. The Justice Secretary, Chris Grayling, stood up in the House of Commons and introduced the Voting Eligibility (Prisoners) Draft Bill. The bill to be considered by a committee of both Houses of Parliament proposed three options: prisoners sentenced to less than four years would be allowed vote; prisoners sentenced to less than six months would retain the franchise; and the final option – a restatement of the existing ban on all sentenced prisoners voting.

In his statement to the House of Commons, the Justice Secretary argued that the court had gone beyond the original intention of the European Convention on Human Rights. He was giving parliament the authority to consider the bill as its response to the ECtHR, because, while he recognised that it was his 'obligation to uphold the rule of law seriously. Equally, it remains the case that Parliament is sovereign' (*Hansard*, HC Debates, 22 November 2012, vol. 553, col. 745). He asked a parliamentary committee to consider the legislative proposals 'and whether there are other options – for example, the Italian system, found to be compliant by the court, which disfranchises prisoners post-release' (*Hansard*, HC Debates, 22 November 2012, vol. 553, col. 746). Asked if there may be consequences to this process, he stated: 'I shall make it very clear to the Court that this is the start of a parliamentary process and an important part of the response to what it has asked us to do' (*Hansard*, HC Debates, 22 November 2012, vol. 553, col. 755). He argued: 'Ultimately, if this Parliament decides not to agree to rulings from the ECtHR, it has no sanction. It can apply fines in absentia, but it will be for Parliament to decide whether it wishes to recognize those decisions' (*Hansard*, HC Debates, 22 November 2012, vol. 553, col. 754). Nevertheless, there were other matters that the government had to contend with: a case was due to be heard in the Supreme Court in summer 2013 on the right to vote in European elections and the nearly 3,000 cases taken by prisoners for compensation, which were on hold pending implementation of the judgment.

The Opposition Labour Party supported the government's approach. This was, according to Shadow Justice Spokesman, Sadiq Khan, 'not a case of our Government failing to hold free or fair elections, or an issue of massive electoral fraud; it is a case of offenders, sent to prison by judges, being denied the right and the privilege of voting, as they are denied other rights and privileges'. He believed that it should be 'within the margin of appreciation that nation states are given by the European Court' (*Hansard*, HC Debates, 22 November 2012, vol. 553, col. 746–7).

While there was overwhelming cross-party support on the rejection of *Hirst*, there were dissenting voices. The Conservative MP, Peter Bottomley, was eager to point out that just 'because there may be a bipartisan consensus does not mean that it is right or rational, and it certainly does not include me' (*Hansard*, HC Debates, 22 November 2012, vol. 553, col. 752). The Labour MP, Paul Flynn, asked if the position taken by the government towards the ECtHR ruling was 'giving an open invitation to other, oppressive countries in Europe to mistreat their prisoners?' He continued: 'I say that we are sending out a signal that other countries may behave in line with their own national interests and traditions, and that those traditions are to oppress their prisoners and to ignore human rights?' (*Hansard*, HC Debates, 22 November 2012, vol. 553, col. 750).

As a draft bill is published to enable consultation and pre-legislative scrutiny, it can take years to reach the statute books. This move by the government, considering its stated hostility to allowing prisoners to vote, was seen by some commentators as an attempt to play for time with the ECtHR and the Council of Ministers of the Council of Europe (Rozenberg, 2012). It was a 'mealy-mouthed compromise' and nothing more than 'intellectual sophistry' (Jenkins, 2012: 43). Nevertheless, the UK government could legitimately argue that it had brought forward legislative proposals and it was now for parliament to decide. It would most likely stay any compensation claims and put off condemnation by either the ECtHR or the Council of Ministers.

In another sign of the cross-party rejection of *Hirst*, the Scottish parliament passed the first reading of the Scottish Independence (Referendum) Bill by 97 votes to 12 in May 2013, in preparation for a referendum on independence in 2014. This included a clause banning prisoners from voting. In their desire to prevent prisoners from voting, the Scottish government relied on legal advice that Article 3 of Protocol No. 1 of the ECHR applied only to elections, not to referenda. Just in case the UK government introduced legislation on the issue, the Scottish government wished to future-proof the bill. This was explained in the memorandum to accompany the bill: '[T]he UK Parliament is considering proposals to alter section 3 of the 1983 Act and the Scottish Government would not wish any alteration to apply for the purposes of an independence referendum'. In preparing to break with the Westminster parliament, Deputy First Minister, Nicola Sturgeon, argued that the government were 'not persuaded' of the case for allowing convicted prisoners to vote. Despite the Howard League for Penal Reform (Scotland) launching a campaign to allow short-term prisoners to vote in the independence referendum, the bill was passed with the following clause: 'A convicted person is legally incapable of voting in an independence referendum for the period during which the person is detained in a penal institution in pursuance of the sentence imposed on the person' (Section 3 (1)).

In April 2013, a Joint Select Committee on the Draft Voting Eligibility (Prisoners) Bill was established by the Westminster parliament and began taking oral and written evidence two months later. Nick Gibb MP, chair of the committee, explained that they would engage in a wide-ranging inquiry to consider the government's proposals on enfranchisement and any others from witnesses to the committee. While accepting that: 'All the main parties in the UK, and the vast majority of Members of Parliament and the public, are opposed to allowing prisoners to vote', the committee would 'examine these issues in great depth, to form a view about the draft Bill and to consider how the public's position on this issue can be squared with that of the European Court of Human Rights'. It was anticipated that they would sit over the summer of 2013 and report back to parliament. However, the final bill may not be passed by parliament before the next election, due in 2015.

Prisoner enfranchisement has led to political debate and legal challenge and engaged public opinion in the UK and US more widely than in other jurisdictions. The attempts to resist enfranchisement generally reflect the more punitive tone of their penal polices (see Garland, 2001). However, even within these jurisdictions, there are deep divisions and opinion is not settled. There is also a distinction to be made between the discourse in the UK and the US as debates in the former concentrate more on prisoners and the franchise, while the focus in latter tends to be on ex-prisoners. In the US and UK, while politicians have opposed prisoner enfranchisement, the domestic judiciary have tended to leave it to the legislature and/or executive to decide on the limits to the franchise, in contrast to the legal rulings in jurisdictions that allow all or some prisoners to vote. However, as both jurisdictions have increased their prison populations in the late twentieth and early twenty-first centuries, and demands are growing from prisoners and their supporters for legislative change, prisoner enfranchisement seems likely to remain a source of some controversy.

Conclusion

This chapter reviewed the jurisdictions where voting rights for prisoners have led to legal and political argument. While it may not enter mainstream political debate, except when court cases arise, the deliberations about enfranchisement of prisoners can reveal as much about judicial culture as a nation's penal policies and democratic legitimacy. While many countries' constitutions, or even statutes, do not specifically mention prisoners' access to the franchise, the jurisdictions that allow prisoners to vote usually did so after court rulings rather than initiatives by the legislature or executive to enfranchise. Nevertheless, whether the debates were conducted in the serene surrounds of the courtroom or the hothouse of the parliamentary chamber, they were influenced by a society's history, culture, penal policy and attitude towards prisoners. The next chapter will examine the Republic of Ireland and how its history, culture, penal polices and jurisprudence impacted on the country's approach to prisoner enfranchisement.

3

Political change, penal continuity and prisoner enfranchisement

Introduction

This chapter examines prisoner enfranchisement in the Republic of Ireland. As with many of the jurisdictions considered in Chapter 2, the issue was historically, socially and politically charged, with the debates and outcomes reflecting local characteristics. The chapter begins with an outline of prisoners' involvement in politics pre-independence, and later in that part of Ireland that achieved independence. Although prisoners were not allowed to vote for much of Irish history, this did not prevent them from engaging with and, at times, challenging the political system, especially during the nineteenth and early twentieth centuries. (Much has been written about political activity among prisoners and former prisoners in Northern Ireland (see McEvoy, 2001; McEvoy and Shirlow, 2009), but relatively little about their endeavours in the Irish Republic (see Behan, 2011; McConville, 2013).) Yet, despite using their prison experience for political advancement, on release, few political leaders became vocal advocates of penal reform in general, or prisoner enfranchisement in particular. This chapter considers why there was relatively little change in the prison system, with almost no penal reform and no desire for enfranchisement from many of those who had experience of imprisonment. The final section examines the low-key introduction of legislation to allow prisoners to vote.

Prior to the passing of the Electoral (Amendment) Act in 2006, prisoners in the Irish Republic were in an anomalous position: there was no law on the statute books which specifically barred them from voting. They were allowed to register, but no facility existed for them to vote. The international jurisprudence and political debates provide a backdrop against which to examine the case of Ireland. However, it was predominantly local influences that prevailed. In contrast to many of the jurisdictions examined in previous chapters, it was politicians, without any instruction from the courts, who enabled prisoners to exercise their franchise.

Despite the legal and political struggle by prisoners and penal reformers, when prisoner enfranchisement was achieved in 2006, it was not in the context of penal reform or a civil rights act, but rather a stand-alone piece of electoral legislation after relatively little discussion and none of the media controversy that accompanied similar debates in other jurisdictions. While similar topics were raised in the Irish debates, such as using the vote to encourage civic responsibility and voting as part of the rehabilitative process, the conclusions reached led to a very different outcome. The Republic of Ireland is a somewhat unique case because in few other countries in the world was there such widespread political support for prisoner enfranchisement.

Political representation and penal politics

'A fit and proper person'

The struggle for the right to vote and, more generally, political representation has been a central feature of modern Irish history. Prisoners and former prisoners have played an important role in the fight for democratic representation, with many political leaders spending time in prison. Well-known nineteenth-century figures imprisoned include moderate members of parliament such as Daniel O'Connell and Charles Stewart Parnell. While an MP, O'Connell was given the title of 'Liberator' for his mass campaign for Catholic Emancipation. Although a powerful advocate of peaceful protest, in 1844 O'Connell spent over three months in Richmond prison for conspiracy (Connolly, 1999: 299–300). Charles Stewart Parnell, MP for Cork City, democratic advocate of Home Rule and the 'uncrowned king of Ireland' spent over six months in jail under the Coercion Acts during the Land War of 1879–81 (Connolly, 1999: 287).

In 1828, William Smith O'Brien was elected Tory MP for Ennis and 20 years later, as an MP for County Limerick, he took part in the Young Ireland rebellion (Connolly, 1999: 398; see also McConville, 2003 for 1848–1922 period). He was convicted of high treason and sentenced to death. After a public campaign, this was commuted to transportation to Australia. Outraged and horrified by his activities, the Prime Minister, Lord John Russell, argued that he could no longer be considered a member of parliament. 'The present case of William Smith O'Brien is one', contended Russell, 'with regard to this House, so far as I have been able to ascertain, without precedent' (*Hansard*, HC Debates, *18 May 1849*, vol. 105, col. 668). He believed:

> that a person guilty of high treason or felony is incapable of sitting in this House. Such is the law of Parliament ... The consequence is, therefore,

that William Smith O'Brien, having been convicted of high treason, is a person who is civilly dead. He cannot be elected to this House, and he could not hold a seat in this House if elected. (*Hansard*, HC Debates, 18 May 1849, vol. 105, col. 668–9)

Smith-O'Brien was subsequently debarred as an MP.

Twenty years later, the Fenian leader, Jeremiah O'Donovan Rossa, who had been in prison since 1865, was elected MP for County Tipperary in a by-election. The Prime Minister, William Gladstone, believed that O'Donovan Rossa's imprisonment removed 'a capacity to receive one of the highest honours that can be conferred on any individual'. He continued: 'the disability attaching to felony is a matter of undoubted principle'. Due to his imprisonment, the writ for the election was null and void (*Hansard*, HC Debates, 10 February 1870, vol. 119, col. 126). During the parliamentary debate, Gladstone put forward a truly appalling vista if the votes of the people of Tipperary stood and O'Donovan Rossa was allowed to become a member of parliament:

> I need only in conclusion point out to the House that the negative of that proposition involves this affirmative doctrine – that a person convicted of felony, and suffering sentence within the walls of a prison in consequence of that felony, is, nevertheless, a fit and proper person – one of the magis idoneos et discretos milites – whom the writ requires the electors to return for the purpose of representing their interests in this House, and of dealing with the highest questions that can be submitted to the judgment of Parliament. (*Hansard*, HC Debates, 10 February 1870, vol. 199, col. 126)

The House of Commons eventually agreed that O'Donovan Rossa, 'having been adjudged guilty of felony, and sentenced to penal servitude for life, and being now imprisoned under such sentence, has become and continues incapable of being elected or returned as a Member of this House' (*Hansard*, HC Debates, 10 February 1870, vol. 199, col. 151). O'Donovan Rossa was released in 1871 and moved to the US where he was involved in fund-raising activities for the Fenian bombing campaign in Britain of 1881–85 (Connolly, 1999: 405). He achieved notoriety in death, with his body being returned home in 1915 for a Fenian funeral, used as a rallying call against British rule in Ireland.

John Mitchel (after whom one of Ireland's prisons was named), was the author of the *Jail Journal* (1854), written about his conviction for treason and transportation to Australia. After escaping from Tasmania, he returned home and on two occasions in 1875 was returned as MP by the electors of County Tipperary. He declared: 'The people of Tipperary have elected me as the most implacable enemy of the British tyranny. I take it that the chief fact about my past life which recommended me to the people of Tipperary was that I made no peace with England'. Discussing his election shortly before his death he asserted: 'There is no man in Tipperary, or in Ireland, who really supposed I was going to creep up to the Bar of the House of Commons, and seek permission to take the oaths' (Mitchel, 1854: xvi).

Neither he nor the people of Tipperary need have worried. In a motion proposed by the Prime Minister, Benjamin Disraeli, the House of Commons agreed that 'having been adjudged guilty of felony, and sentenced to transportation for fourteen years, and not having endured the punishment to which he was adjudged for such felony, or received a pardon under the Great Seal, has become, and continues, incapable of being elected or returned as a Member of this House' (*Hansard*, HC Debates, 18 February 1875, vol. 222, col. 539).

Michael Davitt spent seven years in Dartmoor prison for gun-running as part of the Fenian movement. After his freedom was revoked for involvement in agrarian agitation, he spent a year in Portland jail. During this time, he was elected MP for County Meath but his election was declared void because of his imprisonment. The House of Commons resolved that 'having being judged guilty of felony … and now being imprisoned … is incapable of being elected or returned as a member of this House' (*Hansard*, HC Debates, 28 February 1882, vol. 266, col. 1869).

It is perhaps unsurprising that Davitt, the internationalist, labour leader and advocate on behalf of the Jews of Russia was one of the few political leaders who used his prison experience to campaign for penal reform. According to Radzinowicz and Hood (1979: 1454, n. 146) in their study of the struggle for recognition by political prisoners in English jails, 'Davitt is one of the very few, if not the only one, of the Fenians to show sympathy for the plight of ordinary criminals and to urge penal reform'. While incarcerated, he wrote *Leaves from a Prison Diary; Or, Lectures to a 'Solitary' Audience* (1885), which chronicled prison life and his reflections on penal reform. He was subsequently a member of the Humanitarian League's criminal law and prisons department, which 'sought to humanize the conditions of prison life and to affirm that the true purpose of imprisonment was the reformation, not the mere punishment, of the offender' (Bailey, 1997: 306). On his international tours, he visited prisons in Australia and Honolulu. In 1898, as an MP, Davitt became involved in the inspection of prisons, visiting institutions in Bedford, Birmingham and Bristol. Understandably, he showed particular interest in Portland and Dartmoor prisons, where he had previously been incarcerated (Marley, 2010: 208).

'Put him in to get him out'

The early decades of the twentieth century saw the struggle to end British rule in Ireland intensify and prisoners played a prominent role in these developments. It was in the years immediately after the 1916 Easter Rising that prisoners began to take centre stage in Irish politics, with an upsurge in republicanism and rise in support for Sinn Féin and the Irish Volunteers. It is estimated that the British government interned nearly 2,000 prisoners immediately after the Rising (Lee, 1989: 37). In the period afterwards, many candidates standing at elections wore as a badge of honour their physical force opposition to British rule. Nevertheless, in their struggle to resist the criminalisation of their cause, imprisonment became 'war by other means' (McConville, 2003: 509). Sinn Féin adopted the Reading policy of participating in elections to gain support for its cause. It was given this title because it was devised by prisoners in Reading Gaol in England (Flynn, 2011: 19).

In 1917, the first by-election after the Easter Rising returned former prisoner Count Plunkett (father of executed rebel leader, Joseph Mary Plunkett), as an independent member of parliament for Roscommon North with Sinn Féin support. In the next by-election in May 1917, Joe McGuinness stood as a candidate for the South Longford seat. At the time, McGuinness was serving a sentence in Lewes prison, for his part in the Easter Rising. His election slogan was 'Put him in to get him out. Joe McGuinness, the man in jail for Ireland' (McConville, 2003: 608). He defeated the Irish Parliamentary Party candidate, Patrick McKenna, by 37 votes. Shortly after, in a by-election in East Clare owing to the death of William Redmond during his tour of duty in World War I, Eamon de Valera defeated the Irish Parliamentary Party candidate, Patrick Lynch, by 3,000 votes. Referring to the fact that only a number of weeks previously, Eamon de Valera had been released from Pentonville Prison in London, one leaflet asked: 'Are you giving Patrick Lynch the vote?/He's fat with English pay/For he sat at home in comfort, when de Valera was away' (Flynn, 2011: 21). Recently released from prison, W. T. Cosgrave, future president of the Executive Council, stood as a Sinn Féin candidate in the Kilkenny City by-election in May 1917. His campaign poster encouraged the electorate to: 'Vote for Cosgrave – A Felon of our Land' (Flynn, 2011: 76).

The first post-World War I election held in the United Kingdom (including Ireland) was under the terms of the Representation of the People Act 1918, which increased the Irish electorate from 700,000 during the 1910 election to just under 2 million for the 1918 ballot (Connolly, 1999: 206). Of the 105 seats at stake, Sinn Féin won 73. In keeping with their abstentionist platform, instead of taking their seats in the Westminster parliament, Sinn Féin MPs convened a representative assembly of all elected Irish MPs. The 105 MPs elected to the British parliament in the 1918 election were invited to attend the first Dáil (which later became the Lower House of Parliament). However, participation would have been anathema to the 6 Irish Parliamentary Party and 26 Unionist MPs. At the inaugural meeting in the Mansion House, Dublin on 21 January 1919, only 27 of the 73 Sinn Féin TDs (Teachta Dála – Members of Parliament) were in attendance. Of those who could not attend, four are listed in the official records of the Dáil as 'ar díbirt ag Gallaibh' ('banished by foreigners') and 35 are listed as 'fé ghlas ag Gallaibh' ('imprisoned by foreigners'). Of the 73 constituencies that returned Sinn Féin MPs, four were returned in two constituencies. Thus, over half of the 69 Sinn Féin representatives elected to the first Dáil were in prison or in exile. Former prisoner, Cathal Brugha, presided over the largely symbolic proceedings. In April 1919, after his escape from Lincoln jail, Eamon de Valera was elected as President of Dáil Éireann. Despite the parliament being recognised only by Soviet Russia, this short meeting, 'two of the most momentous hours in Ireland's history', is listed on the Oireachtas website as the first meeting of the first Dáil (www.oireachtas.ie/parliament/about/history/). The British authorities banned the Dáil in September 1919.

Alongside attempts to create a representative assembly raged the War of Independence which lasted from 1919–21. Of the five Irish signatories of the Anglo-Irish treaty that ended the war and established the Free State, four had been in prison. In November 1922, after the Irish Free State came into existence, Kevin O'Higgins, Minister for Home Affairs (with responsibility for prisons), proudly proclaimed in the Irish parliament that there 'is not a member of this present Government who has not been in jail . . . We have had the benefit of personal experience and personal study of these problems'. He continued:

> I think that everyone here would agree that we should aim at improvement and reform in the existing prison system. I think we would be unanimous in the view that a change and reform would be desirable. Personally I can conceive nothing more brutalising, and nothing more calculated to make a man rather a dangerous member of society, than the existing system. But one does not attempt sweeping reforms in a country situated as this country is at the moment. (Kevin O'Higgins TD, Dáil Debates, 1922, vol. 1, col. 2321–2)

Many former prisoners, who had been prominent in the struggle for independence, went on to play a leading role in the new state's penal and criminal justice system. Among those who had been familiar with the inside of a prison cell were Arthur Griffith, Eamon Duggan, Gerald Boland and Sean MacEoin, who all served as Ministers for Justice (or Home Affairs) in the new state (Kilcommins *et al.*, 2004: 88). Eoin O'Duffy had been imprisoned a number of times before becoming the first Commissioner of An Garda Síochána (the Irish police force) and later head of the Free State army (Connolly, 1999: 405). In 1928, seven years after being released, Seán Kavanagh returned to Mountjoy Prison to serve nearly 34 years behind the walls; this time as governor (Carey, 2000: 231–2).

With so many prisoners and ex-prisoners achieving prominent political positions, there may have been an expectation that this might impact positively on the development of penal policy. Nevertheless, on release, few, if any, championed prisoners' rights or enfranchisement. Most of these and future former prisoners sought to make a break with their earlier period and, while taking pride in their penal experience, the released politicians were quick to put their prison past behind them. In rejecting the criminalisation of their cause, and particularly to distance their activities from the deeds of 'ordinary criminals', they sought to distinguish their imprisonment from that of regular prisoners. Some of those who went on to have political responsibility for the prison system became quite punitive, showing little or no interest in penal reform. Despite the new state being built by prisoners and ex-prisoners, penal reform and prisoners' rights would have to wait for another day. There were more pressing priorities. The newly elected and now respectable politicians needed, as O'Higgins suggested, to get on with state building.

Political change
In the period before the majority of the people had access to the vote, due to property and gender restrictions, prisoner disenfranchisement was unlikely to have been of much popular or political concern. When the Irish Free State was formally established in December 1922, electoral laws inherited from the period of British rule still applied. Section 2 of the Forfeiture Act 1870 declared that an individual imprisoned for over 12 months was 'incapable of being elected, or sitting, or voting as a member of either House of Parliament, or of exercising any right of suffrage or other parliamentary or municipal franchise whatever within England, Wales or Ireland'.

The Free State constitution was introduced in 1922 and under Article 14, all citizens 'without distinction of sex, who have reached the age of twenty-one years and who comply with the provisions of the prevailing electoral laws, shall have the right to vote for members of Dáil Éireann'.

The next year, just before a general election, the Prevention of Electoral Abuses Act 1923 provided for a prohibition on voting for those convicted of personation or 'aiding, abetting, counselling or procuring the commission of that offence'. Depending on whether it was a first or subsequent offence, there were various penalties, from two months' imprisonment up to three years' penal servitude. Added to these penalties was an electoral punishment. A person who was found guilty of these practices was barred for seven years from the date of conviction from holding any public or judicial office, being a member of parliament or a local authority, being registered for or voting in general and local elections or voting for any public office (Prevention of Electoral Abuses Act 1923, Section 6 (2–4)). This effectively meant that an individual could be incarcerated for a period of up to three years and on release not be allowed to stand for office or cast their vote for a further four years.

Even before the Irish Free State had been formally established, civil war had begun. There was widespread internment of anti-government opponents with estimates of up to 12,000 detainees, including both sentenced prisoners and internees (Lyons, 1973: 467). The civil war was, by international standards, quite short, lasting for less than a year, but it left a bitter political legacy. Perhaps understandably, the new state sought to prevent prisoners from using their confinement to win support for a political cause. The Electoral Act introduced in April 1923 disqualified from being elected or sitting as a member of the Dáil, prisoners undergoing a sentence of imprisonment with hard labour for a period of six months or of penal servitude for any term. Similarly, if 'any person who has been duly elected a member of the Dáil should, while he is so a member, become subject to any of the disqualifications mentioned ... he shall thereupon cease to be a member of the Dáil' (Section 51 (4)).

Opponents of the new government would soon turn from physical force to politics, but to try to catch them off guard and establish a firmer mandate, the government called an election for August 1923. Even though the civil war had effectively ended in April 1923, by the time of the election there were still up to 10,000 internees, some of whom were on hunger strike. Despite pleas from prominent clergymen, the government refused to contemplate mass releases at this stage (Keogh, 1994: 17). Prior to the August election, there was a debate in the Dáil on a proposal from Farmers Party TD, Michael Doyle, that: 'all political prisoners and internees be afforded an opportunity to vote at the coming elections' (Dáil Debates, 1923, vol. 4, col. 1379). If prisoners were allowed to vote, Independent TD, Alfred Byrne, argued, 'nobody will be in a position to say that they [parliamentarians] were unrepresentative or that the Dáil elected was unrepresentative' (Dáil Debates, 1923, vol. 4, col. 1381). Anticipating government inaction, and arguments about the practicalities of the procedure, the leader of the Labour Party, Tom Johnson, suggested that a postal voters' list could be prepared for this purpose and internees could vote in their home constituencies (Dáil Debates, 1923, vol. 4, col. 1382). If the government felt that it was logistically too cumbersome to create a postal voters list, he had a solution: 'I suggest there is a much better way to meet the grievances, and that is release [the internees], not to wait until after the elections but to release before the elections' (Dáil Debates, 1923, vol. 4, col. 1382). Later in his speech, he foresaw the symbolism discussed in many future debates about prisoner enfranchisement: 'If we are going to encourage the idea that the vote is a matter of importance to the voter, and that he should look upon the vote as something valuable, as symbolic of civic responsibility, then I think we should take this opportunity of adding to the force of that lesson' (Dáil Debates, 1923, vol. 4, col. 1382).

Responding for the government, former prisoner and now Minister for Local Government, Ernest Blythe, stated that this would entail special legislation. Setting the scene for future political priorities, he said that while the government was looking into it, 'this matter is not one of prime importance'. He suggested that while there was no law in place barring prisoners from voting, special arrangements would have to be made and '[t]here is no real reason for that, except the desire to shut mouths' (Dáil Debates, 1923, vol. 4, col. 1383). The proposal was rejected by the governing party that had just been involved in a civil war with those they had interned and it was in no mood to listen to sympathetic pleas on their behalf.

Nevertheless, with many prisoners incarcerated for politically motivated activity, the lack of access to the franchise was unlikely to prevent political engagement. Barring a return to a separate or silent system of imprisonment, the government could not prevent debates about the political situation. During the civil war, prisoners had been politically active. They organised their own prison societies, educational classes and sporting tournaments. Magazines were produced, including *C-Weed* and *The Trumpeter: When Gabriel Sounds the Last Rally* (Carey, 2000: 199). While imprisoned in Mountjoy Prison, republican socialists Peadar O'Donnell and Liam Mellows wrote a number of publications on social and political matters. 'Notes from Mountjoy', smuggled out in secret communications, was a political programme for a republican government (Rogan, 2011: 26–7).

Following in the recent tradition, prisoners were nominated to stand as candidates in the election to try to boost support for the anti-Treaty side. In Mountjoy Prison, mock elections were organised by prisoners as a civic engagement exercise, to teach them about Proportional Representation (PR), the complicated new electoral system introduced in 1920. With a history of civil disobedience, violent political disorder and non-compliance, many prisoners were understandably ignorant of the finer points of the electoral system. One of those in Mountjoy at the time, Ernie O'Malley, explained how anti-Treaty prisoners reacted to news of the calling of an election.

> Meetings were addressed from the landing-rails or empty butter-boxes in the exercise-rings; waves of oratory flowed to and fro on rocks of interruption and hecklings. Businessmen, farmers, imperialists, separatists, educationalists spoke seriously or in mock parody. Rival candidates offered jail utopias for votes ... We discussed the making of box kites carrying election slogans which could be flown from the wings and the strings cut before the Staters could seize them. The kites might have amused the city electors but were never made. (O'Malley, 1978: 237)

Even though O'Malley professed little interest in standing for the Dáil, he was elected for the North Dublin City constituency, rather ironically, as he pointed out, with second preference transfers from the Free State Minister for Defence, Richard Mulcahy (O'Malley, 1978: 238). Another of those elected from prison was IRA leader and socialist, Peadar O'Donnell. His mother had complained in a letter to the *Derry Journal* the week before election day that her son and daughter, Bridget, both in prison, were not on the electoral register and therefore not entitled to vote (Hegarty, 1999: 145).

During the election campaign, leader of the anti-Treaty side, future Taoiseach and President, Eamon de Valera, was arrested at a political rally in his County Clare constituency and imprisoned for nearly a year (Ryle Dwyer, 1980: 73). He was elected to the Dáil from Kilmainham gaol; the same prison where he had been condemned to death seven years earlier by the British authorities. The prohibition on prisoners sitting as members of parliament was somewhat irrelevant in practical terms, as despite the new political dispensation, de Valera's anti-Treaty Sinn Féin continued to stand on a platform of abstentionism. However, he out-polled his Cumann na nGaedheal opponent by 17,762 to 8,196 (Keogh, 1994: 18).

Of 153 members of this Dáil (elected in August 1923), 44 anti-Treaty TDs were elected and 18 were prisoners (O'Malley, 1978: 237). The anti-Treaty side would certainly have received more votes, if not seats, had the thousands of internees been allowed to vote. However, the result provided a morale boost in the prisons. 'We went half wild with delight ... they were whacked', recorded an exhilarated Peadar O'Donnell. 'We hadn't lost ... we felt our release was a remote thing; that there was too much resistance left in the country to risk letting the prisoners loose' (O'Donnell, cited in Hegarty, 1999: 146). After the euphoria of their electoral victory, however, prisoners in Mountjoy returned to more traditional methods of achieving freedom. Once again, they drew up plans for an escape.

At the first meeting of the new Dáil, the president of the Executive Council and former prisoner, W. T. Cosgrave, spoke of the crack-down on political resistance among his former comrades (now political enemies) in the prisons. He complained about the practice of those on the anti-Treaty side of using prisoners as candidates for political gain.

> Is the future political history of this country to be written in this manner: that a man or woman has only to get into jail and has only to stand for election and get elected, and our courts and our institutions, and the order of citizenship that we have established, are to be swept away in order that a number of persons returned in a constituency perhaps under false pretences, can order the Courts to open the doors and demand their freedom and do and say whatever they like? Forty-four of these people have been elected; eighteen of them are in jail. (Dáil Debates, 1923, vol. 5, col. 31–2)

Despite using his imprisonment for political advantage in the past, he asked pointedly: 'What contribution are they going to make to the stability of this State? What apology have they got to make for the wrongs they have done this country?' He concluded: 'Until we get some evidence of a real change of heart I say it is not for us to be swept off our feet by sentimentalism because an actual minority of forty-four people say they are going to determine and mark out the progress of this country' (Dáil Debates, 1923, vol. 5, col. 32). However, despite Cosgrave's protestations, while there was political advantage to be gained from standing prisoners for election, it was likely to be utilised by his opponents.

Penal continuity, electoral reform and prisoner litigation

Many of those who went on to form governments during the 1930s and in the decades afterwards were former prisoners, including Frank Aiken, Oscar Traynor and Sean Lemass. Despite the prevalence of ex-prisoners in Irish political and civic life during the early decades of the state, there was very little discussion of prisoners' rights or access to the franchise. Considering that the state was built on the struggle of both prisoners and ex-prisoners for political rights and representation, prison issues in general and political enfranchisement in particular remained low on the political agenda. On release, few of those political prisoners identified with, or showed much interest in, the rights of prisoners and would have baulked at being associated with those left behind.

In 1932, a new government under Fianna Fáil came to power and five years later, Eamon de Valera, as Taoiseach, introduced a new constitution, Bunreacht na hÉireann. This stipulated that voting for Dáil Éireann was open to every citizen who had reached the age of 21 years and who was 'not disqualified by law and complies with the provisions of the law relating to the election of members of Dáil Éireann' (Article 16). This constitutional caveat would have allowed legislation to bar prisoners from voting; nevertheless, no law was enacted in 1937 or thereafter to specifically prevent prisoners from exercising their franchise.

Penal continuity
The leaders of the new state used their prison past for political advantage rather than to inform a more progressive penal policy. With little or no interest in penal reform, they had no inclination towards prisoner enfranchisement. They had more important issues on their agenda. For decades after independence, much of the legislation governing prisons pre-dated the foundation of the state (McDermott, 2000: 4–5). 'Once the civil war was over', argued Tomlinson (1995: 200), the 'prison service largely faded from view'. The low level of imprisonment was undoubtedly one reason for the absence of discussion about penal policy. By 1926, after political prisoners were released and the closure of a number of prisons, the daily average number of prisoners was 862 (O'Sullivan and O'Donnell, 2012: 34).

Periodically, penal reform was discussed, but this rarely led to more than muted debate among those already involved in prison reform or human and civil rights organisations. Despite penal conditions in general being widely criticised as poor and inadequate (see Rogan, 2011: 60–6), the government 'showed little interest in developing the prison system such as improving conditions or providing education and welfare resources' (Tomlinson, 1995: 200). During the inquest of IRA leader Seán McCaughey who died on hunger strike in 1946, conditions for political prisoners were so bad in Portlaoise Prison, and punishment so severe, that the prison doctor admitted to McCaughey's lawyer, Seán MacBride, that if he had a dog, he would not have been kept in the conditions in which McCaughey had been held (Flynn, 2011: 116).

The 1947 Rules for the Government of Prisons was one of the first attempts by the new state to reform the penal system. It was an opportunity to set out minimum standards of confinement, prisoners' rights and indicate the state's penal priorities. Gerald Boland, ex-prisoner and now Minister for Justice reminded the Dáil as he introduced the new Prison Rules that 'some people in this House know all about prison conditions, first hand, from inside as well as outside' (Dáil Debates, 1947, vol. 105, col. 594). However, the 1947 Prison Rules were an almost Victorian set of regulations which set out the conditions under which prisoners were held and indicated the penal priorities of the Irish State. There was no mention of prisoners' rights or enfranchisement (for the prison rules, see Rogan, 2011: 68–9).

Between 1926 and 1971, there were less than 1,000 prisoners each year. In 1951, the daily average number of prisoners in the Republic of Ireland was 488 prisoners, with an average imprisonment rate of 16.5 per 100,000. By 1971 this rose to 926 prisoners, with an imprisonment rate of 31.1 per 100,000 (O'Sullivan and O'Donnell, 2012: 5–6). With such low numbers, it is perhaps not surprising that successive governments showed little interest in transforming the prison system. Calls for penal reform in general and enhancement of prisoners' rights in particular fell on deaf ears. However, some politicians kept up the pressure. In 1970, Labour Party TD, Noel Browne, addressed the Dáil and criticised the lack of penal reform by successive ministers with responsibility for prisons.

> One of the things that always surprised me ... was that this Dáil had a series of Ministers who were what you might call distinguished jail birds in their time – and I do not mean that at all disrespectfully; quite the contrary – men who for very good reason had spent a long time in jail and very honourably in jail but few of them, who must have known what the inside of a jail was like as few of us do, took up the matter when they got into power and became Ministers. I am referring to both sides of the House. Few of them applied their own personal inside knowledge and showed the House how stupid and futile and degrading is the whole principle of locking up people and how utterly sterile it is and unproductive of any change. It is quite valueless from the point of view of the individual and from the point of view of society. Few of them took the opportunity to introduce changes which were needed. (Dáil Debates, 1970, vol. 247, col. 121–2)

In 1973, a Prison Study Group was established in University College Dublin. Defined as a 'voluntary non-political study group', its purpose was to 'find out the factual situation, not to agitate for prison reform' (Prison Study Group, 1973, cited in Kilcommins *et al.*, 2004: 70). It was made up of community activists, solicitors, a priest and academics. Despite several attempts by the Group, the Minister for Justice, Patrick Cooney TD, and his officials declined to co-operate in any way with the Group's work; nor were they allowed to visit any prisons. The Group described a 'very closed system' that 'imposed severe limitations' on their research (Prison Study Group, 1973, cited in O'Donnell, 2008: 125).

In the late 1970s, ex-prisoner and former Minster for External Affairs, Seán MacBride, chaired a Commission of Inquiry into the Irish Penal System on behalf of the Irish Section of Amnesty International, the Association of Irish Jurists and the Prisoners' Rights Organisation (PRO). Members of the Commission included Michael D. Higgins, Chairman of the Labour Party, and Mary McAleese, Professor of Criminal Law, both future Presidents of the Republic of Ireland; and Michael Keating TD, Fine Gael Spokesman on Human Rights and Law Reform and a former member of St Patrick's Institution (for Young Offenders) Visiting Committee. The government was unreceptive towards the deliberations of the committee, but with high profile and distinguished members, the potential remained that their final report might carry some weight. The Commission endorsed prisoners' right to form associations and unions 'in accordance with Article 40, paragraph 6.1 of the Irish Constitution'. It suggested that: 'Provision should be made in the Prison Rules for the exercise of their franchise by all prisoners in local and national elections and referenda' (MacBride, 1982: 93). Despite the credentials of the chair and members of this Commission, the involvement of the Prisoners' Rights Organisation in its deliberations led the Minister for Justice, Gerard Collins, to refuse to engage with it, because he did not wish 'to be put in a position of appearing to give some form of official approval for an exercise prompted by the organisation' (cited in MacBride, 1982: 108).

In 1983, the Council for Social Welfare (CSW), a committee of the Irish Catholic Bishops Conference, published what they termed an information document, *The Prison System*. While no mention was made of enfranchisement, they set out the rights of prisoners (CSW: 1983). Some debate about the state of Irish prisons and the rights of prisoners surrounded a government-appointed committee's deliberations in the mid-1980s, 'the first full-blown inquiry' (Tomlinson, 1995: 210) into the Republic's penal system. Chaired by T. K. Whitaker, a respected former senior civil servant, senator and government advisor, the subsequent report was a wide-ranging account of conditions in Irish prisons. 'The fundamental human rights of a person in prison', the report asserted, 'must be respected and not interfered with or encroached upon except to the extent inevitably associated with the loss of liberty' (Whitaker,

1985: 12). While there was no mention of the enfranchisement of prisoners, there was recognition of their rights, with a recommendation that prisoners should be allowed access to the Ombudsman (Whitaker, 1985: 16).

Although there were 'moments' when 'republican prisoners brought the prisons into the spotlight' (Tomlinson, 1995: 200), attempts to improve their conditions and status did not always widen out into concern for non-political convicts. As the state responded to protests by republican prisoners, it also 'deflected a large amount of attention, resources and energies from "ordinary" prison matters' (Rogan, 2009: 8). The removal of special category status in 1976 for those convicted of political offences in Northern Ireland led to prolonged prisoner campaigns of resistance, including the no-wash and blanket protest. Eventually, republican prisoners undertook a hunger strike in 1980 to bring their conditions and grievances to public and international attention.

After a disputed agreement to end the 1980 hunger strike failed to deal with the prisoners' demands, another fast began which led to the deaths of ten republican prisoners throughout 1981. This was the moment when prison conditions were perhaps under the most intense spotlight since partition. Hunger striker Bobby Sands was elected to the Westminster parliament in April 1981. He died on 5 May after 66 days fasting. While the election of Sands and two other prisoners in Long Kesh to the Dáil in June 1981 highlighted prisoners' grievances in Northern Ireland and their struggle for political status, this did little to raise penal reform in general. Paddy Agnew and hunger striker Kieran Doherty were elected to the Dáil and they hoped to mirror the support generated by the election of Bobby Sands. Kieran Doherty TD died on hunger strike on 2 August, after 73 days, but his and Agnew's election caused domestic political controversy due to a slender government majority in the Dáil rather than any discussion about political status for republican prisoners or reforms for the general prison population, north or south. (For the 1981 hunger strikes, see Beresford, 1987; Campbell *et al.*, 1994.) While in future decades, some hunger strikers and many former prisoners went on to 'deploy their prison time or previous experience of conflict and violence in the community as a resource' (McEvoy and Shirlow, 2009: 49), after the calling off of the hunger strikes in October 1981, prisons and prisoners faded from popular view for long periods of time.

Electoral reform
Despite the lack of penal reform, there were developments in the electoral code that could impact on the right to vote for those incarcerated

in Ireland's penal institutions. In 1963, a new Electoral Act repealed disqualifications from voting under the 1870 and 1923 Acts. This Act was introduced after a parliamentary committee rejected a suggestion that 'prisoners should be allowed to vote by post or that special facilities for voting should be provided in prisons' (Joint Committee on Electoral Law (Final Report), 1961: 105). The Electoral Act 1963 simplified the law. Section 5 affirmed that: 'A person shall be entitled to be registered as a Dáil elector in a constituency if he has reached the age of twenty-one years and he was, on the qualifying date (*a*) a citizen of Ireland, and (*b*) ordinarily resident in that constituency'. It widened eligibility for a postal vote, which hitherto had been reserved only for members of the Defence Forces, to now include members of An Garda Síochána.

Prisoners were still in limbo, not barred from voting legally, but because of their location and the failure to introduce postal voting or other measures, prevented from voting physically. In a book published by the Prisoners' Rights Organisation in 1981, *Prisoners' Rights: A Study of Irish Prison Law* (Byrne *et al.*, 1981), four pages were devoted to the electoral rights of prisoners. As there had been little legal activity concerning prisoners' access to the ballot box, the authors analysed US jurisprudence and other aspects of the right to vote, concerning age, postal voting and secret ballot. They concluded that if the 1963 Act was challenged, the judiciary 'would have to consider whether Article 16.1.2 [of the constitution, dealing with right to vote] should be considered in isolation or whether, for example, the equality provisions of Article 40.1 [dealing with fundamental rights] have any bearing on the question' (Byrne *et al.*, 1981: 85). They concluded: 'The result of these new provisions appears to be that a prisoner is entitled to be registered to vote'. However, in the absence of legal clarity 'whether this amounts to sufficient compliance with the requirements of Article 16.1.2 has yet to be decided' (Byrne *et al.*, 1981: 82).

As there was little political or legal debate about prisoners' rights in general or enfranchisement in particular, legal commentators speculated that a precedent had been established as to the Irish state's responsibility to voters in the *Draper* judgment in 1984 (Gallagher, 2001: 13–17). This involved Nora Draper, a registered voter who suffered from multiple sclerosis. She could not exercise her franchise because she was unable to access the polling station and there were no procedures in place to allow her to vote. She held that the state was in breach of its constitutional obligation to facilitate her in exercising her franchise by way of postal voting. The High Court found that the legislature could strike a balance between the right to vote and protecting the electoral system against abuse. Justice McMahon held that:

Postal voting cannot be regarded as a privilege under our Constitution. It is the responsibility of the Oireachtas to make laws providing for the manner in which the right to vote at an election of members of Dáil Éireann may be exercised. These laws must provide a manner of voting which as far as practicable will enable the right to be exercised by every citizen who is entitled to vote including those for whom attendance at a polling station is difficult or impossible. Postal voting necessarily involves some risk of abuse and it is for the legislature to strike a balance between the right to vote of the physically disabled and the risks of abuse of postal voting. (*Draper* v. *Attorney General*, 1984)

On appeal, the Supreme Court found in favour of the state. Chief Justice Thomas O'Higgins ruled that the facilities available to allow members of An Garda Síochána and the Defence Forces to vote by postal ballot were justifiable because 'in these two categories, the probability of the ballot paper reaching the designated address by post is high and the possibility of abuse is low'. He concluded, however, that a more general extension of this facility 'obviously contains a very high risk of abuse which could not easily be countered or controlled'. He ruled that in the opinion of the Court, the present law provided a 'reasonable regulation of elections' and concluded:

The fact that some voters are unable to comply with its provisions does not of itself oblige the State to tailor that law to suit their special needs. The State may well regard the cost and risk involved in providing special facilities for particular groups as not justified, having regard to the numbers involved, their wide dispersal throughout the country and the risks of electoral abuses. (*Draper* v. *Attorney General*, 1984)

Shortly after the conclusion of this case, the Minister for the Environment announced that he would introduce legislation to facilitate those unable to attend polling stations due to disability, and certain other categories of voters, although this would not include prisoners. The Prisoners' Rights Organisation protested that if this legislation was passed, 'only one minority grouping in Irish society will be deprived of the right to vote – that is the prison population' (Costello, 1985). While criticising successive ministers for their failure to introduce legislation to allow prisoners to vote, the PRO felt it 'was imperative at this point in time, when the postal vote is being extended, that the Government consider the desirability of extending the postal vote to prisoners' (Costello, 1985). Their plea fell on deaf ears. In 1986, the Oireachtas passed the Electoral (Amendment) (No. 2) Act. It contained no reference to prisoners.

Throughout the 1980s and 1990s there were sporadic parliamentary discussions about prisoners and voting. In 1981, the Minister for Justice,

Gerard Collins, in reply to a parliamentary question said that 'as far as is known from available records' (Dáil Debates, 1981, vol. 326, col. 65), there was never any facility to allow prisoners to vote. Unless electoral laws were to be changed, this would 'involve taking some 1,300 prisoners to polling booths near their normal place of residence. Such a project would be entirely impractical' (Dáil Debates, 1981, vol. 326, col. 65). Some months later, the Minister for Justice replied to the same TD, Fine Gael's Michael Keating (former member of the MacBride Commission), that there was no provision in place to allow remand prisoners to vote and it was not practical to escort approximately 120 remand prisoners to polling booths in their constituencies. While conceding that there was 'no law which prohibits prisoners from voting at local polling booths' the Minister looked for some understanding of the difficulties with such an undertaking. 'I am sure the Deputy appreciates that it would be impracticable and impossible' (Dáil Debates, 1981, vol. 328, col. 1072). If remand prisoners were to be allowed to vote by post, the Minister for Justice replied, then it was the responsibility of the Minister for the Environment to enact legislation. Michael Keating responded angrily that 'the Minister is satisfied that citizens in the circumstances in the question are to be deprived of their right to vote since he does not propose to lift a finger to do anything about it' (Dáil Debates, 1981, vol. 328, col. 1073). Ten years later, the matter was raised in the Dáil again; this time the Minister for the Environment, Pádraig Flynn, outlined those eligible to vote under the Electoral Act 1963 and conceded that 'there are no proposals for special voting arrangements for prisoners' (Dáil Debates, 1991, vol. 404, col. 1824).

In 1992, a new Electoral Act was introduced. A person was entitled to register to vote in Dáil elections if they were over 18 years of age, an Irish or British citizen and were ordinarily resident in the constituency. The issue of voting rights for prisoners was raised during the Seanad (Upper House of Irish Parliament) debates on the bill. Senator Joe Costello, former Chairman of the Prisoners' Rights Organisation, proposed that prisoners should be allowed to register either in prison or at their home address. While this amendment was defeated there was some discussion about the history of prisoner involvement in Irish politics. One reason the government rejected the amendment was that 'the vast majority of prisoners are short term and that, having regard to the fact that a period of 18 months elapses between the qualifying date for a register and the expiry date for that register', therefore, 'registration of prisoners at the prison where they are detained would be a pointless exercise unless special voting arrangements were put in place to allow them to vote' (Dan Wallace TD, Minister for State at Department of the

Environment, Seanad Debates, 1992, vol. 132, col. 1732–3). The government was unwilling to introduce special measures to allow citizens to vote while in prison. Senator Costello foreshadowed many of the discussions that accompanied the enactment of legislation in the next decade, when he argued that enfranchisement:

> would have a very substantial rehabilitation function. The fact that somebody would be encouraged to vote within the prison confines ... would give them an extra interest and awareness that would be beneficial to them, because it would mean they would be taking an interest in what is going on outside; and of course that is one of the greatest means of alleviating boredom and facilitating rehabilitation and a return to the community. (Seanad Debates, 1992, vol. 132, col. 1735)

Senator Maurice Manning, a senior member of the main opposition party, Fine Gael, supported the government in refusing to enfranchise prisoners. He believed that on imprisonment, one should lose 'the right to liberty but also the right to vote'. He continued:

> If we talk to some of the people who are suffering at the hands of criminals at the present time – the victims of crime – and the word goes out from this House that we are so concerned that we actually want to have special polling stations in Portlaoise and Mountjoy where [prisoners] ... will be given the right to vote despite the heinous crimes they have committed, I would find, and I think the ordinary humane person outside would find on this particular issue, that it was a step too far. They would say yes, do everything in your power when it comes to their rehabilitation, but this is a symbolic action and it must stop there. (Seanad Debates, 1992, vol. 132, col. 1736)

Under the Electoral Act 1992, to be eligible for election to the Dáil or Seanad, one had to be an Irish citizen and over 21 years of age. Among those not allowed to be members of the Oireachtas was any individual 'undergoing a sentence of imprisonment for any term exceeding six months, whether with or without hard labour, or of penal servitude for any period imposed by a court of competent jurisdiction in the State' (Section 41). If, while an individual is a member of the Oireachtas, they are sentenced to the above, they forfeit their seat. The registration of prisoners as electors was specifically set out in Section 11 (5), which provided that: 'Where on the qualifying date, a person is detained in any premises in legal custody, he shall be deemed for the purposes of this section to be ordinarily resident in the place where he would have been residing but for his having been so detained in legal custody'. This left open the question, if prisoners were allowed to register to vote, were they allowed to vote? If so, how would they exercise that right? Under the 1992 Act prisoners had a right to register but with little likelihood of ballot boxes being provided in prisons and no procedure to allow postal voting, the registration was somewhat moot.

Prisoner litigation

In 1994, the Irish courts rejected an application from a prisoner, Patrick Holland, to suspend the European parliament election to allow him to pursue constitutional proceedings because he was denied the facility to vote. The Supreme Court rejected the application, because by the time it heard it, the election had taken place. He pursued the case to the European Commission of Human Rights (ECmHR). (Until 1998, there was a European Commission of Human Rights and a European Court of Human Rights. Thereafter the former was abolished and its functions were subsumed into the latter.) In 1998, the Commission considered his contention that both Irish and European law was contravened by the refusal of the government to facilitate his right to vote. While acknowledging that the applicant had not exhausted all legal remedies at a national level, it noted that the European Convention on Human Rights had not been enacted into Irish law (see Behan and O'Donnell, 2008; Hamilton and Lines, 2009).

However, when rejecting the application, the arguments laid out by the ECmHR did not bode well for future litigation. 'The domestic courts recognise', according to the Commission, 'that an inevitable practical and legal consequence of imprisonment is that a great many of the constitutional personal rights of the prisoner are for the period of imprisonment suspended or placed in abeyance' (*Holland* v. *Ireland*, 1998). The Irish government argued that it would be impractical to have hundreds of ballot boxes in prisons throughout the country to facilitate prisoners from different constituencies and it was too much of a security risk and a burden on the prison service to allow the release of all 2,300 prisoners to vote. There was, the government maintained, no constitutional or convention guarantee of a postal vote. Previous opinions from the Commission had found that 'the deprivation of the right to vote, pursuant to a conviction by a court for uncitizenlike conduct' was not arbitrary. In rejecting the application, the Commission felt bound:

> to conclude that the legislator, in the exercise of its margin of appreciation, may restrict the right to vote in respect of convicted persons. Such restrictions could, in the Commission's opinion, be explained by the notion of dishonour that certain convictions carry with them for a specific period, which may be taken into consideration by legislation in respect of the exercise of political rights. Accordingly, the Commission concluded that the suspension of the exercise of the right to vote was not arbitrary and

did not affect the expression of the opinion of the people in the choice of legislature within the meaning of Article 3 of Protocol No. 1. (*Holland* v. *Ireland*, 1998)

In 2000, the position concerning prisoners' right to vote was set out in a book on Irish prison law. Prisoners had a right to be registered in the 'constituencies where they would normally be resident were it not for their incarceration'. They had no right to postal voting or access to a ballot box. There was clearly a degree of arbitrariness to this situation, as under some circumstances, serving prisoners would have been able to vote. If a prisoner 'happens to be on parole or temporary release at the time of an election, he is free to vote where registered' (McDermott, 2000: 335). However, there was no legal obligation on the government to put in place provision for voting for those physically present in prison on polling day.

Two years after the *Holland* judgment, another prisoner, Stiofán Breathnach, challenged the state on its refusal to provide facilities for prisoners to vote and met with initial success. The High Court ruled that prisoners retained the right to vote under the Electoral Act 1992. The Court declared that the failure of the state to provide a means whereby a prisoner could vote breached the constitutional guarantee of equality before the law. It ruled that prisoners enjoyed a right, which had been conferred on them by the constitution, to vote at elections for members of Dáil Éireann, and no legislation was currently in force that removed or limited that right. Drawing on European human rights standards, Mr Justice Quirke stated that failing to provide:

> The necessary machinery to enable him to exercise his right to vote comprises a failure which unfairly discriminates against him and (a) fails to vindicate the right conferred upon him by article 40.1 of the Constitution of Ireland to be held equal before the law and; (b) fails to vindicate the right conferred upon him by article 14 of the European Convention on Human Rights to vote in national and local elections without discrimination by reason of his status. (*Breathnach* v. *Ireland*, 2000)

During the hearing the state had acknowledged that the extension of postal voting to prisoners would not impose undue administrative demands, but Justice Quirke noted that no legislative provisions existed for such a facility. While the government was considering the judgment and the possibility of an appeal to the Supreme Court, opposition politicians sought clarification. The Minister for Justice, Equality and Law Reform, John O'Donoghue TD, acknowledged that 'prison rules do not prohibit the right of a prisoner to vote'. However, under current legislation, 'it would be prohibitive for the Prison Service to provide a means by which prisoners could exercise their constitutional right to vote at their home polling station' (Dáil Debates, 2000, vol. 523, col. 1145–6). There was some discussion in the Dáil about the possibility of legal action being taken to allow prisoners to exercise their franchise should an election be called in the near future. Soon after, the government appealed the High Court judgment.

In 2001, five judges of the Supreme Court unanimously rejected the right of citizens to exercise their franchise while in custody. The court had to consider if the absence of machinery to exercise their franchise while incarcerated violated their constitutional rights. In stark contrast to South African, Canadian and Israeli jurisprudence, the Irish Supreme Court found that while prisoners were detained in accordance with the law, some of their constitutional rights, including voting, were suspended. 'It is of course clear', Chief Justice Ronan Keane ruled, that 'despite the deprivation of his liberty which is the necessary consequence of the terms of imprisonment imposed upon him, the applicant retains the right to vote and could exercise that right if polling day in a particular election or referendum happened to coincide with a period when he was absent from the prison on temporary leave' (*Breathnach* v. *Ireland*, 2001). After outlining the jurisprudence, Susan Denham, future Chief Justice, acknowledged that the law providing voting facilities for those who could not physically access polling stations had developed since *Draper*. However, it did not extend to prisoners. She ruled that imprisonment was only part of the punishment.

> The applicant [Stiofán Breathnach] is in a special category of person – he is in lawful custody. His rights are consequently affected. The applicant is in the same situation as all prisoners: there is no provision enabling any prisoners to vote. Consequently, there is no inequality as between prisoners. The inequality as between a free person and a person lawfully in prison arises as a matter of law. It is a consequence of lawful custody that certain rights of the prisoner are curtailed, lawfully. Many constitutional rights are suspended as a result of the lawful deprivation of liberty. It is a consequence of a lawful order not an arbitrary decision.
>
> The applicant has no absolute right to vote under the Constitution. As a consequence of lawful custody many of his constitutional rights are suspended. The lack of facilities to enable the applicant vote is not an arbitrary or unreasonable situation. The absence of such provisions does not amount to a breach by the State of the applicant's right to equality. (*Breathnach* v. *Ireland*, 2001)

This put sentenced prisoners in a unique but similar situation. They were all prevented from voting, so there was no discrimination against the individual who took the case when the reference group was deemed to be other prisoners, rather than fellow citizens. However, the Chief Justice did point out that remand prisoners were in a different category, as they were not convicted. He suggested that the state might have to consider putting in place some practical arrangements to allow remand prisoners to vote.

The Supreme Court had set out the constitutional position. Nevertheless, even with this legal clarity, there was still some confusion about the rights of prisoners, leading some international and domestic commentators to point out what seemed like an inconsistency of being allowed to register, but effectively denied the opportunity, to cast a vote. Manza and Uggen (2006: 235) included Ireland in the 'No restrictions' section in a table on International Disenfranchisement Laws and the Voting Rights of Prisoners. Rottinghaus and Baldwin (2007: 697) stated: 'Ireland's Constitution, for instance has a provision allowing prisoners to vote but had never in practice established a formal arrangement for prisoners to vote'. The UK Department for Constitutional Affairs (DCA, 2006: 12) claimed that 'Ireland ... prohibits all prisoners from voting' but it recognised that while there was no legal ban in place, there was no mechanism to allow prisoners to vote (DCA, 2006: 20). These observations seemed to concur with the Irish government's position. In response to a parliamentary question, Minister for Justice, Equality and Law Reform, Michael McDowell, pointed out that there was no law on the statute books that prohibited prisoners from voting. However, he noted that the Supreme Court 'held that the State is under no constitutional obligation to facilitate prisoners in the exercise of that franchise' (Dáil Debates, 2004, vol. 586, col. 1345).

With government politicians reluctant to champion the rights of prisoners, and clarification provided by the courts, it seemed the matter was closed. However, despite the Supreme Court judgment, the issue would not go away and there continued to be some muted debate about the enfranchisement of prisoners. In 2002, a report from a government-appointed forum on the reintegration of prisoners recommended that the Department of Justice, and the prison service, should 'develop a Charter of Prisoner Rights (including consideration of extending voting rights to prisoners)' (National Economic and Social Forum (NESF), 2002: 71). In response to the initial *Hirst* judgment, Fine Gael (main opposition party) MEP, Avril Doyle, suggested consideration should be given to the enfranchisement of prisoners. She argued that many prisoners have 'never voted before, and participation in the democratic process may bring home to them the importance of rules and laws to secure freedom for all'. She concluded: 'All citizens shall, as human beings be held equal before the law' (cited in Hennessy, 2004). In 2005, Gay

Mitchell, a senior member of Fine Gael, proposed a private members bill on prisoner enfranchisement. With the possibility of the Fine Gael bill being discussed in the Oireachtas, the Tánaiste (deputy prime minister), Mary Harney, told the Dáil that the 'Government has cleared the legislation to provide for prisoners' voting by way of a postal ballot in their own constituencies' (Dáil Debates, 2005, vol. 612, col. 1115). This was just two months after the *Hirst* judgment in the Grand Chamber of the European Court of Human Rights.

Prisoner enfranchisement

Change comes quietly

In December 2006, the Oireachtas passed the Electoral (Amendment) Act to allow prisoners to vote by postal ballot. The legislation to enfranchise prisoners was introduced by a coalition government made up of Fianna Fáil and the Progressive Democrats, centre-right and right-wing parties respectively, not known for their liberal attitude towards prisoners. During the 1997 election, the main party in the coalition, Fianna Fáil, had stood on a zero tolerance platform (O'Donnell and O'Sullivan, 2003). Introducing the Electoral (Amendment) Bill to the Dáil in October 2006, Minister for Environment, Heritage and Local Government, Dick Roche, stated that the legislation would modernise existing electoral law and meet the government's obligations under the provisions of the European Convention on Human Rights. Referring to the *Hirst* judgment, he argued that while the legal position in the UK differed significantly from Ireland, 'in light of the judgment it is appropriate, timely and prudent to implement new arrangements to give practical effect to prisoner voting in Ireland' (Dáil Debates, 2006, vol. 624, col. 1978).

During the debates in the Oireachtas, other speakers referred to the *Hirst* judgment and the situation in the United States. One parliamentarian encouraged his fellow lawmakers to:

> remember the 2000 presidential election and the actions of George Bush's brother in Florida ... He had many people working for him to disenfranchise all the people who had a previous conviction. It gave a terrible picture of a democracy ... They were pursued to get them off the electoral register because of their race and political situation. (Fergus O'Dowd TD, Dáil Debates, 2006, vol. 624, col. 1987)

In the Dáil that debated the legislation, four TDs had been imprisoned previously. They included two members of Sinn Féin (linked to the IRA), jailed for paramilitary activity, and Socialist Party TD, Joe Higgins, who was imprisoned for a month during the lifetime of the 2002–7 parliament. Arthur Morgan, a former IRA prisoner, argued that 'it is a shame that a judgment was required against Britain in the European Court of Human Rights before the Government brought the law into line with best international civil rights practice'. He continued by asking: '[h]ave the people in our prisons not been penalised enough by their incarceration? One is sent to prison as, not for, punishment' (Dáil Debates, 2006, vol. 624, col. 2000).

Gay Mitchell TD, who had previously attempted to introduce his own bill for enfranchisement, believed that there was not widespread public support for this measure. However, he was keen to assure his parliamentary colleagues this was 'not about being soft on criminals ... People not only have rights but they also have responsibilities. It is time to stop recycling prisoners as if they were some sort of commodity and creating an environment in which prisoners have rights but no responsibilities, which takes from their dignity' (Dáil Debates, 2006, vol. 624, col. 2004). Previously he had argued that giving votes to prisoners 'would acknowledge their rights and also underline their responsibility for themselves and to society'. Echoing other advocates of prisoner enfranchisement he was perhaps overly optimistic, however, when he previously suggested that 'it might encourage politicians to take a greater interest in penal reform' (cited in McKenna, 2003).

One opposition speaker went further than the government and suggested that there was a wider context; the bill concerned not only prisoners but, if enacted, would lead to the enhancement of the democratic system. Fergus O'Dowd TD proclaimed that:

> It is important our prison system forms part of our reform agenda. It is also important that our criminal justice system is framed with the hope that this measure will in some small part go towards the rehabilitation of prisoners. It is an important social step and democratic reform which will, my party believes, strengthen our electoral process. (Dáil Debates, 2006, vol. 624, col. 1984)

In the course of the debates over the bill, no parliamentarian spoke against the enfranchisement of prisoners. Indeed, much of the time set aside for discussion of the bill was used to criticise the government for its failure to update the Register of Electors for the general population. Amendments were put forward to make sure prisoners would have trust in the electoral process. Outside parliament, there was little debate about prisoners and enfranchisement in the lead up to or during discussion of the legislation.

In stark contrast to the role played by the media (especially the tabloid press) elsewhere, particularly when it comes to the issues of crime and prisoners' rights, the Irish media was remarkably silent on the legislation. During the parliamentary debates, very few newspapers even mentioned it. During the passage of the legislation, the three Irish broadsheet daily papers, the *Irish Times*, the *Irish Examiner* and the *Irish Independent*, showed only one reference to it. This was a short parliamentary report in the *Irish Times* (O'Regan, 2006). The tabloid press, which has tended to take a hard line on crime and would generally oppose enhancing prisoners' rights, was silent on the issue. Even Irish editions of British tabloids ignored the story. In the *Irish Sun* and the *Irish Mirror* there were no reports about the legislation, or any outraged editorials or commentary about the 'privileges' of prisoners or the rights of victims. There were no letters to the editor in any of the newspapers about the bill or the significance of such a change in the law. Attempts by the Irish Penal Reform Trust (IPRT) to campaign on the issue (Hamilton and Lines, 2009) failed to generate widespread interest, either for or against the legislation. The press did not pick up a statement issued by the IPRT welcoming the passage of the legislation. There was a surprising lack of interest from the media. The only way to find out about the passage of the legislation was to read through the transcripts of parliamentary debates.

'And the sky didn't fall down ...'

So why did the Irish government decide to introduce legislation to allow prisoner voting, considering neither the prison population nor the general public was clamouring for it, the courts did not require it and little political capital could be expected in return? The impetus came from different sources, including European jurisprudence, human rights standards and the desire to locate Ireland in a progressive European setting. As this rather prosaic measure did not need to repeal any legislation and with limited financial cost, it eased the passage of the bill. The legislation had little impact on other electoral law and it did not affect criminal law. The lack of political and media opposition allowed the bill to pass relatively unnoticed among the general electorate, and therefore it did not need to use up any political capital by the initiators. There was also a desire to create not only the 'rehabilitated' but also the 'responsible' prisoner.

During the debates on enfranchisement, politicians were keen to stress that this legislation could be used to rehabilitate prisoners and encourage them to be more responsible. The 'rehabilitated' and 'responsible' prisoner has come into vogue in international prison policy and management (see Crewe, 2012; Garland, 2001). The concept of individual responsibility pervades prison management discourse internationally

(Bosworth, 2007) and reflects the wider drive towards responsibilisation that is characteristic of attempts to respond to crime in late modern societies (Garland, 2001). While incarcerated and being punished, prisoners are constantly reminded that it is up to them to begin to behave responsibly. Instead of trying to rehabilitate individuals, the late modern prison seeks to make them responsible (see Crewe, 2012). The objective of rehabilitation has morphed into responsibility. The discourse may be different. The sentiment remains the same. Yet this model of responsibility reveals a deeper meaning than at first glance. The concept of individual responsibility has become desirable in a way defined by the state.

At the time of the 2006 Act, the Irish Prison Service (IPS) mission was to help 'prisoners develop their sense of responsibility' and to enable them 'to return to live as a law abiding member of the wider community having reduced the risk to society of further offending' (IPS, 2001: 34). The United Nations Standard Minimum Rules (UNSMR) (United Nations, 1955: 11) state that the treatment of prisoners 'shall be such as will encourage their self-respect and develop their sense of responsibility'. The Council of Europe (2006: Rule 102) suggests: 'the regime for prisoners shall be designed to enable them to lead a responsible and crime-free life'.

Using enfranchisement to encourage prisoners to become more responsible was a clear theme in the discussions that took place. Introducing the bill, Minister for the Environment, Heritage and Local Government, Dick Roche, claimed that to enfranchise prisoners would encourage them to behave responsibly and appreciate the implications of citizenship. He believed that prisoners have not 'ceased to be a citizen or to enjoy the rights of the franchise. We should facilitate that person's exercise of the franchise and encourage responsibility as part of the education process ... There are rights and responsibilities of citizenship' (Oireachtas Select Committee on Local Government, 2 November 2006).

During the debate, Fergus O'Dowd TD, speaking for Fine Gael, was adamant that 'giving votes to prisoners would not only acknowledge their rights but would also underline their responsibility for themselves, and to society' (Dáil Debates, 2006, vol. 624, col. 1989). His position seemed to get some backing from an Irish citizen who voted for the first time from behind bars in the 2007 election and observed that the act of voting: 'brings a bit of pride to yourself ... It brings a sense of equality with the outside. Prisoners are so looked down on, but this is part of taking responsibility for yourself, isn't it?' (cited in Holland, 2007). Voting then, it was hoped, becomes part of the process of developing a pro-social, responsible identity. Uggen and Manza (2004: 214–15) speculated that the opportunity to vote was one of the most powerful symbols of stake-holding in a democratic polity: 'To the extent that felons begin to vote and participate as citizens in their communities, it seems likely that many will bring their behaviour into line with the expectations of the citizen role, avoiding further contact with the criminal justice system'.

There were a number of other reasons for prisoner enfranchisement. This measure could be introduced at virtually no financial cost, which is in contrast to the contention from those who oppose enfranchisement of prisoners that it is 'costly and impractical to allow prisoners to vote' (cited in Dhami, 2005: 239). Even the Chief Justice in the *Breathnach* case, while recognising that legislation would be needed to allow prisoners to vote, conceded: 'No doubt the provision of facilities to enable the applicant to exercise their rights by post or in the precincts of the prison would not be wholly impractical' (*Breathnach* v. *Ireland*, 2001). Prior to 2006, denying prisoners access to the ballot box was, in Ireland, as elsewhere, down to politics rather than practicalities.

During the early years of the twenty-first century, the Irish government proclaimed its desire to create a more progressive electoral system, and voting for prisoners was one such measure, along with a much criticised and subsequently abandoned introduction of electronic voting. In an interview with the author undertaken after the 2007 general election, Dick Roche TD, the minister responsible for enfranchisement, outlined his reasons for so doing. He was personally committed to, and publicly extolled, electoral reform. As a former Chairman of the Irish Commission for Justice and Peace, he believed that 'every citizen has the right to vote, even citizens that found themselves locked up'. Prisoner enfranchisement was, he argued, 'intrinsically the right thing' (interview with author, November 2007).

The influence of European human rights standards (see Griffin and O'Donnell, 2012) was recognised by Dick Roche. While the Irish government was aware there may be implications arising from *Hirst*, Ireland's situation was different from the UK, not having legislation barring prisoners from voting, but 'it was better to deal with it at our pace, of our own volition than have a challenge to us in the Court of Human Rights'. He argued that 'there is an obligation under the European Convention of Human Rights and Fundamental Freedoms which guarantees the right to vote', and there 'is a moral responsibility on members states that if you sign the Charter, you abide by the Charter'. Furthermore, the Minister for Justice, Michael McDowell, was 'very progressive' on the issue and 'saw the worth in this straight away' (interview with author, November 2007).

The lack of legislation banning prisoners from voting also made it easier to pass legislation without repealing any other measures. With no opposition in the cabinet, Oireachtas, media or among the general public, the short piece of enabling legislation initiated by a minister with a commitment to enfranchisement allowed legislation that has been controversial in many other jurisdictions to be passed relatively unnoticed in political or public discourse. The lack of media interest, not to mention opposition, is in contrast to much of the comment in tabloid papers in debates in the UK. So at minimal cost, with little opposition and a welcome from the Irish Penal Reform Trust, Dick Roche believed it was 'one of those serendipitous moments'. He located the issue in a wider context: 'If you take somebody who is marginalised all their lives and you just institutionalise that marginalisation ... they don't feel worthwhile as citizens'. Reflecting on the objectives of imprisonment, he suggested: 'if you believe that prison is not about punishment but is about rehabilitation, surely one of the first things that you should do as citizens, [is to make sure that] they are not cast into the outer darkness, that they have responsibility and obligations'. He acknowledged that 'the course of politics is changed by individual votes', and concluded: 'it just struck me that we had an opportunity to give prisoners the vote. And the sky didn't fall down' (interview with author, November 2007).

Conclusion

While the debates on the introduction of legislation to allow prisoners to vote in Ireland may have made reference to the international situation, the impetus for reform was more complex and local. The Irish case was unlike many other jurisdictions where 'disenfranchisement is a punitive sanction' (Uggen *et al.*, 2009: 64). As Ireland did not have a law barring prisoners from voting – it had legislation specifically setting out the practicalities of their registration – enfranchisement was a more mundane and practical measure. This made it easier to legislate for, rather than having to repeal other legislation. In contrast to circumstances elsewhere, the Irish legislature was not instructed by domestic courts to take action; indeed the courts interpreted the law so as to preserve the status quo. But with no political or media opposition to enfranchisement and at little cost, this eased the passage of a far-sighted and progressive piece of legislation. In an attempt, perhaps, to avoid possible political fallout from such a decision, those who introduced the new law reminded prisoners of their responsibilities and the obligations of citizenship, while reassuring the general public of their abhorrence of crime.

In the course of examining the role of prisoners in Irish politics, this chapter highlighted a number of significant issues around penal reform in general and prisoner enfranchisement in particular. The first was the lack of interest in penal reform by those who had spent time in Ireland's prisons. They promoted their prison past for political credibility, but were keen to distinguish themselves from, and felt little empathy with, those they had left behind. In a state built by prisoners and ex-prisoners, it was not those who had experience of imprisonment who reformed Irish prisons, or extended the franchise to embrace the incarcerated. That was left to future generations of politicians. Significantly, when legislation was enacted to allow prisoner voting, it came about quietly in comparison to the controversy it has caused in other jurisdictions. However, legislation to facilitate voting was a stand-alone issue. While being welcomed as a progressive electoral change, it was not part of a programme of penal reform. The improvement of conditions in Irish prisons and citizenship rights among convicts would, as those who founded the state reminded us, have to wait for another day. Nevertheless, within six months of the introduction of the legislation to allow them to vote, prisoners would get an opportunity to cast their ballot. It is to the 2007 general election we now turn.

4

Voting and political engagement

Introduction

The 2007 general election was the first opportunity for Irish prisoners to cast their ballots. This chapter examines their political engagement and voting behaviour. The first part briefly sketches some key characteristics of the Irish penal landscape, gives a description of the three institutions where prisoners were surveyed and then sets out the research process. Using data collected in these institutions, the second part outlines the results of the first survey of its kind among prisoners. It examines voting behaviour, party preference, political involvement and wider issues around levels of trust in political institutions and concludes with an analysis of who votes in prison. The final section examines the level of voting among prisoners in subsequent polls, to try to determine preliminary trends.

The Irish penal landscape

This section begins by briefly outlining some key features of the Irish penal landscape and then introduces the three prisons where research was undertaken. There are 14 prisons in the Republic of Ireland, including one dedicated women's prison – the Dóchas Centre (and accommodation for women in Limerick Prison) – and one juvenile facility, St Patrick's Institution. Historically, Ireland has had a relatively low level of imprisonment. By 2007, the rate of incarceration was at the lower end of the European scale, at 3,321 prisoners or 76 per 100,000, although by 2013 it had risen significantly to 4,306 or 94 prisoners per 100,000 (International Centre for Prison Studies, 2013). There are two open prisons holding just under 6 per cent of the prison population (IPS, 2009: 16). In contrast to many other European jurisdictions there is no open prison for women and the only open prison for juveniles was closed in 2002 (Warner, 2009).

There are a number of distinguishing features of the Irish penal system, including large numbers of short sentences, with a high turnover of prisoners and, consequently, pressure on space. In 2007, the majority of sentences were for less than six months (IPS, 2008: 12) and by 2012 over 60 per cent of committals received a similar sentence, with over 80 per cent of committals under sentence for less than 12 months (IPS, 2013: 21). Despite the relatively low (although increasing) incarceration rate, the high turnover indicates that alternatives to custody are underutilised, with prison 'used as the default sanction in many cases, rather than being held in reserve for the most serious offences' (O'Donnell, 2011: 84–5).

Pressure on space has led to overcrowding, which has become 'an over-riding characteristic' (Jesuit Centre for Faith and Justice (JCFJ), 2012: 1) of the prison estate. With a doubling of the prison population between 1995 and 2011, by 2012 nearly every institution was detaining greater numbers of prisoners than its 'original design capacity' and 60 per cent of the prison population were sharing a cell (JCFJ, 2012: 26). Overcrowding has a detrimental impact on the conditions of confinement in prison, human rights for those held there, prisoner–staff relations, access to programmes and is especially harmful for the prisoners who continue to 'slop out'.

By 2010, the practice of 'slopping out' was the 'norm for 30 per cent of the prison population' (Rogan, 2011: 204) and was still in operation in a number of institutions, including Cork, Limerick, Portlaoise and Mountjoy Prisons. It has been condemned regularly in both national and European Committee for the Prevention of Torture and Inhuman or Degrading Treatment or Punishment (CPT) reports. Conditions in Ireland's largest prison – Mountjoy – especially overcrowding and 'slopping out' in shared cells, have been criticised by the Inspector of Prisons (2009a: 26) as amounting to 'inhuman and degrading treatment'. Despite efforts to tackle some aspects of the conditions of confinement and improvements in the prison estate, especially the ending of 'slopping out' in Mountjoy, the practice remained one of the blights on the Irish penal landscape in the first and second decades of twenty-first century.

With so much of the debate in the Irish prison system on space, other issues 'receive significantly less attention but are no less important or indeed pressing' (Rogan, 2011: 203). Prison accountability and oversight mechanisms remain below international standards (see Owers, 2004 and 2006). There is no prisoner ombudsman – the first Inspector of Prisons was only appointed in 2002 and given statutory effect under the 2007 Prisons Act. It was also in 2007 that new Prison Rules were instituted, with prisoners and staff governed by an antiquated and almost Victorian set of rules dating back to 1947. The Visiting Committees, criticised by prisoners in this study and in various reports into the Irish penal system (examined in Chapter 6) still operate under legislation from 1925. The panacea to the problems in the penal system has been to suggest the building of new prisons. While new buildings may indeed be necessary this is only part of the solution and a deeper examination of the penal system is necessary. However, this has been inhibited because for long periods there has a 'poverty of thought' in the development of penal planning (O'Donnell, 2005: 105) and a 'lack of imagination to "do" punishment differently' (Rogan, 2011: 205). (For a more in-depth analysis of Irish penal policy, see O'Donnell, 2008 and 2011, and Rogan, 2011; for coercive confinement, see O'Sullivan and O'Donnell, 2012; and for the prison system, see JCFJ, 2012 and www.iprt.ie.)

Three institutions were chosen for the research. All three are adult male prisons, but have little else in common. Arbour Hill is a closed prison, the Training Unit is a semi-open institution and Shelton Abbey is an open prison.

Arbour Hill

Arbour Hill prison architecture reflects a more punitive and austere period, built as it was in 1842 to house British army personnel in Dublin. It closed down in 1922 after the establishment of the Irish Free State and was re-opened in 1975. By 2007 it was an adult prison for males over 18 years serving two or more years. It had a 'bed capacity of 139' and the 'daily average number in custody was 138' (IPS, 2008: 34). All cells have in-cell sanitation and television facilities. The vast majority of cells are for single accommodation and by 2007 it had generally avoided overcrowding.

Arbour Hill has a wide range of facilities and professional services, dealing with 'offending behaviour'. These include a Thinking Skills Programme, Group Skills Programme, Sex Offenders' Treatment Programme, Lifers' Programme and an Alternative to Violence Programme, in addition to a well-equipped education centre (Arbour Hill Visiting Committee (AHVC), 2008). According to the Inspector of Prisons (2007b: 73–4), Arbour Hill had 'a very settled population with little turnover'. He stressed that all of the prisoners to whom he spoke emphasised the positive environment. 'The staff/prisoner relationship is very good. There is a relaxed and homely atmosphere about the place', the Inspector concluded. 'Most of the prisoners are serving long sentences and consequently the staff and prisoners know each other very well ... All in all it appears to be a well-run prison'.

Training Unit

The Training Unit was established under the Prisons Act 1970 for 'the purpose of promoting the rehabilitation of offenders' and to provide places 'other than prisons for the detention of persons who have been sentenced to penal servitude or imprisonment'. It opened in 1975, with a more modern building, erected within the Mountjoy Prison complex, specifically as a pre-release centre. It is a semi-open, low security prison for males aged 18 years and over. It houses those serving sentences up to life imprisonment. Prisoners with long sentences are usually nearing the end of their time in prison when they arrive at the Training Unit. It has accommodation for 96 prisoners in single rooms. During 2007, 177 prisoners were transferred to the Training Unit. The average daily prisoner population was 91 (IPS, 2008: 38).

The Training Unit was designed to facilitate long-term prisoners' return to the community. In keeping with its semi-open status, the regime is less restricted than traditional prisons. Reflecting the idea that prisons can have different ethos and regimes, in the Training Unit there are no 'landings', just 'units', 'cells' are called 'rooms' and 'prisoners' are referred to as 'offenders'. Officers wear civilian clothes. The modern building reflects a more functional exterior and the interior reflects a different philosophy from a more traditional prison. Out-of-cell time is rather more than allowed elsewhere. Unusually for an Irish prison, meals are taken communally in the canteen. Up to a quarter of the prisoner population were released on a daily basis (Monday to Friday) to attend community based work and educational initiatives. Other activities included vocational training courses (Training Unit Visiting Committee Report, 2007: 1–2). There is an education department offering classes from literacy to music and computers to philosophy (Irish Prison Education Service, 2007: 29).

Shelton Abbey

Shelton Abbey, from the outside and within, betrays none of the security attributes associated with a prison, still bearing many of the hallmarks of its previous existence as a stately home. Originally it was the residence of the Earl of Wicklow and subsequently a hotel, before it was turned into a forestry school. It became an open prison in 1976. Shelton Abbey houses male prisoners from 19 years of age upwards, predominantly long-termers from closed prisons, who are coming towards the end of their sentence. Out-of-cell time is longer than even the semi-open Training Unit. The regime is relaxed and flexible as might be expected in an open prison. In 2007, it had a bed capacity of 60 with a daily average of 55 prisoners. It has a school, which covers a range of subjects, from mathematics to woodwork to history. It also has a farm where prisoners work. It is almost unique among Irish prisons with sleeping accommodation mainly in dormitories (IPS, 2008: 37).

The research
There were a number of components to this study. Through personal correspondence with official sources, data were collected from both the Irish Prison Service and the Department of the Environment, Heritage and Local Government about the numbers who had registered and voted in the 2007 election and subsequent polls. These data were not always complete but confirmed registration and voting trends in the various prisons. To piece together a general picture about the motivation behind enfranchisement, an interview was conducted with Dick Roche TD, who as Minister for the Environment, Heritage and Local Government introduced legislation to allow prisoners to vote. This was particularly useful in examining the government's stated reasoning behind the initiative and provided information that was used in the survey and interview questions. A content analysis of Irish newspapers was also undertaken.

A quantitative survey was carried out in three institutions and qualitative interviews in one. The questions for both the survey and interview were chosen after a review of political science and penology literature, prison writings, political science surveys and a pilot study. The questions were devised using a combination of material from the Eurobarometer poll conducted regularly by the European Commission (2007 and 2008), the Economic and Social Research Institute Irish Election Survey (2002 and 2007) and opinion polls in the *Irish Times*. As far as possible the questions replicated those used in surveys among the general public to allow for comparative analysis. However, some modification was necessary because of the uniqueness of the setting and awareness that literacy difficulties can be an issue among some members of the prison population.

Surveying was undertaken between November 2007 and March 2008. As this was a prison-wide survey in three institutions, every individual was offered the opportunity to participate. In order to replicate the survey administration across each of the institutions it was necessary to adapt to different prison routines, giving the survey to prisoners as they entered their cell, and picking it up on opening up for recreation or work. With Shelton Abbey having mostly dormitory accommodation, prisoners were approached throughout the day and waited on while they filled in the survey. Over 90 per cent of all prisoners were spoken with at least once. Arbour Hill Prison was surveyed first. With an average of 138 prisoners while the research was being undertaken, 91 completed surveys were returned, yielding an overall response rate of 66 per cent. In the Training Unit there was an average daily population of 84. In total, 57 prisoners, or 68 per cent, returned the completed survey. In Shelton Abbey, there were 58 prisoners and 39 surveys were returned, a response rate of just over 67 per cent. There were 280 prisoners in the three prisons. In total, 187 surveys were filled out and returned; overall a high completion rate at 67 per cent. Despite the different institutions, and regimes, there was remarkable similarity in the response rate.

Qualitative interviews were conducted in Arbour Hill between January and May 2008. Participation was voluntary. Over one third (50 prisoners) of those in the institution at the time agreed to be interviewed and 46 agreed to be audio recorded. Each was offered – and signed – a consent form. While there was a smaller number interviewed than surveyed, the topics covered were wider and more in-depth. It also provided an opportunity to sample the views of some of those who may not have responded to the survey because of literacy difficulties. In order not to put any burden on staff it was agreed that interviews could be conducted in a room in the education department. This allowed space to carry out interviews, access to interviewees (as officers called students for classes, it was straightforward for an interviewee to be added to their list) and without placing a burden on the prison in terms of time or resources.

No inducement or compensation was offered for participation in either the survey or interview. To respect the privacy of the individual, no official files on prisoners were consulted and during interviews participants were not asked the crime for which they had been convicted, only their sentence length and time served. All names used are pseudonyms. In order to protect their anonymity in such a small population, the only distinguishing feature included is sentence length and where there was only one interviewee on a particular sentence, this is given as an approximate duration.

Prisoners go to the polls

Registration

The passing of the Electoral (Amendment) Act in December 2006 allowed prisoners to register for a postal vote. Advertisements appeared in national newspapers in late January 2007 asking prisoners to register, with a closing date of 14 February. For this study, information was collated from the 14 prisons in Ireland and while the data is somewhat patchy as records vary between institutions, there are discernible trends in registration and voting patterns.

Overall, the level of registration was quite low, at just 451 out of approximately 3,359 prisoners (see Table 4.1). There were a number of reasons for this. There was a short time span (less than a month) from the issuing of registration forms to the closing date, which was unrealistically tight for both prisoners and prison authorities, bearing in mind that this was the first time voting could take place behind bars. The level of registration in different prisons may also indicate the institutional support, not only from the Irish Prison Service but also within individual prisons. Those with management, officers and education centres that were more proactive in encouraging prisoners to register would undoubtedly have led to a greater level of awareness, likely leading to increased registration and subsequent voting. There were also a number of prisoners who placed their names on the supplementary register which was open until a few weeks before the election. The best informed estimate is that there were 57 prisoners aged under 18 and therefore ineligible to vote and another 100 prisoners who were unable to vote due to nationality, leaving approximately 3,202 eligible prisoners. Thus, approximately 14 per cent of those eligible to vote registered to do so (see Table 4.1 and Behan and O'Donnell, 2008).

Other reasons for the low level of registration include the fact that the majority of sentences in Ireland are short. In 2007, 35.5 per cent were for less than three months and the majority for less than six months (IPS, 2008: 10 and 12). Those who had a short sentence and could have registered in February 2007 (closing date for registration) may not have been in prison three months later during the May general election, thereby removing the incentive to register, even if an individual was eager to vote. The parliamentary term is for a legal maximum of five years; however, it is at the discretion of the Taoiseach when to call an election. For short-term prisoners, there would not be the same urgency to register, considering the date of the election usually remains (albeit a

Table 4.1: General election 2007: voting in Irish prisons

No. in prison 15 May 2007	3,359
No. eligible to vote	3,202
No. registered	451
No. who voted	322
Percentage of eligible prisoners who voted	10.1
Percentage of registered prisoners who voted	71.4
Percentage of registered national population who voted	67.3

Source: Personal correspondence with Irish Prison Service and Department of the Environment, Heritage and Local Government, April–July 2007.

sometimes open) secret until the dissolution of the Dáil by the President. A number of prisoners who had been sentenced after the closing date for the supplementary register would not have been in time to register for a postal ballot. There is a clause in the legislation that allows a prisoner to vote at a Garda (police) station if released before polling day. Considering the rather ambiguous, indeed hostile, attitude many prisoners have towards the police, this is unlikely to draw many to vote in the event that they registered for a postal ballot and were released before polling day.

There were generally greater levels of registration in those institutions that housed long-term and more mature prisoners. Portlaoise Prison, with the largest percentage registered at 50 per cent (see Figure 4.1), housed those convicted for more serious crimes and paramilitaries from the dissident republican movement, who would be more politically active. They also tend to serve longer sentences. In 2006, out of a total of 115 prisoners in Portlaoise, 28 per cent were serving between four and seven years and nearly 30 per cent were serving over seven years; 57 per cent were over 30 years of age (Inspector of Prisons, 2006: 13–14). In 2004, nearly 60 per cent of prisoners in Arbour Hill were serving over seven years (AHVC, 2005: 1) and in 2005, nearly 60 per cent were over 40 years of age (AHVC, 2006: 1). Nearly 40 per cent of the Arbour Hill Prison population registered to vote.

The Dóchas Centre is the main prison for women in the Irish Republic with a number of non-Irish women incarcerated there. Just over 35 per cent of the population registered to vote. In the Training Unit, just over 10 per cent registered. St Patrick's Institution is for young offenders aged from 16 to 21 years. A number of its prisoners would be ineligible to vote due to age restrictions and it had a low rate of registration at just 15 per cent. Cloverhill is a remand prison with a transitory population, with a higher proportion born outside the state, most of whom would be ineligible to vote. It had a very low level of registration at less than 1 per cent. Shelton Abbey is an open institution where prisoners tend to spend a very short time, with three registering out of approximately 56–60 prisoners (see Figure 4.1).

The Inspector of Prisons made a number of visits in late January 2007 to review preparations for registration. Prison officers in the Training Unit informed him that each prisoner had received a form that was 'left on his bed in his room' (Inspector of Prisons, 2007a: 35–6). They expected a good response with five out of approximately 90 prisoners registered by the time of his visit, 10 days after advertisements had appeared in newspapers. Arbour Hill had notices on landings and forms were available in English and Irish. Officers were in liaison with two

Voting and political engagement

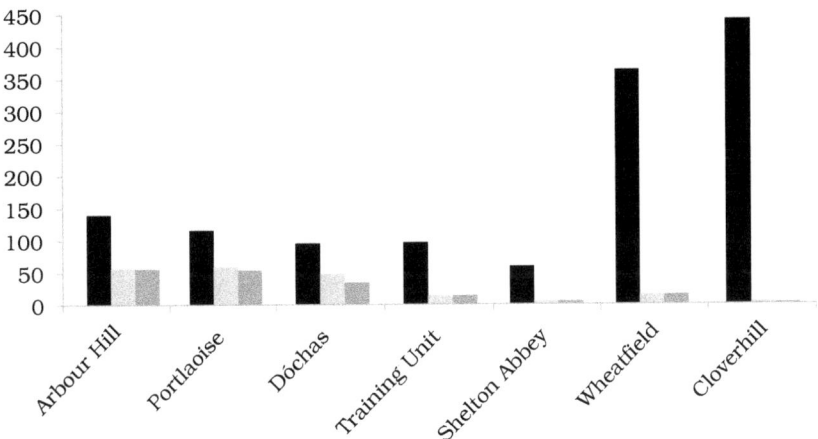

■ Number in Prison 15/05/07   Number who registered   ■ Number who voted

Figure 4.1: General election 2007: registration and voting patterns
Source: Personal correspondence with Irish Prison Service, April–June 2007.

officials from Dublin City Council and as it had a more settled community they anticipated that at least 50 per cent would vote (Inspector of Prisons, 2007a: 36).

Captive citizens
Given the low, but variable, level of registration what do we know about how eligible prisoners behaved on polling day? The evidence is somewhat sketchy as not all institutions reported full details of numbers incarcerated, registered and voting. Table 4.1 sets out the overall percentage of those registered who voted. This was relatively high at 71.4 per cent. This is a minimum estimate as some of those who had registered would have been discharged before polling day. This compares favourably with the national turnout in the election at 67.3 per cent of registered voters (Gallagher and Marsh, 2008: 234–5).

Figure 4.1 sets out details of seven prisons, those at either end of the registration and voting spectrum. There were interesting inter-institutional variations. For example, the turnout of registered voters in Arbour Hill Prison was 98 per cent and in Portlaoise Prison it was 91 per cent. Data from some other prisons was incomplete with imprecise numbers for registration. In Cloverhill remand prison (which, as noted, is characterised by a very high turnover of prisoners), one prisoner voted out of a population of 427 prisoners. In the Training Unit, 12 prisoners voted out of a prison population of 95. In Shelton

Abbey, three prisoners voted out of a population of between 56 and 60 prisoners.

Seanad Éireann is the Upper House of the Irish parliament and voting takes place subsequent to the Dáil election. It has 60 senators, of which 43 are elected in panels by local and national politicians. Six are returned by graduates of the National University of Ireland and University of Dublin and 11 are nominated by the Taoiseach. The method of voting for Seanad Éireann has been by postal ballot since its inception in 1937. Therefore, serving prisoners who were registered would always have been in a position to cast a vote if their ballot paper had been forwarded to them (Gallagher, 2001: 3). A jailed county councillor, Michael Fahy, was on the electoral register for Seanad Éireann (Office of Public Works, 2007) and according to one newspaper report, the first ever to vote in the Seanad elections from behind bars (*Irish Times*, 2007b). What makes this even more notable is that the councillor was serving a 12-month prison term for fraud and attempted theft from the local authority of which he was a member (Sheridan, 2007). Michael Fahy had previously served as a member and then chair of a prison visiting committee. In 2011, the Court of Criminal Appeal quashed his conviction after it was deemed unsafe.

Electoral outcomes
However variable the turnout, could the enfranchisement of prisoners alter the outcome of an election in Ireland? Given the relatively small number of prisoners it is unlikely that their impact would be as great as it might be in countries with larger custodial populations. Uggen and Manza (2002: 794) estimated that felon and ex-felon disenfranchisement 'may have altered the outcome of as many as seven recent U.S. Senate elections and at least one presidential election'. Even though the numbers incarcerated are substantially lower, the nature of the Irish electoral system – Proportional Representation, Single Transferable Vote (PR-STV) – allows for a small number of voters to exercise a more decisive influence, especially in local or general elections.

PR-STV is designed to give smaller parties and minority interests the opportunity to be represented in parliament. The vagaries of the system mean that a small number of second, third or fourth preferences can decide the outcome of a particular constituency and in a close-run poll can influence who gets elected. During the 2002 general election a handful of votes separated the winners and losers in a number of constituencies. In Limerick West, one vote (out of 35,669 cast) was enough to give victory to Fine Gael's Dan Neville over his party colleague, Michael Finucane. John Dennehy's victory over Kathy Sinnnot in Cork

Voting and political engagement

South Central was by just six votes. In Wicklow, Mildred Fox defeated Nicky Kelly (a former prisoner who was later given a presidential pardon) by 19 votes after a marathon election count. We can only speculate how the outcome might have been different if the 174 Wicklow men and women committed to prison in 2002 had been allowed to vote (IPS, 2004: 16). Of course not all would have been inside on polling day, but potentially, many would have wanted to show solidarity with a former prisoner.

The 2007 election was not as tight with only two candidates winning by less than 100 votes (*Irish Times*, 2007a). Data available for registration patterns for prisoners is recorded by the Department of the Environment on a county by county basis. While few counties share boundaries with constituencies, the margins in the 2007 election meant that even if all registered prisoners voted as a bloc in a given constituency they would not have altered the outcome. However, in the event that the tight contests of 2002 were repeated in future years, it is possible that prisoners, like all citizens, could influence who gets elected and, ultimately, forms a government.

Political participation and civic engagement

We know little about prisoners' political preferences, participation rates and levels of civic engagement (for ex-prisoners, see Farrall *et al.*, 2011). A limited number of studies give indications about prisoners' attitude towards, and understanding of, politics (Manza and Uggen, 2006), the level of turnout where allowed to vote (Storgaard, 2009), and civic engagement inside prison (Solomon and Edgar, 2004). Having set out the national data, and to probe deeper into the politics of prisoners, the following are the results from surveys in the three institutions outlined above. Prior to the election, prisoners were not included in opinion poll data, either as part of surveys among the general public or a distinct group. This is the first comprehensive study of their voting preferences and their attitudes towards voting and political engagement in any jurisdiction.

The politics of prisoners

In the 2007 election, 451 prisoners registered and 322 prisoners voted, indicating a turnout of 74.1 per cent. In the three prisons surveyed, 154 of the respondents (out of 187 surveyed) were in prison in May 2007 and of these, 70 voted. Figure 4.2 indicates the level of party support among prisoners. Of those who expressed a preference (not necessarily first preference), Fianna Fáil (centre-right) polled 28 per cent,

Sinn Féin (republican) got 24 per cent and the Green Party (environmental) received 17 per cent support. The largest party in the state in the 2007 election, Fianna Fáil, was the most preferred party among prisoners.

Among the whole population in the general election, Fianna Fáil got 41.6 per cent of the total first preference vote, Fine Gael (centre-right) 27.3 per cent, Labour (centre-left) 10.1 per cent, Sinn Féin received 6.9 per cent of the first preference votes and the Green Party 4.7 per cent. The Progressive Democrats (right wing) got 2.7 per cent and the Socialist Party (left wing) won 0.6 per cent. Others received 6.6 per cent (Gallagher and Marsh, 2008: 234–5). If the prison vote were replicated among the Irish electorate, those who would benefit most would have been the Green Party and Sinn Féin, as they were supported in much greater numbers by prisoners than among the whole population. Figure 4.2 compares party preference among prisoners and the general population for the 2007 general election.

While the survey was not directly comparable with election results as it asked for voting choice rather than first preference, responses to other questions revealed that there was a greater level of support for Sinn Féin and the Green Party among the prisoners than the general population. Asked which party, if any, best represented their views, of those who answered this question in the affirmative, nearly 14 per cent believed

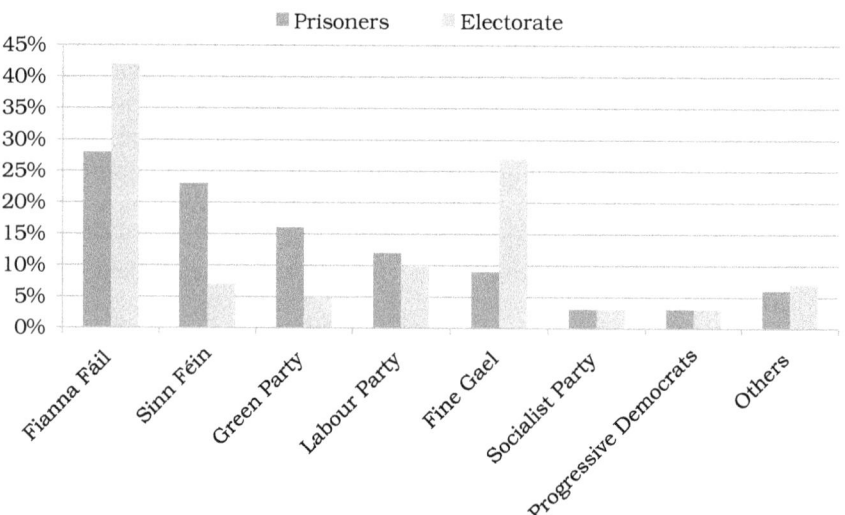

Figure 4.2: General election 2007: party preference
Sources: Irish prison election survey and Gallagher and Marsh (2008: 234–5).

the Green Party and just over 25 per cent believed Sinn Féin represented their views 'reasonably well'. Some respondents, nine in total, gave two parties as their answer. Of these, five included the Green Party and four included Sinn Féin.

There was a low response to the question as to whether any party was more honest, which may reflect a certain cynicism towards politics and politicians. Only 60 respondents indicated that any one political party 'was more honest than others'. Of these, only 8 per cent believed it was Fianna Fáil; at the other end of the spectrum, 25 per cent believed the Green Party were more honest and just under 17 per cent believed that Sinn Féin were more honest than other parties. Of those surveyed, 16 had been members of political parties. The largest number, five, had been members of Sinn Féin. Other parties included the Labour Party, Fianna Fáil, Sinn Féin, the Workers Party and two were members of political parties outside the state.

The support for and trust in Sinn Féin and the Green Party may reflect the fact that prior to the 2007 election, the Green Party had not been in power nationally, nor had Sinn Féin been part of a national government since the foundation of the Irish Republic. Lack of power can increase support for a political party that has been untainted by the (either real or perceived) trappings of office. Those parties that stood on a left-wing and green agenda are taken for the purposes of this study as representing an anti-establishment platform. They fared better among the prison, than the wider, population. Taking Sinn Féin, the Labour Party, the Green Party and the Socialist Party together, they achieved 54 per cent of the prisoner vote compared to just over 23 per cent among the general population.

Tradition of voting
Asked if they had ever voted prior to the 2007 general election, 52 per cent said they had. Just 33 per cent replied that they had not, which may be related to age, as 14 per cent were in the 18–24 age group, most of whom would not have been eligible to vote in the previous election, which took place five years earlier. The remainder did not answer this question. There were minor inter-institutional variations to this figure, with 48 per cent of the Training Unit prisoners surveyed having voted previously, 51 per cent of Shelton Abbey prisoners having voted previously, and Arbour Hill, possibly because of the older and better educated population, having the highest level of prior voting at 57 per cent.

Despite the low level of turnout in the election, an overwhelming majority believed in prisoner enfranchisement. Even if it was not utilised, there was a belief among prisoners that they have a right to vote: 91 per cent believed all prisoners should have the right to vote, 6 per cent believed only some had the right and 3 per cent believed prisoners should not have the right to vote (see Chapter 5 for further analysis).

Political prisoners?
Interviewees were asked a number of questions related to their attitude to politics and civic engagement. This section began by asking them to self-determine whether they were political. Four options were offered and, as indicated in Figure 4.3, 10 per cent described themselves as very political, 26 per cent as political, 39 per cent as not very political and 25 per cent as not political at all. Many prisoners lack belief in and trust of political institutions as outlined later in this chapter. If politics, as some believed, had negative connotations they may have been hesitant to identify with it by defining themselves as political.

Political knowledge
Having asked interviewees about how they would describe themselves, a series of questions was used to determine their level of political knowledge. It began with what might be considered a relatively easy question, who is the Taoiseach? As can be seen in Figure 4.4, at 90 per cent there was a high level of knowledge of that office holder. No respondent got this answer wrong; the other 10 per cent did not answer.

While only 31 per cent correctly identified the Tánaiste as Brian Cowen, the same percentage answered the question incorrectly. All but eight of those respondents identified Mary Harney as Tánaiste. As Mary Harney had been Tánaiste from 1997 to 2006, and was a high profile

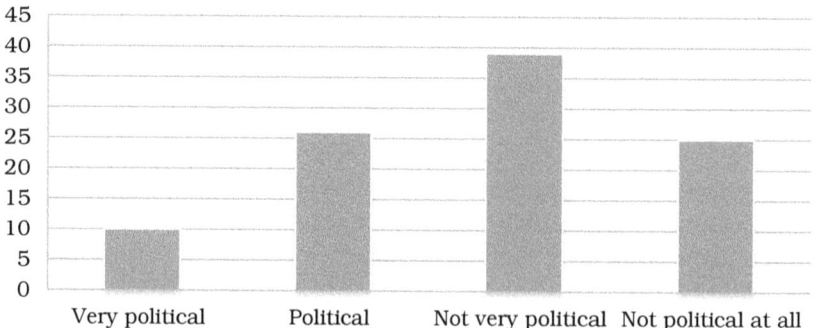

Figure 4.3: Are you political?

Voting and political engagement

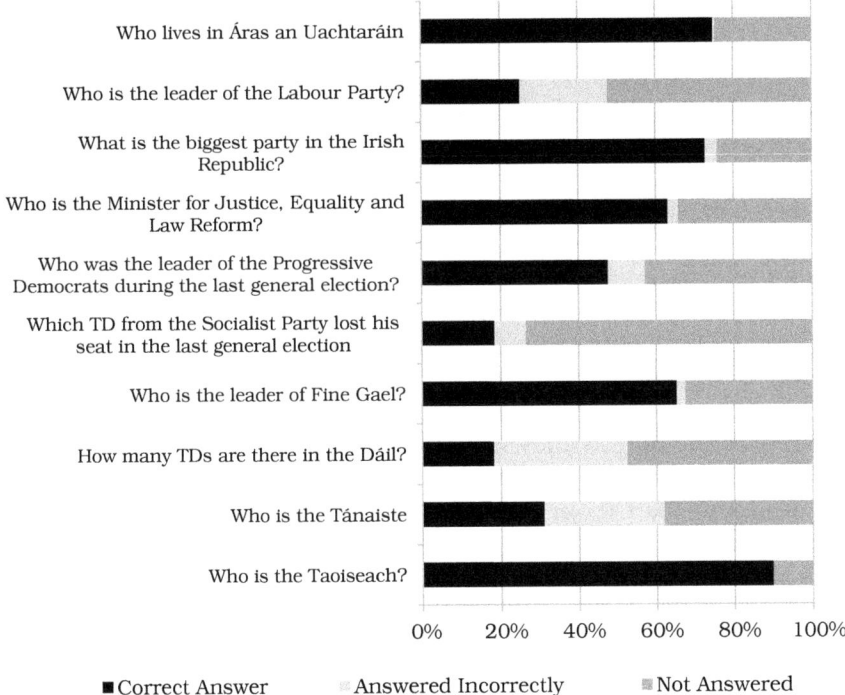

Figure 4.4: Political awareness among prisoners

minister for health from 2004, this indicated a good level of political awareness, if a little dated. This was a trend running through many of the answers. Rather ironically, the survey revealed at times as much about political awareness from the wrong answers, as from those that were correct.

Some room for flexibility was allowed in the answer about the number of TDs. The correct number was 166, but those who answered between 160 and 170 (18 per cent) were deemed correct. At 65 per cent, there was strong recognition that the leader of the main opposition party, Fine Gael, was Enda Kenny. Interestingly, while there was a low level of awareness, at 18 per cent, that Joe Higgins was the leader of the Socialist Party, who lost his seat in the 2007 election, nine respondents suggested that it was Joe Costello, former head of the Prisoner Rights Organisation, a Labour Party TD at the time of the survey. It was also noted by some respondents that Joe Higgins had been a former prisoner, having spent one month in prison for a political campaign against non-payment of local council charges.

There was a relatively high degree of recognition at 48 per cent that the leader of the Progressive Democrats during the 2007 general election was Michael McDowell. This may have been influenced by their present circumstances; not only had he been the leader of one of the government parties, he had also been Minister for Justice, Equality and Law Reform, with responsibility for penal policy. However, 18 respondents, or nearly 10 per cent, identified Mary Harney as Progressive Democrat leader during the 2007 election. She had a high profile over a prolonged period of time as Progressive Democrat leader from 1993 until 2006; again this showed some political awareness, despite an incorrect answer.

Considering the importance the justice system plays in the life of a prisoner, it is understandable that 63 per cent of respondents were aware of the identity of the Minister for Justice at the time, Brian Lenihan. There was widespread knowledge that Fianna Fáil was the largest party in the state, with nearly 73 per cent getting this question correct. While the leader of the Labour Party had little recognition, this may be due to the change in leadership in September 2007, shortly before the survey was initially carried out; 25 per cent answered correctly that it was Eamon Gilmore. However, like other questions that related to a relatively recent change of personnel, there were some dated answers; 15 per cent suggested that the leader of the Labour Party was Pat Rabbitte (the previous leader), four of those stating that he 'was' and five putting a question mark beside the name. Finally, three quarters of those questioned knew that the President lived in Áras an Uachtaráin. Only one respondent gave an incorrect answer, believing that the Taoiseach, Bertie Ahern, lived there. This was an incorrect, but not uninformed answer, as many international heads of government have their own residence. Ireland does not.

While some respondents' knowledge was a little dated, the survey revealed there were varying degrees of awareness about politics and current affairs. Higher levels may indicate an interest in current affairs and political engagement. Of those surveyed, 10 per cent got all the answers wrong or did not fill them out. This suggests that 22 per cent had a low level (1–3 questions correct) of political knowledge, 43 per cent (4–7 correct) had a fair knowledge and 25 per cent (8–10 correct) had a good level of political knowledge, including 5 per cent who got all ten questions correct.

Once an election or referendum is called, there are legislative safeguards to guarantee fairness of coverage in traditional media, especially television and radio news. There are also election rallies, campaign buses, keynote speeches and various informal opportunities to discuss the impending vote. Other methods of propagating a candidate's/party's message include posters, election literature, media debates and personal canvassing. Only 12 per cent of those interviewed had received political literature (mostly those who had not been in prison at the time) for the 2007 election. During the debate on the introduction of the Electoral (Amendment) Act 2006, there was some discussion about the dissemination of election literature to prisoners. It was agreed that as the postal register is open to the public, it would not be desirable to reveal that a particular elector is in prison. The only person who would know about the voter's incarceration would be the returning officer, not individual political parties.

An elector registers at the address they lived at prior to their incarceration. Election literature is sent to the home address and it is up to the people at that address to pass it on to the prisoner. While the legislation does not bar politicians from visiting prisons, ultimately it would be up to either the Irish Prison Service nationally, or each prison governor locally, to facilitate or refuse a visit by a candidate if they wished to engage in electioneering inside prison (see Chapter 5 for further discussion).

Informed citizens are in a better position to contribute to the democratic polity. Information comes through a variety of fora, including education, political engagement, discussions about current affairs and from newspapers and television. During the 2007 election campaign, those held in Irish prisons did not have access to the internet. Politicians were aware of the importance of not only allowing prisoners to vote, but also giving them the opportunity of making an informed choice when casting their ballots. The Minister for the Environment, Heritage and Local Government, Dick Roche, pointed out during the parliamentary debates that prisoners 'have access to media and the coverage of political matters in the general course of events' (Oireachtas Select Committee on Environment and Local Government, 2 November 2006). The Irish Prison Service pointed out that: 'Prisoners have access to a range of media forms including newspapers, radio and TV' (personal correspondence with IPS, 2008). In the decade prior to the election, televisions were installed in Irish prisons. Virtually every cell now has a television, allowing prisoners to keep up to date with news and current affairs. The vast majority of Irish prisoners also have radios in their cells.

Of those surveyed, 81 per cent watched television news every day, 10 per cent once or twice a week, 4 per cent less frequently and nearly 2 per cent did not watch television news at all. The remainder did not answer. The survey found that 50 per cent read a newspaper daily, with another 29 per cent reading newspapers once or twice a week, and 6 per cent on Sundays only. A further 6 per cent did not read newspapers at all and 9 per cent did not answer this question. The latter two categories include those who have literacy difficulties and whose English was not their first language and therefore might not be in a position to understand the printed media. Of those who read newspapers, 32 per cent read tabloids, which are lighter on political news and current affairs, and 23 per cent read broadsheets. Another 25 per were somewhat less discriminating and read both tabloid and broadsheet. The remainder did not answer this question.

In 2008, prisoners in Ireland received €2 a day as a gratuity payment. Daily newspapers cost from €1 to €1.80 each. Some prisoners paid for their newspapers from their own resources. Others got a copy (especially local newspapers) from visitors. Despite receiving such a modest amount, some bought newspapers daily. However, as might be expected in a closed community, there was a lot of second-hand distribution of newspapers and therefore much greater readership, especially of Sunday newspapers. Prison libraries also carried newspapers. (For an analysis of the impact of, and engagement with, the media among prisoners in the United Kingdom, see Jewkes, 2002.) With 91 per cent of respondents watching television news at least once a week and 85 per cent reading newspapers at some stage over the course of the week, Irish prisoners seemed to have relatively easy access to various media to keep themselves informed about current affairs and events outside the prison walls.

Political issues among prisoners
It is often argued that the electorate decide who to vote for out of self-interest. Yet this survey seems to challenge this contention: 62 per cent of respondents said they would not vote for Fianna Fáil or the Progressive Democrats simply because they introduced the law allowing prisoners to vote, arguably a far-sighted and progressive advance in the rights of prisoners. Only 34 per cent answered that this would influence their decision. Two respondents suggested that they would vote for Fianna Fáil (centre-right) but not for the Progressive Democrats (right wing). Many were more nuanced in their answers, some arguing that because they had been given access to the franchise, this alone was not a good enough reason. Unfortunately for the politicians and parties that introduced the legislation, there was a widespread belief among prisoners that the Irish government had not voluntarily initiated legislation to facilitate prisoners in their right to vote. There was a perception that the European Court of Human Rights forced this change on the government. One respondent wrote on his survey: 'the right of prisoners to

Voting and political engagement

vote was a previous European Court Judgement'. Another elaborated: 'Both parties fought hard to stop prisoners having the power to vote. Prisoners can now vote, because a prisoner took the above mentioned parties to court'.

The political concerns of prisoners mirrored somewhat those in wider society. They suggested that polices other than those related to their location were more important in terms of determining political preferences. As can be seen in Figure 4.5 there was widespread interest in matters other than what might be considered 'prisoner' or 'criminal justice' issues. When asked to identify the most important political issue, 32 per cent listed the health service. The next most important issue was the economy at 17 per cent and political corruption came next at 12 per cent. Others included drugs and the environment. Only 4 per cent mentioned what might be categorised as 'prisoner issues'.

During the 2007 general election campaign, polls found that the 'quality of health service was the issue most often cited as important to respondents' (Ó Muineacháin and Gallagher, 2008: 152). In the Eurobarometer survey of the community outside prison taken in autumn 2007 (fieldwork conducted between September and November), interviewees were asked for the two most important issues facing Ireland. The highest was crime at 57 per cent. Health care was next at 45 per

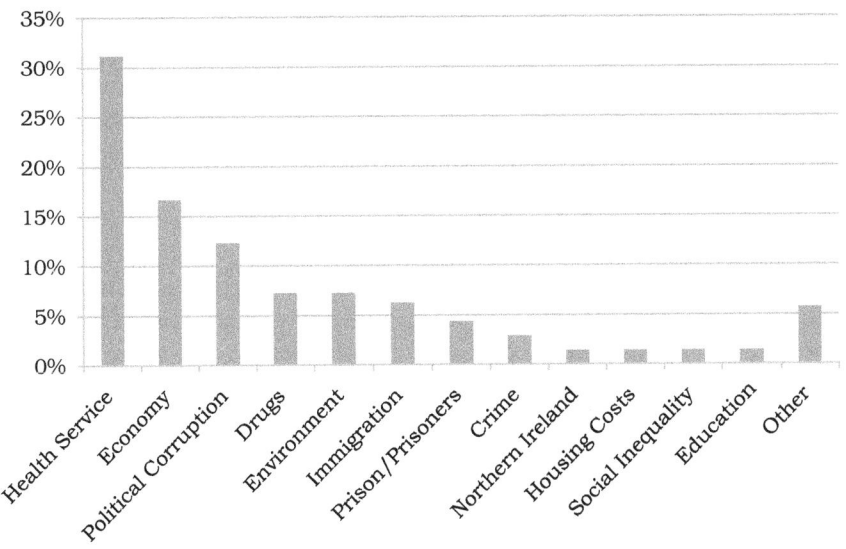

Figure 4.5: Political issues
Note: The following were mentioned once in the 'other' categorisation: globalisation, homelessness, sovereignty, neutrality, the European Union, Travellers rights, transport and taxation.

cent. Inflation was one of the two most important issues for 22 per cent. Immigration was a priority for 14 per cent, unemployment for 14 per cent, the economic situation 8 per cent, education 6 per cent and protecting the environment 4 per cent (European Commission, 2007: 19). By the spring of 2008 (fieldwork conducted between March and May 2008), there had been a change in the top two, with health care (53 per cent) overtaking crime (51 per cent), and other matters lagging behind, with the economy at 14 per cent, immigration at 5 per cent and education at 5 per cent (European Commission, 2008: 6).

The survey indicates that prisoners, while being cut off physically from the rest of society, remained affected by the political issues outside. During the four-month period of surveying, the major political issues being reported in the Irish media were the health service and the downturn in the Irish economy after an unprecedented period of growth. Access to various media and educational classes give prisoners the opportunity to keep themselves up to date with current affairs. Considering that, in some respects, the most important issue among prisoners was the same as for those outside, this shows how much prisoners are affected by external influences. However, there was one major exception. The worldview of those interviewed was shown to be in sharp contrast with the wider public in their concern – or relative unconcern – about crime. Less than 5 per cent saw crime as a major issue, yet by the spring of 2008, 51 per cent of the Irish people felt that crime was the most important issue. It is possible that because many of those interviewed may feel safe as they are young, male (the group most likely to be victimised) and – ironically – behind bars, crime is of little immediate concern at this moment in their lives. It is also possible that because of their actions they do not attach the same importance to crime as those outside prison.

Democratic deficits
The numbers that vote, define themselves as being political, join political parties or become informed about the institutions of power can reveal the level of interest and/or confidence in the democratic process. Other indicators as to whether individuals engage politically might include an understanding that voting matters and can effect change. A belief that there are duties and responsibilities that accompany the rights of citizenship is also important.

To try to unravel the attitudes to, and perceptions of, democracy among Irish prisoners, the following statement was offered for consideration: 'Whatever I think about the parties and candidates, I really do think it is my duty to go out and vote'. Respondents were given a scale

Voting and political engagement

of one to ten. Of the 180 who answered this question, 14 per cent strongly disagreed with this statement (1–3 on the scale of 1–10), 38 per cent were uncommitted (4–7 on the scale), but 48 per cent believed strongly that they had a duty to vote (8–10 on the scale). This line of questioning was developed further with the statement that: 'So many people vote, my vote does not make a difference to who is in government'. Of those who answered, 47 per cent strongly or moderately disagreed with this standpoint, 31 per cent neither agreed nor disagreed and 22 per cent strongly agreed. A final statement in this section put forward the proposition: 'It doesn't matter which political party is in power, in the end things go on much the same'. Of those who answered this question, 27 per cent strongly disagreed, 28 per cent neither agreed nor disagreed and 45 per cent strongly agreed. From the above figures there seemed to be a belief in the importance of voting, even if a large section of the prison population did not avail of this opportunity, and did not believe that their votes would contribute to meaningful political change.

An important element of a healthy democracy is a belief by citizens that the government listens to or takes seriously what is pressing to voters, their voices are heard and they can influence those who hold the levers of power. Only 18 per cent believed that there was a high level of interest in the concerns of the electorate by the government. Another 32 per cent believed that the government was not interested in the concerns of the electorate and 50 per cent believed they were neither interested nor uninterested. While there were no comparative findings available with the general public, prisoners were clearly sceptical that the government was interested in the concerns of the electorate.

How much did Irish prisoners feel they had to contribute to the development of Irish society? While not all respondents answered this set of questions, when asked how often the government listened to views of prisoners, only 3 per cent believed that they always listened and 84 per cent believed that they never or almost never listened to their perspective. In answer to a question about how interested Irish society was in the plight of prisoners, 68 per cent believed that they were not interested at all, 13 per cent believed that they were neither interested nor uninterested and 5 per cent believed that they were very interested. Given the statement that: 'The government protects the rights of prisoners', 16 per cent agreed (totally or tending to) with this statement, 71 per cent disagreed (totally or tending to) and the remainder were undecided. From these responses, a large majority of prisoners did not believe that the government was interested in their views generally or in safeguarding their rights. This could have consequences in terms of non-engagement with authorities in which they had little faith, and political and civic institution more generally.

Trust

Lack of trust in civic and political institutions can be transformed into non-engagement. Low levels of trust can lead to high levels of disengagement, with little confidence in the possibility of change either by an individual, group or society. Putnam (2000: 137) believed that 'people who trust others are all-round good citizens, and those more engaged in community life are more trusting and more trustworthy'. On the other hand 'the civically disengaged believe themselves to be surrounded by miscreants and feel less constrained to be honest themselves. The causal arrows among civic involvement, reciprocity, honesty and social trust are as tangible as well-tossed spaghetti'.

A belief in human agency, the opportunity to influence those in power and participation in civic society are essential for a healthy democratic polity. Among the ten Guiding Principles for active citizenship are 'openness, accountability and trust', which 'will help maximise participation in the democratic and decision-making process' (Taskforce on Active Citizenship, 2007c: preface). With slight variations, there were generally low levels of trust among prisoners across a range of political and civic institutions (see Figure 4.6). Trust may have been depleted by reports from the then ongoing tribunals of inquiry to examine various

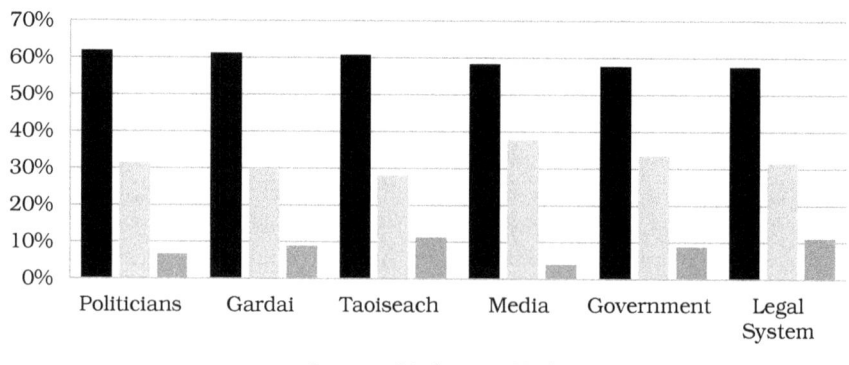

Figure 4.6: Levels of trust

The following questions were asked: On a scale of 1–10, what is your level of trust in 1) Politicians; 2) Government; 3) Taoiseach; 4) Legal System; 5) Gardai; 6) Media. On this scale, 1–3 is low, 4–7 is medium and 8–10 is high.

allegations of corruption in Irish political, civic and business life (see Byrne, 2012 for corruption in Irish politics). These were mentioned by a number of respondents and elaborated in interviews outlined in the next chapter.

There were low levels of trust in various civic and political institutions. Those trusted least were politicians, who scored 62 per cent in the 'low' category. The legal system was 58 per cent in the 'low' category. All the major civic and political institutions and the Taoiseach fared badly in levels of trust, with only 4 per cent of those surveyed with a 'high' level of trust in the media, while 11 per cent had a 'high' level of trust in the Taoiseach.

According to the autumn 2007 Eurobarometer poll, 33 per cent of the Irish population had trust in the Dáil/national parliament, 32 per cent in the national government and 22 per cent had trust in the political parties. Regarding the media, 68 per cent had trust in radio, 68 per cent in television and 40 per cent had trust in the press (European Commission, 2007: 16–17). By the spring of 2008, 42 per cent of the Irish population had trust in the the Dáil/national parliament, 37 per cent had trust in the national government and 27 per cent had trust in political parties. Furthermore, 72 per cent had trust in radio, 68 per cent in television and 40 per cent in the Internet (European Commission, 2008: 3). Clearly prisoners are less trusting than society at large, perhaps reflecting what they perceive as their treatment by the gardai, courts and media and the way they tend to be referred to in political discourse. Citizens with low levels of trust are less likely to vote and participate in political and civic society. Civic engagement needs trust; it lubricates its progress.

Who votes in prison?

To examine the voting patterns among prisoners, T-tests and Chi-square tests were used to test for the differences between those who voted and those who did not. Significant variables were then entered in a logistic regression model, where the dependent variable was voting or not voting in the 2007 general election while in prison.

Age, education, sentence length and institution

Voters and non-voters were compared on three variables – age, education attainment and sentence length – to determine if they could be used to understand voting patterns. Age was divided into three categories; 'under 35', 'between 35 and 55' and 'over 55'. Older citizens are were more likely to vote. Of those aged under 35 years, 32 per cent voted;

in the 35 to 54 years category, 49 per cent voted; and 55 per cent voted in the over 55 years category. Using a Chi-square test ($X^2 = 5.56$, $p = .06$, ns), the result was not statistically significant (although it was very close to being so).

The respondents were divided into three different levels of education: those who had 'primary education or less', those who had 'completed the Junior or Leaving Certificate Examinations' (high school examinations) and those who had 'completed a third level course', whether diploma or degree. Among those with primary education or less, 36 per cent (16 out of 44) voted; those who completed a Junior or Leaving Certificate examination, 38 per cent (30 out of 78) voted and among those who had completed a third level qualification, 57 per cent (23 out of 40) voted. Although people with a higher level of education are more likely to vote, the difference was not significant across the education range ($X^2 = 4.88$, $p = .09$, ns).

Examining the relationship between sentence length and voting, 39 per cent (26 out of 66) of those with shorter sentences (less than five years) voted in 2007. Of those with longer sentences, 45 per cent (42 out of 93) voted. This difference was not significant ($X^2 = 5.25$, $p = .47$).

The test to find if there were significant differences among the three prisons for those who voted and those who did not in the 2007 election indicated that the inter-institutional variations were not statistically significant ($X^2 = 2.15$, $p = .34$).

Voting history and representation
To examine if factors such as voting history and an element of self-identification with a political party distinguished voters and non-voters, the responses to two questions were analysed. Asked if they had voted before, 20 per cent of those who voted in 2007 had not voted previously. There were significant differences between those who had and had not voted previously ($X^2 = 10.54$, $p < .001$) in determining if they voted in the 2007 election. Those who had voted before were more likely to do so again. Respondents who identified with a party that represented their views were more likely to vote. This factor had a significant impact ($X^2 = 10.90$, $p = .004$) in determining whether they voted.

Politics, duty to vote and trust
To examine if those who considered themselves political, felt they had a duty to vote and had trust across a range of civic and political institutions were significant among voting and non-voting prisoners, t-tests were carried out.

It is perhaps understandable that those who described themselves as political were more likely to vote (M = 2.41, SD = .825) (1–4 on a scale from very political to not political at all, see Figure 4.3). Of those who described themselves as non-political, the reverse was true (M = 3.04, SD = .901). This was highly significant (t = 4.57, p < .001).

Respondents who felt they had a 'duty to vote' were more likely to have done so (M = 8.39, SD = 2.261), compared to those who rejected the concept of a duty to vote (M = 5.88, SD = 3.085). This difference was highly significant also (t = 5.915, p < .001).

Respondents were asked if they felt that voting counted. Those who voted (M = 4.10, SD = 3.608) were no more likely than those who did not vote (M = 4.61, SD = 3.211) to believe that voting counted. This was not significant (t = .933, p = .352). In other words while supportive of the right to vote and keen to exercise it, they were realistic (or sceptical) about the impact it may have on policy changes.

The survey asked prisoners if they believed all political parties were similar. Comparing those who voted (M = 5.90, SD = 3.361) with those who did not vote (M = 6.63, SD = 3.314) there was no significant difference (t = 1.365, p = .174).

In terms of trust in Irish civic and political institutions, there was a significant difference among voters and non-voters. Those who voted (M = 22.9, SD = 10.98) were more likely to trust these institutions than those who did not vote (M = 16.98, SD = 9.97). This difference was statistically significant (t = 3.59, p < .001).

Predicting voters
The preliminary analysis revealed five significant variables that differentiated between voters and non-voters. These were trust in institutions, self-identification as political, previous voting history, belief in a political party and feeling duty-bound to vote. They were entered into a logistic regression model to discover which variables might be used to predict whether a prisoner voted in the 2007 election in the three prisons surveyed. Using the NagelKerke R Square, the model explained 28 per cent of the variance. As shown in the Table 4.2, only duty to vote was significant.

There were a number of findings that were of note in the above tests. Usually older people who are better educated tend to have greater levels of civic engagement, tested in this analysis by voting or not voting. This was similar across the three prisons. The lack of inter-institutional difference is surprising, considering that Arbour Hill has an older, better-educated population and a greater proportion serving longer sentences. The tests indicate a pattern of results and a consistency with the inter-

Table 4.2: General election 2007: regression analysis of voters in prison

Variable	B	Wald	Sig.	Exp (B)
Trust in civic and political institutions	.029	2.006	.157	1.029
Are you political?	−.235	.834	.361	.790
Have you voted pre-2007?	.482	.880	.348	1.619
Does any party represent your views?	−.041	.179	.673	.960
Do you have a duty to vote?	.252	7.223	.007	1.287
Constant	−2.588	4.723	.030	.075

pretations across a range of answers. It reveals that it is not where prisoners were located that indicated if they voted, more who they were in terms of identification with politics, and in particular, duty to vote, levels of trust and prior voting behaviour.

Prisoners at the polls: 2008–11

The 2007 general election was the first opportunity for prisoners to exercise their franchise. With any initial exercise, it is perhaps understandable that the process of registration and voting would take time to find an equilibrium with voters, politicians, prison staff and electoral officials. The next section examines levels of registration and voting among prisoners in polls subsequent to the 2007 election.

Lisbon Treaty referendum, 2008

In June 2008, prisoners had the second opportunity to vote when the Irish government held a referendum on the Lisbon Treaty which provided for changes in governance of the European Union. Table 4.3 shows that the total number in custody on 15 February 2008 (date on which the voting register was published) was 3,491. At the publication of the 2008/9 electoral register, 21 prisoners, 0.6 per cent of the prison population, had registered. The electoral register is compiled

Table 4.3: Lisbon Treaty referendum 2008: voting in Irish prisons

Number in prison on publication of register: 15 February 2008	3,491
Number of prisoners registered	21
Percentage of prisoners registered	0.6
Number in prison on polling day: 12 June 2008	3567
Number eligible to vote	3228
Number of prisoners who voted	27
Percentage of eligible prisoners who voted	0.8

Source: Personal correspondence with Irish Prison Service and Department of the Environment, Heritage and Local Government, June–July 2008.

annually in November and published the following February. Prisoners, like all other voters who wish to be included, have to register for a postal ballot each year. That they were registered in the prison previously is of no consequence. They must re-register annually for a postal vote, to allow for those changes to the register because of release or transfer. Like other postal voters, prisoners can apply to be included in the supplementary register. The closing date is two days after the order being made for a referendum or election. Some prisoners obviously availed themselves of this opportunity. By the time voting took place in the referendum, more prisoners had registered. The total number in custody on referendum day, 12 June, was 3,567, of whom 27 voted. As voting for referenda is only open to Irish citizens, the best informed estimate (using data from Irish Prison Service, 2009: 15), is that there were 38 prisoners under 18 and 301 non-Irish prisoners, with 3228 eligible prisoners. With no data available for the numbers registered, 0.84 per cent of the eligible prison population voted. This compares to 53 per cent turnout among the general population (Sinnott, 2008).

Table 4.4 shows the breakdown of the numbers who voted in each prison. No prisoners voted in six prisons. The highest turnout was in Arbour Hill and Portlaoise, consistent with the 2007 poll (Figure 4.1), even if the numbers were markedly lower. However, with an overall low

Table 4.4: Lisbon Treaty referendum 2008: voting by prison

Prison	Total No. Voted
Arbour Hill	7
Castlerea	1
Cloverhill	0
Cork Prison	0
Dóchas	0
Limerick	5
Loughan House	0
Midlands	3
Mountjoy Prison (male)	1
Portlaoise Prison	6
Shelton Abbey	0
St Patrick's Institution	0
Training Unit	2
Wheatfield Prison	2
Total	27

Source: Personal correspondence with Irish Prison Service, July 2008.

level of registration, this meant that the vast majority of prisoners were unable to vote in the referendum, no matter how strongly they felt on the issue. By the close of the annual registration period (Table 4.3), only 21 prisoners had registered, less than 1 per cent of the prison population. It is unlikely that there was a surge in numbers for the supplementary register, which meant that approximately 99 per cent of the prison population was unregistered and therefore ineligible to vote.

The calling of an election or setting of a date for a referendum signals the beginning of the campaign when there is a heightened awareness of the impending vote. This usually prompts potential electors to consider whether they are registered or not. In the lead up to this referendum, the government was criticised by opposition politicians for not allowing a longer period between the calling of the referendum and closing date for registration for all categories of postal voting, which is only two days. Fine Gael TD, Leo Varadkar (cited in Hennessy, 2008) was critical of the procedures the government had put in place. 'Instead of encouraging these [postal] voters to exercise their rights', he claimed, they had 'effectively disenfranchised a great swathe of them. At least 50,000 voters will be denied their right to vote'. The government rejected this criticism and argued that it was a complicated procedure with many checks necessary. Therefore, time was needed to verify the register (cited in Hennessy, 2008).

Other reasons for the low numbers who voted are similar to those outside prison. Traditionally, there is lower turnout in referenda among the general electorate. Among the population outside, there was also much confusion about the Lisbon Treaty and the relevance, and role of, the European Union. As prisoners have access to various media, these factors likely impacted on their decision on whether or not to cast their ballot.

Local, European and by-elections, 2009
In June 2009, local and European elections as well as two by-elections were held. Taking as a best informed estimate (using data from Irish Prison Service, 2010: 15), there were 39 prisoners under 18 and 112 ineligible to vote due to nationality, which reduces the potential voters by 151 to 3744 eligible voters. As shown in Table 4.5, the number of prisoners voting was up on the 2008 figure, although (while not directly comparable in measurement) it did not reach the numbers for the 2007 general election (see Tables 4.1 and 4.3). As all registered residents of Ireland are allowed to vote in local elections and EU citizens in European elections and UK citizens in the by-election, there would have been a greater potential number of voters in this election.

Table 4.5: Local, European and by-elections 2009: voting in Irish prisons

Number in prison on publication of register: 15 February 2009	3714
Number of prisoners registered to vote	282
Percentage of registered prisoners	7.6
Number in prison on Polling Day: 5 June 2009	3895
Number of prisoners eligible to vote	3744
Number of prisoners who voted	220
Percentage of eligible prison population who voted	5.9

Source: Personal correspondence with Irish Prison Service and Department of the Environment, Heritage and Local Government, June–July, 2009.

Table 4.6: Local, European and by-elections 2009: voting by prison

Prison	Total registered	Total No. voted
Arbour Hill	21	17
Castlerea	4	2
Cloverhill	0	0
Cork Prison	3	3
Dóchas	1	1
Limerick Prison	37	35
Loughan House	0	0
Midlands Prison	34	31
Mountjoy Prison (male)	59	34
Portlaoise Prison	47	40
Shelton Abbey	1	1
St Patrick's Institution	0	0
Training Unit	15	12
Wheatfield	60	44
Total	282	220

Source: Personal correspondence with Irish Prison Service and Department of the Environment, Heritage and Local Government, June–July 2009.

General election, 2011

In 2011, the coalition government of the Green Party and Fianna Fáil fell apart acrimoniously. The poll that followed was a watershed election as it 'displayed one of the highest levels of volatility ever seen in post war-Europe' (Courtney and Gallagher, 2011: 3). The number of prisoners registered was 344, or 7.6 per cent of the eligible prison population (Table 4.7). Following the format for the 2007 general election, those under 18 years and the majority from outside the state were not eligible to register. The number who voted was 254, or 76 per cent of the registered prison population, compared to just over 69 per cent of the general population (Courtney and Gallagher, 2011: 12).

Table 4.7: General election 2011: voting in Irish prisons

Number in prison on publication of register, 18 February 2011	4607
Number of prisoners eligible to vote	4400
Number of prisoners registered	334
Number who voted	254
Percentage of eligible prisoners who voted	5.8
Percentage of registered prisoners who voted	76
Percentage of registered national population who voted	69.2

Source: Personal correspondence with Irish Prison Service, March 2011, and Courtney and Gallagher, 2011: 12.

While the percentage and numbers registered was lower than the 2007 general election, the trends were somewhat similar. Those prisons with stable populations, such as Arbour Hill, had a high turnout, if a low level of registration. Institutions with a high turnover such as the remand prison at Cloverhill had a low turnout. St Patrick's Institution with a number of prisoners under 18 years and all of them under 21 years had one registration and one voter. The one major difference between 2007 and 2011 was Portlaoise Prison, which had one of the highest registrations in 2007 and subsequent polls. In 2011, only 8 out of 268 prisoners registered.

Voting turnout among prisoners

The data from the second, third and fourth polls in 2008, 2009 and 2011 (Tables 4.5–4.7) combined with the 2007 election turnout (Figures 4.1 and 4.7 and Table 4.1) indicate preliminary trends in voting among prisoners. In 2011, there was a lower registration and subsequent turnout in practically every prison (Table 4.8). In 2009 there were no voters in three prisons, Cloverhill, St Patrick's Institution and Loughan House. The populations may help explain the reasons behind this. Cloverhill had one voter in 2007 and none in 2008 or 2009 and seven out of a population of 456 in 2011. It is a remand prison, with a high turnover of prisoners and many would not be in the prison for long periods of time. Even if they registered in the institution, they would be unlikely to vote there. It also contains many non-Irish prisoners, some of whom may have been detained on their arrival and therefore have no address in Ireland. St Patrick's Institution is for young offenders, some of whom are under 18 years (and not entitled to vote) and most with little tradition of voting. It had the same level of voting, zero, for both 2008 and 2009. It had one voter in 2011. Loughan House is an open prison with a high turnover, where no voters exercised their

Table 4.8: General election 2011: voting by prison

Prison	Total registered	No. who voted
Arbour Hill	20	19
Castlerea	10	5
Cloverhill	29	7
Cork Prison	12	10
Dochas	5	5
Limerick Prison	42	22
Loughan House	2	2
Midlands Prison	36	21
Mountjoy Prison (male)	65	46
Portlaoise Prison	8	7
Shelton Abbey	3	1
St Patrick's Institution	1	1
Training Unit	60	43
Wheatfield	95	65
Total	334	254

Source: Personal correspondence with Irish Prison Service, March, 2011.

franchise in 2008 or 2009 and two out of a population of 145 voted in 2011.

At the other end of the spectrum, 20 prisoners were registered in Arbour Hill for the 2011 election and 19 voted. This reflects an older, better educated population, serving long sentences in a stable environment. The most noticeable change was the fall off in voting in Portlaoise between the 2007 and 2011 elections, with only eight registering out of a population of 268. However, seven out of the eight voted. There was a marked increase in the numbers voting from Mountjoy Prison, which went from one voter in 2008 (Table 4.4) to 31 in 2009 (Table 4.6) and 46 in 2011.

These data seem to confirm Rottinghaus's (2005) conclusion in his study of voting patterns among prisoners internationally, that the crucial time in preparing prisoners for voting is the period leading up to registration. This can be a difficult time to encourage interest when an election or referendum may be months or potentially years away. Nevertheless, the registration period is crucial in getting prisoners on the electoral roll, especially as obtaining a postal vote involves a more complex procedure. This is particularly important for those who have little tradition of voting or political engagement. Many prisoners indicated they were unaware that they had to register in the prison for a postal vote annually. However, with little publicity or discussion at registration time compared to the hype that surrounds elections, it is

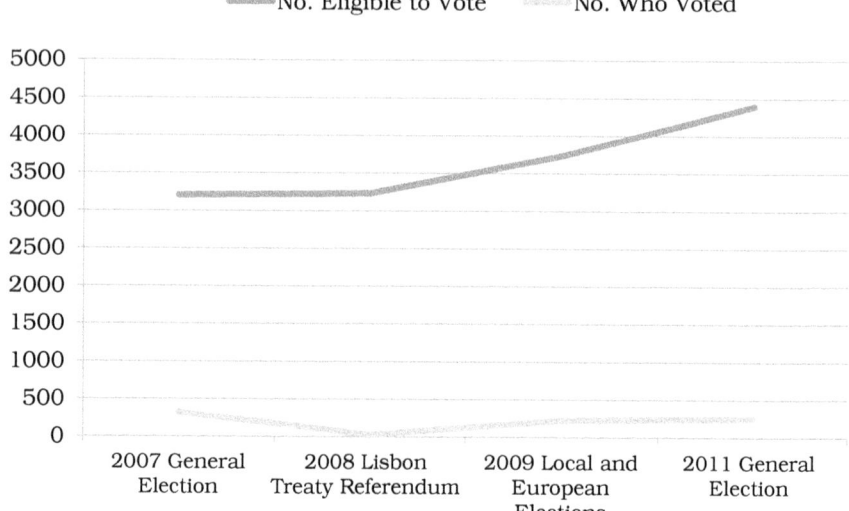

Figure 4.7: Voting in Irish prisons 2007–11
Sources: Personal correspondence with Irish Prison Service and Department of Environment, Heritage and Local Government, 2007–11 and Irish Prison Service Annual Reports, 2007–11.

more difficult to encourage either prisoners or prison authorities of the immediacy or importance of registration. Figures from the first four polls in which prisoners participated indicated that one variable remained constant – if prisoners take the time and effort to register, they are likely to vote.

Conclusion

This chapter began by examining the level of voting among Irish prisoners during their first election. Details of the research setting were outlined and the political preference from survey data in three prisons, at either end of the voting spectrum, was reported. While knowledge of politics, political preference and the perception of politics varied, levels of trust among confined citizens were low. Many of those interviewed felt their concerns were neglected, their voices silenced and believed their actions will not influence or effect change. The latter may indicate why so few turned out when they had the opportunity to exercise their franchise. For policymakers, this requires some consideration, because a healthy polity is created by citizens who participate and have confidence that their activities can effect change. Trust in the institutions of state is an integral part of a functioning democracy, as is a belief in the regulatory bodies to observe and protect the rights and interests of all citizens. In a number of areas, there was lack of engagement with those institutions. Low levels of trust lead to a high degree of disconnect and this impacts on the confidence of those who might seek to effect change, both inside and outside prison. This has a bearing on the levels of political engagement and, subsequently, voting and indicates the depth of disconnection from the political system and civic institutions, which will be examined in the next chapter.

The first comprehensive survey among prisoners about politics and civic engagement found that the characteristics of those who voted during their first election had somewhat similar characteristics to those who vote and civically engage outside: those who are older, in more stable penal environments, and particularly those who identify with a party, who believe voting is a duty and have voted previously were more likely to cast their ballot. Predicting voting among the prison population was a combination of factors: the attributes brought into the institution by an individual and the prison environment where they were located. Significantly, even though the registration rate was low, those who took the time to register tended to go on to vote. Comparing the data for those registered and those who voted, this indicates a higher turnout – at over 71 per cent in 2007 and 76 per cent in 2011 – among the Irish prisoner population than the general electorate. The next chapter examines in more detail some of the reasons why confined citizens decided to vote and participate and why many were reluctant to do so.

5

Enfranchisement – the prisoner as citizen

Introduction

This chapter examines the experience of enfranchisement based on interviews with 50 prisoners. Their narratives are used rather than the raw statistical data, usually associated with opinion polls and electoral surveys, which was analysed in the last chapter. It begins with an examination of topics such as prisoners and the vote, motivation behind political participation and the government decision on enfranchisement. The experience of postal voting, the facilities available, the election campaign (or lack of) within the prison walls are discussed. It concludes with some suggestions from prisoners about the desirability of deeper political and civic engagement. As this was the first occasion to interview prisoners after the 2007 general election, the decision to vote and identification with the electoral process were prominent themes (Behan, 2012). The perspectives of prisoners are rarely heard in public policy discussions, especially criminal justice debates (see Healy, 2009; Mauer, 2011; Richards and Jones, 2004). The purpose of this chapter is to allow prisoners to give their perspectives on politics and civic engagement with the emphasis on their voices being heard. All names used are pseudonyms.

'It was a historic thing to do'

For those included in the franchise, it is difficult to imagine the immense impact the denial of the right to vote – the cornerstone of citizenship – has on some individuals, and conversely the profound effect the restoration of the franchise can have on them. For Deirdre Cruz (cited in Brennan Center for Justice, 2009: 6), an ex-prisoner from California, who voted in her first presidential election in November 2008, it was an intense, emotional experience. She explained that after filling in her postal ballot:

I closed the envelope, removed the edges, and I flattened it very gently with a prayer for social and spiritual change in the world. As I ran my hands over the envelope, I truly felt the energy and weight of the small line of choice I made inside. I felt chills ...

My vote is equal to everyone else's and it connected me to the rest of the United States ... Voting isn't entirely about the candidate who wins; it's about the inspiration and hope people feel when they have a voice they can use to bring real change.

Interviewees in this study were asked what the opportunity to vote meant to them. Some agreed with Cruz; they were participating in a momentous event. Rory had served over ten years of a life sentence. (By 2009, a life-sentenced prisoner in the Republic of Ireland could expect to serve at least 17 years before release. See Griffin and O'Donnell, 2012.) He had missed the opportunity to vote. 'When I was convicted, I lost that right ... It was a historic thing to do ... I had a chance, a choice and I wanted to vote once in my life'. Having completed one third of his near 15-year sentence, Cian 'couldn't believe it. I thought it was great, the first time in history that prisoners had the right to vote. And I am actually inside it, in that history'. Killian who was serving four years, was aware of the significance of voting because he was 'a history student. And I know how difficult it was to get the vote. I am also inclined to believe that if a person doesn't vote, they don't have a right to criticise'. He drew lessons from Ireland's history:

> I believe it is good that Irish prisoners are allowed to vote. As a person who never missed an opportunity to exercise my franchise, I would have felt very powerless if this right had been denied to me. However, this brings to mind the time when so many people were excluded from voting on the grounds of property, education, etc.

Uggen and Manza (2004: 195) found the 'right to vote' was 'one of the defining elements of citizenship in a democratic polity and participation in rituals such as elections affirms membership in the larger community for individuals and groups'. They concluded: 'Because of all that voting represents in society, voting can be viewed as a proxy for other kinds of civic engagement'. Recognising the importance of voting to embracing citizenship, Aidan, who was serving a life sentence, suggested that, 'not being allowed to vote brought you down. You weren't a citizen'. He believed the right to vote 'helps me to respect myself. Being a voter means being respected in society'. Matthew had served over ten years of his life sentence and admitted that at previous elections, he did 'feel a little left out ... If you couldn't vote, it felt like you weren't important. If you couldn't take part, it took something out of it. If you felt you couldn't participate, you would be less interested'. Conor, serving life, believed that 'what prisoners' voting has done is to allow prisoners at election time to feel they are part of society and can play their part in the democratic process'.

Oisin, serving life, believed voting would influence government policy. 'I'm in prison. Prisoners, in my experience are always talking about rights and privileges and prison being unfair. If they vote, they can obtain some power and that will eventually influence their environment'. He was aware of the importance of participation in the electoral process. Giving prisoners the opportunity to vote was a two way dynamic; it was a positive sign from government and was also indicative of change, albeit a subtle one in the attitude of the prisoner:

> If a person wants to change things, he has to vote. Enough votes can make a difference. If enough prisoners vote, it can make a difference. At the start it mightn't, but gradually.
>
> It would probably give them a sense of self-worth and usefulness. Prisoners can be very angry with authority. It's a start, showing the prisoner that the government don't hate you. There is a sense of hatred of authority from prisoners. It's the beginning, where the system is embracing the prisoner, instead of judging.

Ross, serving nine years, was cynical about the utility of giving prisoners the vote. However, he conceded: 'The only difference it would make, would be to make prisoners aware that there is some little they can do if they are unhappy with the government. The main good that can come out of giving prisoners this right is that it may make the government more aware of the existence of prisoners'.

A belief that there are duties and responsibilities that accompany the rights of citizenship was also important as many interviewees believed they had a civic obligation to vote. Minister for the Environment, Dick Roche, argued that: 'Once we have created this right, we should encourage prisoners to see it as part of their duty as citizens to exercise that right' (Oireachtas Select Committee on Local Government, 2 November 2006). Adam, coming to the end of his five-year sentence, agreed with the Minister. 'It is a very important part of our civic duty to influence things'. Hugh concurred. He had spent over ten years in prison and during that time, 'thought we had a right to vote. It was a duty to do so'.

Bernard, who was one third through his near ten-year sentence, believed so strongly that voting was an 'obligation' that he 'would make it compulsory'. This was because 'coming from the North [Northern Ireland] . . . we believe in voting. It will make a difference, having tried everything else. Bobby Sands [republican hunger striker who was elected to parliament] showed us that anyway'. Gavin, who was serving life, argued that voting mattered: 'Because it was new for prisoners. I value it, even though I am a prisoner and will be for some time to come, I think my vote counts'. Liam, serving just over a year, voted because it 'is a very important part of our civic duty to influence things. If we don't put in our own little impact, we can't be blaming other people if things go wrong afterwards'.

'They are still citizens, aren't they?'

During the parliamentary debates on enfranchisement, both government and opposition politicians argued that to enfranchise prisoners would encourage them to behave responsibly, adopt a pro-social role and appreciate the implications of citizenship. Daniel agreed. Serving life, he believed that having the right to vote will give prisoners 'a sense of responsibility [that] they are doing something in the formation of the government. It will also give them back a bit of dignity'. Fionn, serving life, had already spent over ten years in prison and believed it was essential for prisoners to vote. 'We are governed by the same political system as anybody else. In fact we are probably ... governed by it even more. So, if there are going to be changes to the political system we should be able to influence it'.

In a study of US prisoners, parolees and probationers, Uggen *et al.* (2004: 276) found that many felt that without the right to vote, they were 'outsiders'. As one of their participants, Rachel, suggested, it made her feel 'less than the average citizen'. In another study of ex-felons, 74 per cent felt that losing the right to vote affected them negatively. There was a feeling that they were outsiders, rejected from society, and it impacted on their view of themselves, with expressions of frustration, alienation and anger (Cardinale, 2004: 7–11). For one respondent, Julius: 'Just the word bothers me, disenfranchisement. It's like "As a matter of fact, you're nobody, you don't count. We don't respect your opinion". It's somewhat of a guilty feeling' (cited in Cardinale, 2004: 8).

Interviewees in this study were asked how they felt when they had previously been denied the opportunity to vote. Did they consider this an oversight, benign neglect or something more deliberate and sinister? Many felt that other than the denial of liberty, prisoners should retain their rights. Echoing the oft-quoted sentiment from English Prison Commissioner, Alexander Paterson, Luke, who was serving three years, believed: 'Prison is the punishment. You are not put in here to be punished'. He continued: 'If you take away their right to vote, you are punishing them twice'. Exercising the franchise had wider implications for Peter, who was serving just less than 15 years. 'At the end of the day ... denying somebody the right to vote is a form of rejection from society ... by giving a prisoner a vote gives them some sort of dignity in their lives. And it could help them change for the better as well'.

Many interviewees argued that imprisonment does not, and should not, mean being cut off from society. Cathal, a lifer who had served over ten years, argued that 'imprisonment is depriving people of their liberty, not all their rights. If you want to reintegrate people into society, the best thing is not to isolate them altogether. They are still citizens, aren't they?' Aidan, who was serving life, maintained that 'all prisoners will return to the outside community and this helps prepare them for release. Prisoners will leave prison one day and they will be back in the community'. Citizenship confers certain rights that imprisonment cannot take away, believed Charles, who was serving life. 'We are all Irish citizens. We'd all like to have a say, at least a little bit of a say ... [we] weren't born criminal, [we] weren't always criminals. [We] were good one time as well'. As Gerard, who was serving four years, pointed out that, if prisoners are not allowed to vote, they will be excluded and their concerns will be neglected by politicians and society. 'Without the prisoner's vote this country would be excluding the views of a lot of people'. For Jake, serving life, to take away the right to vote from any group undermines the polity. 'There is a right that everyone has in a democracy to vote and reducing someone's right will weaken the strength of that democracy'. Cathal, who was serving life, while welcoming enfranchisement, put it in a wider context:

> It is a good idea [allowing prisoners to vote]. Unfortunately, it is only one aspect of a democracy. Others include being able to contact your politician in confidence: not permitted; access to the media: not permitted; free speech: not permitted.
>
> It is difficult to see how the provision of a vote, only when forced to by the courts, of itself will help make better citizens of prisoners, when it is made clear by every aspect of the justice system that prisoners are second class citizens. Until prisoners are provided with some form of a 'voice' to address issues of concern, little progress will be made.

There was a belief that the right to vote confers dignity, humanity and promotes inclusion. Issues raised by interviewees included the social contract, collateral consequences of punishment, civil death and penal policy, often mentioned in the debates on prisoner enfranchisement. Reintegration and maintaining connections with the outside world was a prominent theme running through the interviews. Jeff Manza (2009: xiii) has argued that: 'Encouraging offenders to think of themselves as full citizens with the right to participate in democracy's most important exercise – the casting of an election ballot – underscores one of the major benefits of being a citizen. It encourages offenders to think of connections to those outside of the prison'. According to Stern (2002: 135), 'retaining the right to participate as a citizen in the life of the community is symbolised in democratic societies by the right to vote'. There was an overriding belief that all prisoners should retain their right to vote. Interviewees were keenly aware that the decisions to grant or deny them the franchise spoke to profound themes about how a society, through its legislators, viewed the human rights and, for some, dignity of prisoners. Gavin, serving life, suggested that if prisoners are given the opportunity to vote, their voices should be listened to and, he hoped, would make better citizens:

> I think the opportunity for prisoners to vote is largely a good one. Voting allows for the prisoner to feel part of a wider community, something incarceration takes away. It also allows the prisoner to vote for and against changes which may affect his/her time in custody and upon release. I do hope that our vote is not a wasted one – if we are valued enough to be asked to vote, then I hope our wants, needs and requests are listened to.
>
> Being in custody takes away a large part of a person's feeling of self-worth, being allowed to vote gives back some of that lost feeling. This in turn will make better citizens.

'Prison is a very negative place'

In total 451 prisoners registered and 322 voted out of approximately 3,202 eligible voters in the 2007 general election. At over 71 per cent of registered prisoners, this compares favourably to turnout of just over 67 per cent among the registered electorate (Gallagher and Marsh, 2008: 234–5). Nevertheless, nine out of ten Irish prisoners did not vote in 2007. If so many prisoners believed in enfranchisement, why was there such a low level of registration, essential for voting? Were the reasons for non-voting similar to the electorate outside or were the conditions unique to the institution or the group? Psephologists have identified different reasons for non-voting. 'In the analysis on non-voting it is also very important to distinguish between what has been described as non-voting by accident vs. non-voting by design ... or circumstantial vs. voluntary abstention' (Marsh et al., 2001: 172).

There were various reasons for the high levels of non-voting and abstention rates among prisoners, both circumstantial and voluntary.

Many prisoners did not theoretically abstain because they had not registered to vote. However, for this study, abstention was taken as either non-registration or non-voting. As set out in Figure 5.1, some related to the impact of imprisonment, others were for the same reasons that citizens outside prison do not vote. The motivation behind voluntary abstention ranged from apathy, the fact of their imprisonment, especially for those with long sentences who believed that a new government would not change penal policy, little tradition of political engagement,

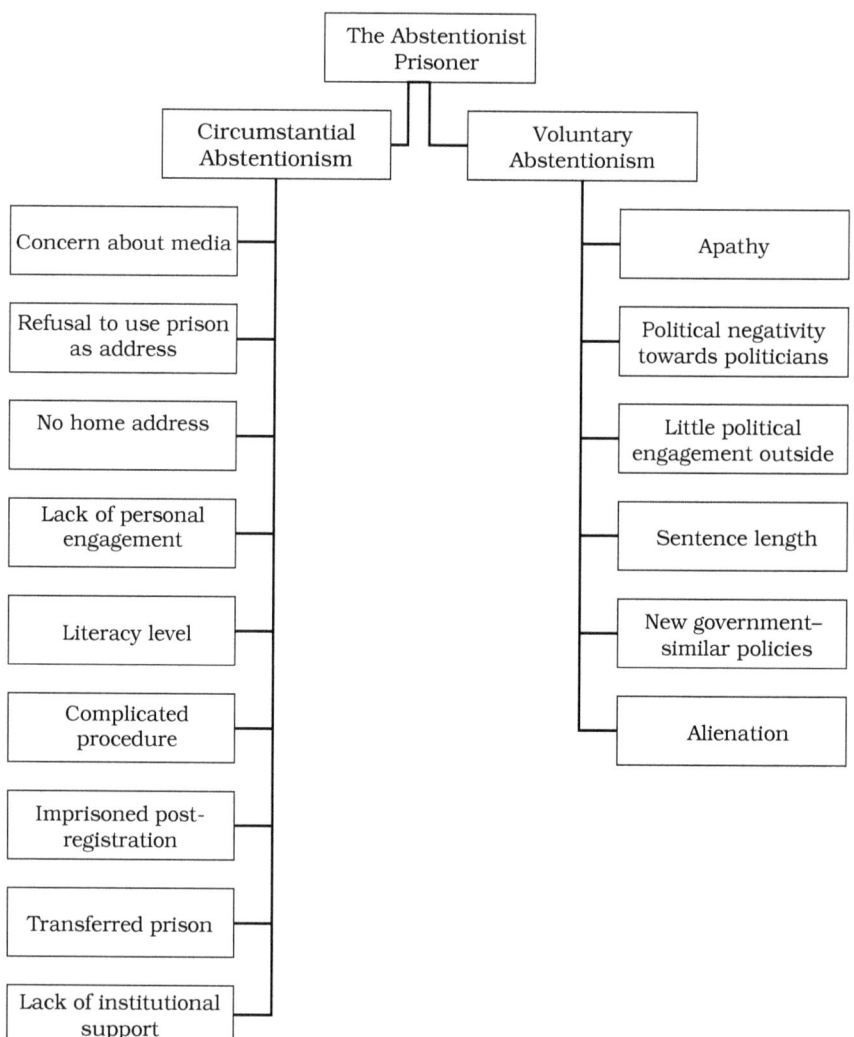

Figure 5.1: Abstentionism among prisoners

lack of trust in politicians and alienation from civil society. The reasons behind circumstantial abstention included refusal to register due to the possibility of media attention, being homeless prior to incarceration, refusal to use the prison as their address (as some mistakenly believed), lack of institutional support, prison transfers and a more complicated registration procedure (especially problematic for those with literacy difficulties). The belief that prisoners were neglected by politicians in general and parliamentary candidates in particular was a prominent theme reflected in the low turnout among the prison population. Some, as is their right in a democratic polity, simply refused to vote.

When interviewees were asked why so many prisoners did not vote, parallels were drawn with the general population, focusing on the relationship between age, education and voting behaviour. Fionn, serving life, believed that many prisoners did not vote because they had no faith in the political system, with the majority of prisoners coming from a social class with a weak tradition of voting. 'Young prisoners would feel totally disconnected' and 'lack of education means they're less likely to vote', according to Adam who was serving five years. In their analysis of punishment, social deprivation and the geography of reintegration, O'Donnell *et al.* (2007) found that 1 per cent of electoral districts accounted for nearly 24 per cent of prisoners, but less than 5 per cent of the population. In general, 'prisoners were at least three times as likely to come from the most, as compared to the least, deprived areas' (O'Donnell *et al.*, 2007: 2). Breen (2010: 58) concluded that 'the bulk of prisoners in Irish prisons are young, male and from deprived urban areas'. This group has a low tradition of voting on the outside and it is therefore unlikely that they would vote inside. As Chapter 4 showed, having voted previously was a significant indication to future voting. Internationally, 'the marginalised groups in any society are invariably over represented in prisons' (Coyle, 2005: 11), with similar levels of social and economic deprivation found among those imprisoned in the UK (PRT, 2013) and the US (Barak *et al.*, 2007).

The educational level of citizens has an impact on interest in politics, civic engagement, registration for elections and voter turn-out. Putnam (1995: 3) concluded that education is 'the best individual-level predictor of political participation'. Prior to this study, the latest research on literacy levels among Irish prisoners showed that nearly 53 per cent were in the level one or pre-level one category (highest is five) and that the average literacy level of the prison population was much lower than the general population (Morgan and Kett, 2003: 35–6). Active citizenship, including voting, is 'positively related to age, educational background, marital status and socio-economic status' (Taskforce on Active

Citizenship, 2007b: 3). This suggests that citizens who find themselves in prison are unlikely voters.

Jack, who was serving a life sentence and was not very political, decided to abstain. He believed that many prisoners did not vote, because 'prison is a very negative place'. Peter believed that prisoners feel marginalised. The government was not doing enough for them and many believed they 'are being treated too harshly'. Aidan, who was a lifer, suggested that the reason many prisoners did not vote was because, 'maybe they were angry because they were in prison'. While believing that prisoners were sceptical, Louis, who was serving life, pointed out that 'a lot of prisoners believe the government has them locked up'. However, 'realistically, it is not. We have ourselves locked up'. Dylan, serving just over five years, was scathing of all politicians and did not vote for quite deliberate reasons. He had described himself as very political, and non-engagement while in prison was a political act. 'I felt that my vote would make no difference while in prison. I felt they [parties/politicians] didn't deserve a vote, any of them'. The government, in enfranchising prisoners, was putting on a 'show for the European Parliament, Amnesty International and other human rights groups'. As he saw it, they were only interested in giving the impression of promoting equality, so he refused to participate in the charade.

Enda, serving six years, had 'no interest out there... so I'm not going to get interested because I am in prison'. Brandon, serving 14 years, was similarly apathetic: 'I just had no interest at the time'. This was the case for Louis, who did not vote and had served over five years of a life sentence. He was angry at government policy towards prisoners and did not want to legitimate it by voting: 'I genuinely didn't believe my vote would have made any difference... My attitude is that this environment doesn't allow us a proper input... It was a gesture to prisoners... I don't see what impact it would have made'.

'It's a different society in here'

Some refused to vote because they felt the outside world had no bearing on prisoners, individually or collectively. This was, understandably, a prominent theme, with the majority of interviewees serving long sentences. Nearly 20 per cent (n = 9) were serving over 10 years and 40 per cent (n = 20) were serving life sentences. Many interviewees, while believing they should maintain rights, had resigned themselves to the denial of many of them, including voting, during imprisonment. This was especially the case for those serving long or life sentences. It appeared to lower expectations, to create a feeling of resignation. It seemed to reduce, not just their sense of autonomy, but also their responsibility. Lack of political rights and, subsequently, diminished civic engagement were merely part of this experience. Killian felt that many long-term prisoners questioned the utility of voting. 'There are a lot of long-term prisoners in here. I suppose they feel that it wouldn't make any difference whether they vote or not'. Describing himself as fairly political and having spent 12 years in prison, Hugh also seemed rather accepting of his position:

> *Did it bother you that you were not allowed to vote before the new law was introduced by the government?*
> I can't say that it did.
> *Why not?*
> Because you are in prison. You have this perception that you are cut off from the outside world. Therefore, a lot of your rights and privileges are taken away from you.
>
> I say that within the present environment. It's a different society in here than it is outside. That's my perception of it. It's a totally different unreal world to what it is outside. It is an enclosed group. Only for the radio and media and visits and that, we are totally cut off from what goes on outside anyway. I think that is one of the reasons why people wouldn't vote, that lack of interest. It is an unreal world here. It is totally different than what is going on outside. It is our little community in here.

Evan, a life sentenced prisoner, believed that prisoners with long sentences were unlikely to vote because of 'the length of their sentence – politicians can do nothing for them', and furthermore, there was a 'lack of interest by politicians in prisoners'. This cynical view of politicians was compounded by their imprisonment. Jason, serving life, did not find the low turnout among prisoners surprising at all. 'I suppose it's just the mentality of prisoners. Career criminals wouldn't vote. They don't give a shit about the government'. Diarmaid, who described himself as non-political, believed that there was an element of self-interest. Prisoners 'don't care. At the end of the day, prisoners are not getting nothing out of it. If they started getting time off, they'd vote'.

There was a high level of non-voting and circumstantial abstentionism, especially among the more politically aware. Some were unwilling to register (even before consideration of voting) because of what they saw as shortcomings in the legislation and some refused to register because of their location. Cathal, who was serving life, was self-described as political, refused to register because he had been the subject of negative media attention in the past. He felt that the mere fact of registration would become known because the electoral register is publicly accessible. 'I would expect some kind of media coverage. They use everything else'. As he could not get a guarantee that his name would not appear on a public voting list, he refused to register. 'I know a few I have spoken to are of the same view as myself. We couldn't get an answer whether our names would be on the electoral register. We didn't want attention for ourselves, our families'.

This was a particular concern as some prisoners had been demonised frequently and received widespread media coverage. A number of these were household names and favourites of the tabloid press. There was a fear that if a journalist, individual or politician accessed the electoral register and was aware of the previous address of the prisoner, the mere fact of registration could be used as a media story or to gain political advantage. While the latter scenario might be unlikely, since no politician spoke out against, or used the enactment of the legislation for political gain, it was another reason why some people would not register and were therefore, due to their circumstances, ruled out from voting.

A desire to protect their privacy was an understandable concern of prisoners, of which lawmakers who debated the legislation were mindful. There was some consideration given to whether candidates and parties would know if voters were incarcerated. All categories of postal voter are recognizable merely by the letter 'p' beside their name on the electoral register. The Minister for Environment, Dick Roche, pointed out that 'the address would only be known to the returning officer. It would not, for example, be subject to the Freedom of Information Act'. However, echoing prisoners' concerns about their privacy, the location of electors would be confidential for that reason and not 'made available to political parties for the purpose of a leaflet' (Oireachtas Select Committee on Local Government, 2 November 2006). However, each candidate's election agent is entitled to a copy of the Register of Electors for his or her electoral area or constituency (Whelan, 2000: 4) and therefore the potential remained for the fact of registration at their home address to be made public. Despite assurances from and the good intentions of politicians, prisoners' concerns were obviously not allayed.

The authors of the legislation also took into account the concerns raised in previous debates about protecting the integrity of the vote and the possibility of influencing electoral outcomes in constituencies with large prison populations. Prisoners should, therefore, vote in their home, rather than prison constituency, because 'the reasons that inform the discussion on where you register on the outside are good reasons and they apply to prisoners too' (interview with author, 2007).

The requirement to have a home address caused difficulties for some interviewees. Section 11 (5) of the Electoral Act 1992 states that a prisoner should be registered 'in the place where he would have been residing but for his having been so detained in legal custody'. Those involved in campaigning for prisoner enfranchisement argued during the passage of the bill that 'a lack of a consistent address prior to imprisonment should not preclude prisoners from exercising their basic rights as citizens' (Hamilton and Lines, 2009: 218). There is a higher proportion of homelessness among the prison than the general population. A 2005 report on homelessness in Dublin prisons found that 54 per cent of prisoners had been homeless at some time in their life, and 25 per cent had been homeless on committal (Seymour and Costelloe, 2005: 50). The 'issue of homelessness among ex-prisoners is an ongoing problem' according to the Irish Prison Service and during 2007, the Homeless Persons' Unit of the Health Service Executive provided in-reach community welfare service to 10 prisons and 570 prisoners availed of the service (IPS, 2008: 22). Therefore, Irish prisoners as a group had the potential to be excluded from the electoral register in greater proportion due to their level of homelessness. This corresponds to the experience among prisoners and ex-prisoners internationally. In the UK, 15 per cent of prisoners were homeless prior to custody (PRT, 2013: 8). A US study found the rate of homelessness among adults in prison was '4–6 times the annual rate' than among the general population (Greenberg and Rosenheck, 2008: 95).

Andrew, who was serving 14 years and described himself as very political, explained that 'they would not give me the right to vote ... I had applied to be added to the Register of Electors and was turned down because I no longer lived at the address that I lived before I came to jail, [I was told] that I couldn't vote there'. For some life-sentenced prisoners who had served a long time, the institution had become their home. Their previous residence was no longer an option, either being unwelcome at their previous address, or their family had moved on, possibly due to the crime of the prisoner.

Legislators were not unaware of the challenges posed with registration by those with no regular home prior to conviction. Arthur Morgan, Sinn Féin TD, proposed that if prisoners were not able to 'prove their previous ordinary residence to the satisfaction of the Registration Authority, arrangements shall be made ... to vote in the constituency in which they are incarcerated'. This amendment was necessary because many people in prison 'come from a homeless background or from a background where they were moving from house to house and simply did not have what would be considered a permanent residential address'. He was concerned that such people 'would stand to lose their franchise – their right to vote – on foot of their previous circumstances' (Dáil Debates, 2006, Vol. 628, col. 846).

Another legislator, Labour TD Eamon Gilmore, suggested an alternative to overcome the requirement for an elector to have to register in the place where they lived prior to their incarceration. He proposed an amendment to delete 'place' and substitute 'constituency' in which they would have been residing had they not been imprisoned. This amendment was based on a submission the Labour Party received from the Irish Penal Reform Trust, drawing attention to the possibility that 'many prisoners were homeless before they were committed to prison'. The rationale for the proposed change was twofold: 'Firstly ... it is possible that people might not be capable of being registered if they were homeless before they were imprisoned. Second, it may not be appropriate in some cases for people to be deemed to have been resident in a place prior to their incarceration' (Dáil Debates, 2006, Vol. 628, col. 848–9).

Neither amendment was accepted. When the bill became law, the address prior to imprisonment was taken for registration, to be determined by the registration authorities. The use of a home address was designed to prevent prisoners skewing the results of the poll if they were registered in the constituency of the prison. It was also argued that, as prisoners have a connection with their home constituency, they are better equipped to make informed decisions about casting their vote. There is also a misplaced fear of prisoners acting as a voting bloc, used by some politicians and anti-enfranchisement advocates who argue that if prisoners register in the constituency of the prison, they will all vote for the same pro-prisoner, anti-law candidate (see Chapter 1).

There are alternatives to prisoners registering at their last address. In Canada, for voting purposes, there are a number of options for 'place of ordinary residence' including place of residence before incarceration; residence of spouse or partner; the place of his or her arrest; or the last court where the elector was convicted and sentenced (Division 5 of the Canada Elections Act 2000). In Australia, eligible prisoners are registered at the address where they were last eligible to be registered (usually the last place they lived). Other alternatives include the residence where their next-of-kin is currently registered; or where they were born; or where they had the closest connection. In Germany, prisoners with a permanent residence in a municipality are usually placed on the electoral list there. However, prisoners without a permanent residence in a municipality are registered in the electoral area of the prison. In France, prisoners are registered according to their last area (commune) of residence. The registered address is the last home or place where he or she normally lived when not imprisoned or detained (HKSAR, 2009a: 24–5; see also Ispahani, 2009).

Other reasons for non-voting included confusion about the technicalities of the legislation and how to go about getting one's name on the electoral register and postal voters list. Clarity was lacking around the procedure for registration and voting. Some participants questioned what location could be used if one had no permanent address. One interviewee refused to register because he had no fixed abode outside and 'it begs the question if your address is the prison?' Some were unaware that they had to register with their outside address, with a number under the impression that the prison address would be on their polling card. Due to the negativity associated with prison, Dylan, despite his interest in politics, would rather forsake his right to vote because there was 'no way' he going to apply for inclusion on the register, 'if the prison address was on my voting card'.

There were other circumstantial reasons for non-voting among prisoners. Some were not incarcerated prior to the closing date for regular or supplementary registration. And even for those who had been sentenced recently, it is unlikely that registration was top of their priorities in adjusting to prison life. Those on the postal list must register every year and therefore it was seen as another layer of red tape by a population that tends to shun bureaucracy.

While postal voting is most common in European countries and those states in the US that allow prisoners to vote, exceptions include Romania where election officials bring a 'special ballot box' to the prison. In Belgium and France, eligible prisoners vote by a form of proxy. In Luxembourg, eligible prisoners leave the prison to vote, sometimes without an escort, and in Malta, police escort eligible prisoners to their respective polling stations. In Australia, mobile voting teams visit prisons in the ten days before the election and in New Zealand, prisoners can vote by mail or when returning officers visit the prison (Ispahani, 2009: 50–4).

Postal voting was not without complications. Some interviewees were sceptical that their ballot would be secret. Censoring of mail was raised and some expressed a lack of confidence that their ballot paper would be sent unopened. When the election took place in 2007, the 1947 Rules for the Government of Prisons were in operation, which stipulated that virtually all mail could be examined prior to leaving the prison. Even though only the election officer and returning officer would have details of postal voters in prison, there was fear that this could be made public. Dylan asked, 'So how do I know that they won't release it [name and political preference]?' The sense of alienation from all 'authority' was so strong that some prisoners refused to accept that the prison would not examine their postal voting envelope or that the returning officer would protect their privacy.

'If we didn't deserve their time'

A recurrent theme in the discussions about political participation was that many prisoners' felt politicians had neglected them, before and during the election campaign. Interviewees responded that their lack of political knowledge, the absence of party manifestoes, election literature and personal discussion with candidates militated against the desired outcome – meaningful political engagement – regardless of where the citizen happened to be living at election time. They felt that they now had the right to vote but did not have the same opportunity to engage in the electoral process as citizens outside. Voters, whether prisoners or not, decide who to vote for by participating in the election process, such as through public debates, discussions among friends/colleagues, posters and election literature. Participation in elections is not just about casting a ballot; it is making an informed choice about who should govern.

The lack of understanding of the issues and the differences between the parties and candidates meant many felt ill-equipped to vote. Gavin, a lifer, explained: 'I had nobody explain to me about what people were proposing'. 'Some didn't know how to vote' and it would be beneficial if somebody took the 'time to help them', suggested Gerard, who was serving four years and had been politically active prior to his imprisonment. He continued: 'There needs to be somebody in the prison service to encourage people to vote. Somebody needs to be a point of contact with prisoners in informing them about elections . . . I don't know if it's the responsibility of the education system or the prison service'.

Thomas, serving over 15 years, argued that while it may not be feasible to send political literature to every individual in prison, there was no reason why party representatives could not visit the prison at regular intervals. 'Otherwise this causes alienation, because you feel excluded. There is no reason why political parties cannot come here every five years'. Conor, who was serving life, went further. While election literature had not been available in the prison, there was no personal contact either. 'There was not one TD who ever took the time to visit the prison'. He believed it was essential politicians engaged with prisoners in between elections. 'At least once a month TDs could give a day, to come in to the prison to see what grievances prisoners have'. Liam was annoyed that 'nobody sent us any literature'. He was willing to accept that 'the prison authorities would be careful if you had people canvassing one way or another in the prison, there could be division in the prison, that would not be good'. However, he made some positive suggestions about how to rectify this. 'Some posters, leaflets, maybe a panel of some kind [from political parties]' would be helpful. Dylan was very angry: 'I felt that if they weren't decent enough to canvass in the prisons, send in candidates, leaflets, information, run a seminar or a talk, then they weren't worth voting for . . . if we didn't deserve their time'. Aidan suggested: 'If TDs want your vote, they should come in and give a talk, with what's on offer from each party'. Geoff, who was serving life, echoed the opinion of the majority; there was neither political interest, nor motivation to participate in such an event. He continued:

> I suppose a lot of people wouldn't understand politics. A lot of them wouldn't be interested in politics. If more people came in and had a talk, let them know what politics means to them . . . But I don't think that any party wants to be seen to be coming into prison and saying 'vote for me, I'm Fianna Fáil, I'm Fine Gael [Irish political parties], I'll help you out'.

Oran, serving life, believed that, even though 'we are viewed as third-class citizens, [we are] still entitled to our say'. Conceding that 'it's a new experience, prisoners having the right to vote', Liam thought that 'so many knew so little about it'. Many did not vote due to 'a lack of civic education about their right to vote, that they maintain their rights as citizens'.

Perhaps understandably, prisoners were not only acutely aware of the difficulties posed by embracing the right to vote, they also provided some solutions. Dylan pointed out perceptively that 'no prisoners' group was ever consulted, prisoners' rights groups or lobby groups'. Despite being directly affected, there is no evidence that any of the policymakers sought advice from prisoners; they had not been given advance briefings, let alone examination of the bill. Had prisoners or ex-prisoners been consulted it may have allayed some of their concerns and overcome some of the challenges the implementation has revealed. Fionn, who was serving life, agreed: 'I'd say we would be best placed to tell politicians what parts of the prison work and what parts don't'.

Despite enfranchisement, prisoners believed they had little impact on parties' policies on what might be considered prisoner or criminal justice issues. When politicians mentioned prisoners, it was usually in an attempt to gain political advantage. 'There are no votes in it for them', believed Daniel, who was serving life. Thomas agreed and went further. The government was not interested in prisoners 'because it is not politically advantageous to be seen to be supporting the rights of prisoners'. Niall, who was serving nine years, agreed: 'It is not a vote-winning tactic to be interested in prisoners'. Louis, who was serving life, believed that politicians were penal populists: 'The only time politicians mention anything to do with prisons or anything like that is when they are looking for the public's votes . . . "We are going to enforce longer sentences." They are going to do this, that and the other [to prisoners]'.

While there might be limited electoral return for a candidate to visit an institution with many voters from outside their constituency, it appeared the individual neglect of prisoners seemed to confirm the general lack of engagement from politicians. There was a feeling of less eligibility. Despite enfranchisement, many still felt distanced from the electoral and political process. They believed it was up to candidates and parties to engage with them. Personal engagement between candidate and electorate and door-to-door canvassing is an 'essential feature of campaigning in Ireland' (Ó Muineacháin and Gallagher, 2008: 152). While it might be argued that is impractical in prison, political scientists have identified personal access to politicians as essential in connecting with voters and garnering votes. 'It provides a vital link between citizen and state, reduces alienation and provides feedback on the effects of government policies' (Gallagher and Komito, 2005: 243). While their disgruntlement was somewhat conventional and similar to voters outside prison, the failure of politicians to personally canvass within prison signalled to prisoners that they were still 'less than the average citizen'.

Politicians were aware of the challenges of trying to spread their message and to win votes among prisoners. However, during the parliamentary debate to introduce the legislation, none of the political representatives seriously suggested entering prisons to canvass. Minister Dick Roche replied to a question from an opposition member with the quip: 'I presume he was not proposing cell to cell canvassing. It is hard enough to get to all the doors in one's constituency' (Electoral (Amendment) Bill 2006: Committee Stage, 2 November 2006). He pointed out that political parties can encourage prisoners to vote for them by sending election literature to the home addresses to be passed on to prisoners, as 'it might not be very wise to have politicians of any persuasion, wandering around the place ... They cannot go to knock on the gates of Mountjoy [Prison] for canvassing' (interview with author, 2007).

Election literature is sent to the address where an individual is registered and it is the responsibility of the householder to pass it on to the registered voter. Not only had no candidate visited any of the prisons, no interviewee who had been in prison during the election had received election literature and this was a source of anger. Election literature is used to encourage party identification and canvass support leading to an increase in votes for a candidate or party. Parties and candidates spend vast sums of money promoting their programme during election time. Some of this funding comes from the exchequer. Under the Electoral Act 1997, Irish political parties are publicly funded, in proportion to electoral support at previous elections (sections 16–21; Whelan, 2000: 97). In 2007, nearly €13 million was paid to political parties from exchequer funds (Standards in Public Office Commission, 2008). Dáil election campaign expenses up to €8,700 are reimbursed if a candidate is elected and for defeated candidates who reach a specified proportion of the quota. During Dáil, European and presidential elections, candidates are entitled to send, free of charge, one item to each elector. This activity is similarly funded from public resources (Whelan, 2000: 108).

If the goal of legislators was to encourage active citizenship, then it seems from these interviews that more needs to be done to engage with prisoners. While it may not be feasible for all candidates to campaign within prison, interviewees believed there was little justification for no contact at all during the election campaign. Mauer (2011: 558) suggests that 'anecdotal evidence regarding prisoner input on public debate suggests that enfranchisement may in fact encourage candidates to engage prisoners in dialogue'. While this did not happen in Ireland, internationally the practice of canvassing in prison varies. In Canada, candidates are permitted, after appropriate security clearance, to canvass for votes in prison. In Australia, candidates or their agents are not allowed to canvass in person inside the penal institutions. In Belgium, candidates may send election advertisements to prisoners but no electoral display is allowed in prisons. In France, candidates or their agents are not allowed to canvass in person inside prisons, but prisoners are allowed to receive mail, and posters informing them of their rights must be displayed inside the prison. In Germany, candidates or their agents are not allowed to canvass inside prisons and in some federal states, election-related information is made available by prison personnel (HKSAR, 2009a: 26). In Denmark, prisons accept literature from political parties and candidates and display this in a common area, usually the library. In her survey of Danish prison management, Storgaard (2009: 253) found: 'In general, the prisons would not deny applications by parties or candidates to visit the prison, but they have no experience in arranging election meetings'. In a Canadian provincial election in 1998, Raóul Duguay from the Parti Québécois went to Cowansville Penitentiary to canvass the support of the 92 prisoners registered there (Mauer, 2011: 558).

Interviewees believed the participation rate would undoubtedly be improved with political engagement between prisoners, political parties and candidates. It would also indicate interest in their concerns. It would certainly send a message to prisoners that their vote is equal to the citizens outside. However, this would require deeper engagement by politicians personally to achieve improvements in the participation rate, including a willingness to go further than changing the law and actively encourage political engagement among prisoners.

Conclusion

When the Irish parliament enfranchised prisoners, there was a near universal belief that the legislation would not only allow them to vote but also lead to their engagement with civic society, encouraging them to adopt a more responsible ethos. However, low levels of registration and voting indicate that enfranchisement alone did not encourage political participation and civic engagement. If prisoners are given the right to vote, they should also have the opportunity to participate in elections on an equal basis as citizens outside. Widespread abstentionism reflects something deeper than not voting. It indicates disengagement from the political system and civic society. A robust and healthy democracy is built on participation among all sections of society. Despite the walls that separate prisoners physically from society, those politically engaged outside made attempts to continue that by voting inside. Even with the low turnout, there was a general welcome for enfranchisement, and a deeply held view from the vast majority of prisoners that while incarceration should remove liberty, it should not necessarily limit all other rights.

These interviews indicate disillusionment with civil society and a deep disconnection from government, politicians and the political system in general. The lack of personalised candidate engagement discouraged a greater participation rate within prison and it seemed to reinforce the alienation felt by many prisoners. Citizenship is not just about voting; it is about participation in the electoral process in an educated and informed manner. As many of the interviewees suggested, voting gave them a sense of belonging and ownership in society but while it was now open to them to vote, they felt there were still impediments to embracing the franchise.

The lack of positive interest from politicians was seen to confirm the marginality of the prisoner and the gulf between political rhetoric about inclusion and the reality that they remained ignored and uncanvassed. This reflected a deeper mind-set towards prisoners as they felt the government and politicians have no interest in their issues because it is politically unpopular. The perception that the political establishment neglected prisoners, especially during election time, as demonstrated in the lack of canvassing, election meetings and campaign literature, led many to abstain and opt out of the electoral and, ultimately, the political process.

The first election was a novel procedure for election officials, prison administrators and confined citizens. However, while it might have been expected that lessons drawn from the experience would strengthen the process and increase voting in subsequent polls, the turnout has not increased. Some of the reasons for non-engagement are similar to the population outside and others are unique to the location. The solution to low turnout must come from a combination of the prison service (who cannot be expected to take sole responsibility for electoral matters), electoral authorities, political parties, politicians, NGOs, education departments, the Inspector of Prisons, visiting committees, civic society and others within the wider penal sphere and electoral environment. As agents in this process, it also requires greater engagement by prisoners. Suggestions from prisoners and canvassing their views on possible solutions would likely enhance the numbers who register and vote. However, without the opportunity to engage in the electoral process on an equal footing with citizens outside, prisoners are given the chance to vote without the opportunity to fully engage in the political process. Unless there are opportunities for greater political and civic engagement among prisoners, the near universal welcome for enfranchisement might be dissipated, and the intent of enfranchisement – inclusion – could be lost in the reality of marginalisation and possibly further exclusion. Participation in political and civic society behind bars is the subject of the next chapter.

6

Civic engagement and community participation

Introduction

This chapter examines the level of active citizenship in prison and, similar to the last chapter, is based on the interviews with 50 prisoners. Recognising that citizenship encompasses more than just rights and responsibilities but is intertwined with participation, it considers their activities prior to imprisonment, the opportunities for participative citizenship behind bars and outlines some reasons for involvement in what are characterised as citizenship activities inside. The chapter concludes by reviewing the impact of an institution that limits agency, freedom of choice and movement, and restricts individuals' involvement in civic society. While engaging in activities traditionally associated with freedom is problematic in prisons, 'the ultimate places of social exclusion' (Stern, 2002: 138), different institutions provide opportunities for various levels of purposeful activity, programme participation and civic engagement. What impact, if any, does prison have on civic engagement and activities associated with citizenship among those who are sent there?

Citizenship as participation

Active citizenship

Citizenship remains a contested concept (Honohan, 2005; Ignatieff, 1989; Riordan, 2003 and 2004; Stewart, 1995). There are generally considered to be two forms of citizenship – state citizenship and democratic citizenship. The former is associated with a legal status in a nation state, the latter, involves *'shared membership of a political community ... [where] citizens are political actors constituting political communities as public spaces'* (Stewart, 1995: 65; emphasis in original). Inclusiveness, universality, equality and participation inform the modern understanding of citizenship. Inherent in these are the right to vote, to contribute to public debate, make educated and informed choices, participate in community governance and become involved in wider civic society.

In his seminal essay on citizenship, T. H. Marshall (1950: 28–9) described it as 'a status bestowed on those who are full members of the community. All who possess the status are equal with respect to the rights and duties with which the status is endowed'. However, he conceded that there is 'no universal principle for what those rights and duties shall be'. By the early twenty-first century, the concept of active citizenship had become so popular that it had 'leaped from the pages of legal and political texts into the everyday language of politicians, journalists and public servants' (Honohan, 2005: 170). Active citizenship is 'fundamentally about engagement and participation in society', focusing on the formal political sphere and the more informal community activity and volunteering (Nelson and Kerr, 2006: 12). Governments and political activists have become so concerned about the decline in levels of voting and civic engagement, two of the 'many indicators that all is not well with citizenship' (Riordan, 2003: 60), they have established commissions to examine the role of citizenship in wider society (Harris, 2005; Taskforce on Active Citizenship, 2007a).

Active citizenship has been defined as extending 'the concept of formal citizenship and democratic society from one of basic civil, political and social and economic rights to one of direct democratic participation' (Department of Social, Community and Family Affairs, 2000: 14). In a modern polity, citizenship is more than just about enjoying the legal right to vote, it is about the opportunities available to participate in, and contribute to, a democratic society. When citizenship is narrowed down to a legalistic concept with rights guaranteed by law and courts, this reduces the agency of the citizen. If legal rights of citizens are privileged, disputes can end up in courts, reducing the power of the citizen and the opportunity to participate in and influence decisions that affect their lives. The importance of the 'political forum is emasculated', reducing the role of citizen as a human agent and consequently there is an 'undermining of the distinctly political activity of participation' (Riordan, 2004: 53).

In prison, laws, rules and regulations predominate. This has led to the examination of prisoners as citizens in the context of their rights and the state's obligations and duties to them (see Easton, 2011; Livingstone *et al.*, 2008; van Zyl Smit and Snacken, 2009). Others have explored the opportunities for prisoners to participate as citizens and the obligations and duties that accompany their rights (Burnett and Maruna, 2006; Faulkner, 2002 and 2003; Levenson and Farrant, 2002; Pryor, 2002). However, citizenship is about more than just rights, entitlements and obligations; it is about the opportunity to participate in, and contribute to, the civic life of a community. This chapter examines prisoners as participative citizens.

Prisoners and social capital

Social capital is intrinsically linked with citizenship activities. It is built up through participation in civic activities and 'networks of civic engagement'. These 'foster sturdy norms of generalized reciprocity and encourage the emergence of social trust' (Putnam, 1995: 67). Social capital is a rather ambiguous concept, but essential to the co-operation necessary for engaging citizens. 'People are connected', according to Halpern (2005: 3), 'with one another through intermediate social structures – webs of association and shared understandings of how to behave. The social fabric greatly affects with whom, and how, we interact and co-operate. It is this everyday fabric of connection and tacit co-operation that the concept of social capital is intended to capture'.

Prisoners generally lack social capital, either because of their crime or background. The results from this study reflect the experience outside: as many prisoners came from neighbourhoods traditionally associated with imprisonment, with low levels of education, high unemployment and social deprivation, they were less likely to vote. Undoubtedly, committing a crime and subsequent conviction likely reduce the social capital of any individual.

Prison isolates and separates, not only physically from friends, family and trusted companions, but psychologically by creating regimes and discipline that do not enhance communication and co-operation, essential to active citizenship. Under the 1947 Prison Rules, communication among prisoners was a privilege and only allowed, 'if such intercourse is conducted in an orderly manner and does not impede the work on which prisoners are engaged'. It could be 'withdrawn by the Governor should he consider it necessary to do so in the interest of good order in the prison' (Rule 65). While it was generally recognised, even by the Minister for Justice, that the 1947 Prison Rules were 'outdated and in some cases obsolete' (Dáil Debates, 1998, vol. 495, col. 806), by the time of the 2007 general election, they still had legal effect. Four months later, a new set of prison rules, years in gestation, replaced them. Under the 2007 Prison Rues, all written and telephone communication with family, friends and acquaintances can be monitored. This makes the building up and maintenance of social capital more difficult.

While the incarcerated may not have large stores of social capital, it is rare (if ever) that an individual has absolutely none. In order to understand the level of social capital within any social formation, it is important to appreciate the reserves of trust that will encourage co-operation, build mutual alliances and engender reciprocity. Structure and environment can affect levels of social capital. The lack of unfettered contact with the outside world reduces social networks built up through past alliances and activities. The enclosed nature of the community means that individuals are forced to connect and work with people who they may have avoided outside. It might be too much to expect a level of mutuality from people who have little in common other than their convict status and the fact of their imprisonment. For many prisoners, their main, possibly only, objective is to do their time quietly and get away from the institution, both physically and psychologically.

Participation prior to prison
To begin to understand participative citizenship behind bars, it is important to determine the level of co-operation, reserves of social capital and civic engagement prior to imprisonment, and the traditions of civic and political activity citizens bring with them to prison. Active citizenship includes the more formal 'civic-political' sphere and the informal 'civic' sphere. As regards participation in the latter, of the 50 interviewees, 38 per cent (n = 19) had been members of sporting and community organisations, ranging from the local Gaelic Athletic Association (amateur sports) club to the Irish Traveller Movement, from the Campaign for Nuclear Disarmament to Age Action. Moreover, 42 per cent (n = 21) had been a member of a trade union prior to their imprisonment. As many, although not all, of these organisations were specific to a locality or workplace, there was no realistic chance of staying involved, a point with which all interviewees were in agreement. This was not necessarily because of their imprisonment, rather their location. Nonetheless, by this measure, imprisonment disrupts citizenship.

For the purposes of this study, eight activities were designated as 'civic-political engagement'. These ranged from the firmly committed, members of a political party to less intense activity such as signing petitions and wearing campaign badges. As indicated in Figure 6.1, 12 per cent (n = 6) had been members of a political party with 20 per cent (n = 10, including the six who were members) having worked with one at election time; 46 per cent (n = 23) had previously contacted a politician; 28 per cent (n = 14) had worn a campaign badge or sticker; 30 per cent (n = 15) had been a member of an action group; 42 per cent (n = 21) had signed a petition; 42 per cent (n = 21) had taken part in demonstrations and 38 per cent (n = 19) had boycotted products for a political cause.

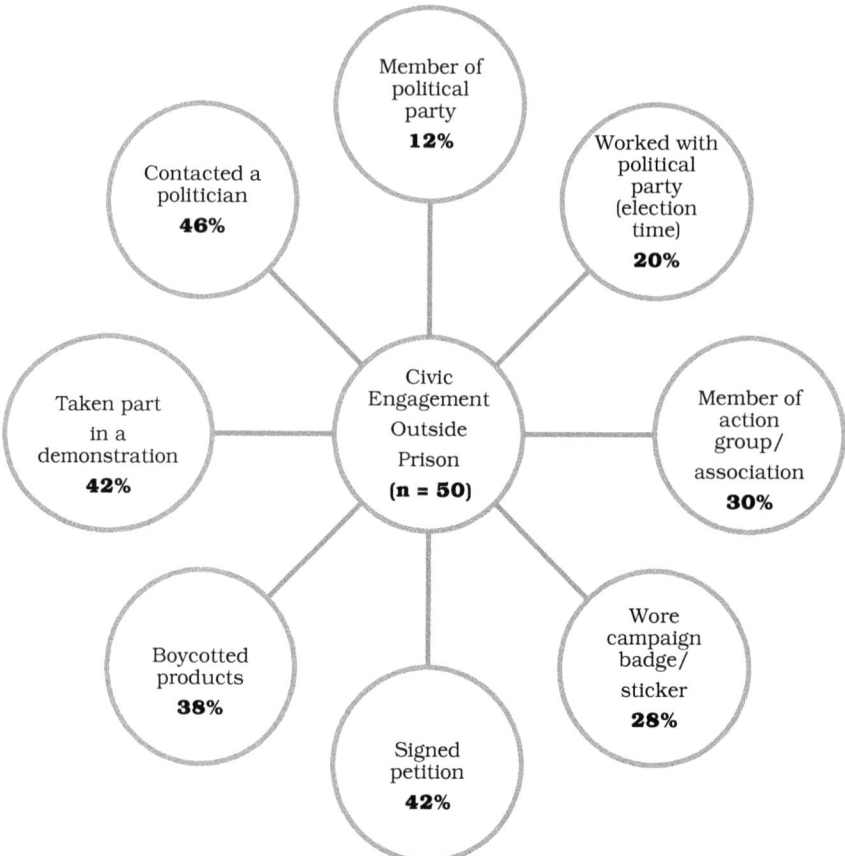

Figure 6.1: Civic participation prior to prison

In comparison, a survey among the general population, published in 2007, found that 29 per cent were involved in at least one community activity and 2 per cent had been actively involved in a trade union in the previous year (Taskforce on Active Citizenship, 2007b: 9–10). Nearly 19 per cent had attended a public meeting, 15 per cent contacted a politician, 2 per cent were members of a political party, with just under 1 per cent involved in local community action on poverty, employment or housing. In total, just over 37 per cent engaged in one type of civic-political engagement during the previous year (Taskforce on Active Citizenship, 2007b: 7–9).

The higher level of civic engagement among the interviewees represents a group of adult males, older and better educated than the general prison population. As active citizenship is 'positively related to age, educational background, marital status and socio-economic status' (Taskforce on Active Citizenship, 2007b: 3), the higher level of political engagement among the interviewees is perhaps unsurprising. An alternative explanation is also possible, despite vigorous attempts to include a representative group of prisoners, it is still feasible that the interview process attracted those who were more interested in putting their point across to a researcher on political engagement, even exhibiting a desire to engage in what may be seen as a civic activity. However, with nearly half (n = 23) of the interviewees not voting in prison, a key indicator of civic engagement and probably the most popular form of political activity, the group was reasonably evenly divided among voters and non-voters.

Citizenship inside

From citizen to prisoner?
A social organisation such as a prison operates within a unique dynamic. It is an environment capable of influencing the attitudes and activities of individuals or groups who live therein and in return being shaped by its inhabitants (see Crewe, 2012; Sparks et al., 1996; Sykes, 1958). Imprisonment, by its very nature, confines, restricts and prevents an individual from voluntarily participating in activities that they may have undertaken prior to their incarceration. Nevertheless, Goffman (1997: 90) believed that a common feature of closed institutions is the practice of an individual reserving something of him or herself 'through the little ways in which we can resist the pull' of the institution. He argued that this 'recalcitrance is not an incidental mechanism of defence but rather an essential constituent of the self' (Goffman, 1997: 89). Even in the most coercive institutions, individuals maintain a sense of individuality. 'It is precisely the struggle to maintain a sense of personal agency in the face of overweening institutional constraint', argued Sparks et al. (1996: 81), 'which motivates and sustains some of the prisoners most intractable contests with the system, long after they would seem to have "lost"'.

By engaging in pursuits associated with their previous life, some prisoners try to move beyond identification with the institution and assert their autonomy, to overcome the constraints, and resist the potential to transform their identity from citizen to prisoner. Nevertheless, the scope for being an active citizen is limited when freedom is taken away. While opportunities to remain autonomous are rare within prison, as Giddens (cited in Sparks et al., 1996: 67) pointed out in his comments on agency, 'even the most rigorous form of discipline presumes that those subjects are capable human agents'. Some prisoners find practical expression of their autonomy in their new community by rebelling through riotous behaviour (Scraton *et al.*, 1991), others through legal activism, the 'peaceful equivalent of a riot' (Jacobs, 1980: 459). Involvement in charitable activities by prisoners is 'now held up as examples of good citizenship' (Burnett and Maruna, 2006: 85). Some prisoners organise and participate in sporting activities to keep themselves active and mirror their community and political involvement outside (Korr and Close, 2008). Education can be an 'intelligent riot' (Davidson, 1995: 9), a transformative process, an opportunity to become a better informed and more critically aware citizen. Others spend their time in prison seeking solace and redemption in religious belief, whether pre-existing or acquired. Some use their sentence to deal with personal issues, by participating in programmes organised by Alcoholics Anonymous (AA), Narcotics Anonymous (NA) and the Alternatives to Violence Programme (AVP). For many, these activities are about surviving imprisonment through maintaining individuality and identity. Some have a more instrumental purpose, being seen as necessary for parole. In the course of the interviews it emerged that for some, non-engagement in any of the above and choosing not to vote was a political act. Non-participation was an act of defiance against the political and prison system.

Internationally, there is little data about prisoners' civic activities. In a series of interviews with 33 Minnesota prisoners, parolees and probationers, Manza and Uggen (2006: 160; generally see pp. 137–80) were 'struck by the degree to which time in prison encourages reflection on civic duty and responsibilities'. Among the activities that the respondents wished to undertake included volunteering, coaching youth sports and giving talks in public, especially about their 'experiences and mistakes'. Edgar *et al.* (2011: 5–6) in their study of active citizenship in UK prisons pointed out that active citizenship can be both challenging and rewarding in 'an environment in which there tend to be very few such opportunities'. However, they identified five types of active citizenship roles in prison. These were peer-support schemes – prisoners helping other prisoners; community support schemes – helping people outside prison; restorative justice programmes; democratic participation in prison life – for example prisoner councils; and arts and media projects such as prison-based radio stations and newspapers or prison arts programmes.

A 'community is often (but not necessarily), the context or framework in which the rights and responsibilities of citizenship can be given practical expression' (Faulkner, 2003: 290). What opportunities exist in the prison community for the rights and responsibilities of citizenship to be expressed? For practical reasons and sometimes for penal objectives, prisoners are not in a position to engage in the same activities inside prison as outside. 'Not surprisingly, there is no clear or convenient statement of what treating prisoners as citizens should actually involve as a matter of theory or practice' (Faulkner, 2002: 1). For the purpose of this study, a list of six activities was drawn up to embrace those that allowed for participation within prison. These are the more informal activities: participation in prison programmes, involvement in education, volunteering for charitable events, to the more formal political and community engagement: voting, contacting a politician while in prison and interaction with the various bodies that monitor and oversee prisoners' rights and conditions.

Putnam (1995 and 2000) found that a civically engaged society was characterised by high levels of voter turn-out, newspaper readership, membership of choral societies, football clubs and other such activities. Nearly half of those interviewed (n = 24) were participating in prison programmes, with just over half (n = 26) volunteering, mainly in some type of charitable activity. The vast majority (n = 45) were attending school. Chapter 4 showed that Arbour Hill had the highest level of voting among the registered population of any prison in 2007 and this study found that just over half (n = 27) of those interviewed had voted in prison; 50 per cent (n = 25) had communicated with one of the prison monitoring bodies; and over one quarter (n = 13), had contacted a politician. As indicated in Figure 6.2, this shows a rather high level of civic activity among participants in what is a restricted and regime-focused institution.

Prisoner participation

The following section sets out the opportunities for activities associated with citizenship and explores the experience and meaning of participative citizenship behind bars. Voting has been examined in detail in Chapters 4 and 5. This section concentrates on why prisoners participate in other civic-political activities. It considers how prisoners engaged with the limited opportunities open to them and if they retained any sense of agency which is necessary for the building up of social capital and participative citizenship.

Prison programmes

There are a number of programmes and groups operating in Irish prisons; some organised by prison staff, others by outside bodies. Some of the programmes are offence focused. The Psychology Service (IPS,

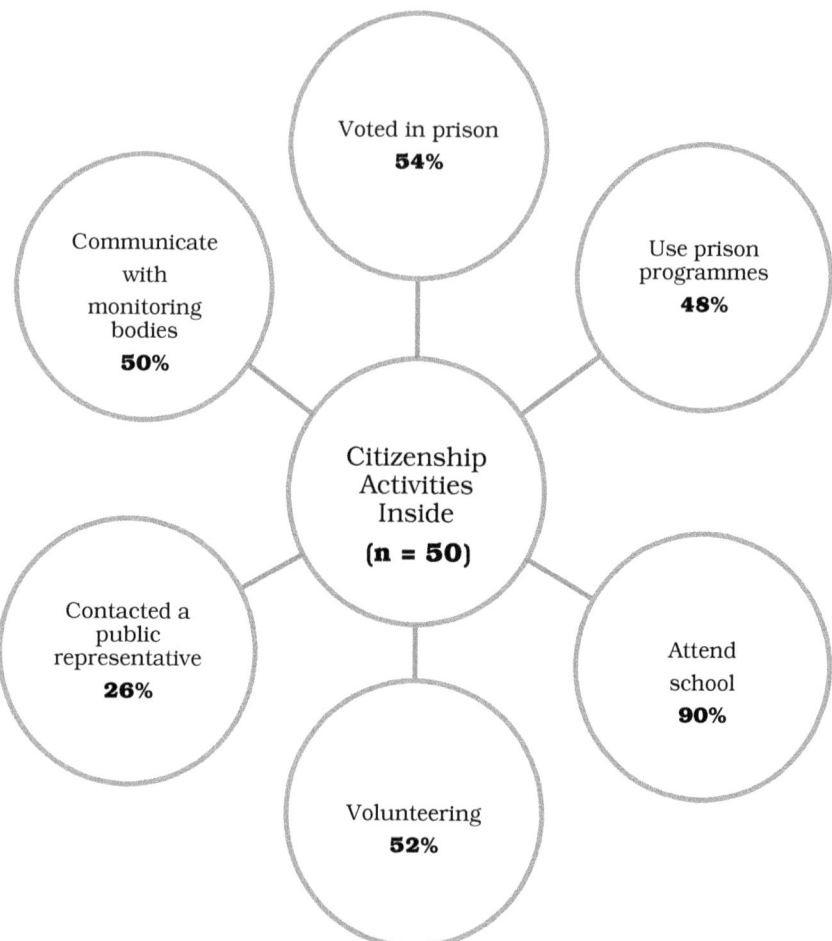

Figure 6.2: Civic participation inside prison

2007: 20) 'addresses those factors that put offenders at risk of reoffending, participates in the development of group programmes for particular offender groups'. Arbour Hill provided programmes such as the Group Skills, Thinking Skills and Sex Offender Treatment Programme and subsequently, in 2009, the Building Better Lives (BBL) programme which 'is a therapeutic programme for men who acknowledge that they have committed a sexual offence and who have a desire to build a better live for themselves' (Inspector of Prisons, 2011: 15). Others programmes reflect the sentence, such as the Lifers Programme. Alcoholics Anonymous, Alternatives to Violence and Addiction Studies deal with addiction or personal issues. Grow (Get rid of worry: mental health charity) was also active in the prison (AHVC, 2008: 3–4; IPS, 2007: 45). Shelton Abbey runs, among other activities, courses in Alcohol and Drugs Awareness, and Anger Management (IPS, 2007: 57). The Training Unit provides courses in Drug and Offending Behaviour and the Breakthrough Programme (IPS, 2007: 57).

Some of these 'offender-focused' programmes, especially those run by prisons, have been criticised as attempts by the state to 'responsibilise', 'redeem', or 'normalise' the socially excluded (Ryan and Sim, 2007: 697). Participation in 'offence-focused' programmes ordered by the courts can give the appearance of change through conformity, rather than an authentic personal transformation. These courses offer prison the opportunity to bend prisoners into compliance, as they attempt to slavishly correspond to the wishes of the institution and show willingness to do what is expected of them. Costelloe and Warner (2008: 137) argue that concentration on 'so-called criminogenic factors' by prison regimes and focusing on prisoners' shortcomings is a 'limited and negative approach'. It follows, they argue, the 'discredited medical model of imprisonment', with a culture that 'views the prisoner primarily as something broken in need of fixing or as an object in need of treatment'. It is no longer just about doing prison time. Individual agency and choice are reduced and prisoners participate in these programmes and comply to be seen to conform. The demands of the institution become all encompassing, with prisoners 'exhorted to practice their freedom in ways that are defined by the dominant party, but then coercively policed to make sure that they decide to do so. The illusion of pure choice is more obvious' (Crewe, 2012: 143). For long-term prisoners, especially lifers, participation in these courses is essential, and the process of achieving freedom early has become more complicated, even perplexing, with those with 'psychological power' (Crewe, 2012) wielding enormous influence.

Under the 2007 Prison Rules, Irish prisoners could theoretically benefit from an increase in remission from one quarter to one third (the 1947 Prison Rules entitled men to 25 per cent and women to 33 per cent remission) 'by engaging in authorised structured activity and the Minister is satisfied that, as a result, the prisoner is less likely to re-offend and will be better able to reintegrate into the community'. Interviewees claimed this reduction was not forthcoming. Their view was substantiated by the data. By the beginning of 2009, one person had been granted increased remission, despite hundreds applying for it (Foxe, 2009).

While aware that there are 'serious questions of justice to be asked about relating the length of time a person spends in prison to the degree to which he or she co-operates with or is involved in such activities' (Coyle, 2008: 230), these programmes are included in this study because participation is voluntary. They can express the autonomy of those who participate, demonstrating a desire to move away from activities that hurt others as well as criminal activity. They can also give individuals the possibility of dealing with personal issues at the same time, or before they can move on to other fora in which to participate as citizens. Active citizenship 'implies an orientation to challenge infringements not only of one's own rights, but also those of others' (Honohan, 2005: 175). For some prisoners, attending these courses is not only challenging their 'offending' behaviour as desired by the state but helps them in facing up to their transgression of the rights of other citizens. The effect may be far more liberating for both the individual and society than the intention. Nearly half (n = 24) had or were currently engaged in some type of activity related to their crime or personal issues through their involvement with prison programmes.

Education
Adults engage in education for a variety of reasons. Some do it to acquire knowledge and learn a skill. Others embrace the opportunity of a second chance education or to continue lifelong learning. A number get involved to pass the time, take their mind off other issues or in the hope of personal transformation (Thompson, 1996). Education is 'central to active citizenship' (Honohan, 2005: 178). An educated population is more informed and participative because, according to Marshall (1950: 26), 'education is a necessary prerequisite of civil freedom'.

Attending school in Irish prisons is voluntary. Arbour Hill Prison school 'is one of the major areas of this facility and it accounts for a large proportion of the prison's daily activity'. It had a high participation rate at over 85 per cent (AHVC, 2008: 4). In the Training Unit, 66 per cent participated in education and in Shelton Abbey, it was 79 per cent (IPS, 2008: 19). Reflecting this high level of attendance, 90 per cent (n = 45) of the interviewees were currently frequenting classes, with four of the remainder having previously attended school.

The promotion of an educational ethos within a prison can make the regime seem less harsh and normalise institutional routine. One of the four objectives of the Irish Prison Education Service is to 'help people cope with their sentence'. The other objectives are to help those in custody 'achieve personal development, prepare for life after release and establish the appetite and capacity for lifelong learning' (Irish Prison Education Service, 2007: 4). Prison education is provided, primarily by Vocational Education Committees (local education authorities), public libraries and the Open University and staffed by non-prison personnel. Drawing on the Council of Europe's recommendations in *Education in Prison* (1990: 4), it aims 'to develop the whole person bearing in mind his or her social, economic and cultural context'.

Education can provide an opportunity for prisoners to make meaning of the world they live in, become critically reflective learners, maybe leading to personal transformation, and the adoption of a pro-social citizen role (Behan, 2008; Costelloe and Warner, 2008; Duguid, 2000). Irish prison education 'employs a liberal adult education model ... voluntary student participation, a broad curriculum, student autonomy in subject choice' (Irish Prison Education Service, 2003: 16–17). This is important because education is not just what goes on in the classroom, but 'in particular, the structure, culture and wider curriculum of schools will affect people's attitudes and behaviours as much as formal education for citizenship' (Honohan, 2005: 178).

Attending school may be a way of not just surviving the prison, resisting the influence of the institution, but also of asserting human agency (Behan, 2008; Costelloe and Warner, 2008). The example of Malcolm X is often used to show prison education as 'a dramatic example of prisoners' ability to turn their incarceration into a transformative experience' (Davis, 2003: 56). Educational activities can allow for responsibility among prisoners, encouraging a more democratic ethos within the prison regime (Duguid, 2000; Eggleston and Gehring, 2000). In a prison context: 'Education acts as a buffer against the nihilistic threat', argue Wright and Gehring (2008: 335) in their reasoning for the prison school as a critical public sphere:

> It provides structures of meaning, feeling and mutuality between the teacher and student that resists the prison ethos. As civil spheres, schools can be restorative and transformative because they counter the stripping away of identities and distorted forms of interaction in prisons. When ethical conversations appear, the potential for critical thought and democratic participation is likely to follow, if not in prison, then perhaps on the outside.

Did prisoners use the opportunity to attend school to find a space for critical reflection and a place to become more informed citizens? A range of motivations prompted interviewees to attend school, sometimes depending on how much of their sentence they had served. Many used education to escape the monotony of the regime or, if they were unfulfilled in their workshop, the boredom of their daily grind, essentially to help them cope with their sentence. Diarmuid was serving seven years and had completed primary education outside. He attended school while in prison simply 'to pass the time'. Enda, serving six years, who had a similar level of education prior to incarceration, attended school because it's 'a change. It passes the time. You haven't too many options in here'. Louis, serving life, had completed his Junior Certificate, and attended school as part of adaptation within prison, to try 'to fill up time. To settle into a routine and fill up' his days with classes. Peter, serving nearly 15 years, was 'thrown out of school' when he was 13, but was attending school because, 'it's a different learning process than I went through when I was a kid. I feel safe with teachers now rather than back then'.

The desire to use their time constructively and prepare for release was a frequent theme. 'I go to school', replied Gavin, a lifer who had completed a Leaving Certificate (final high school examination) equivalent prior to incarceration, 'to equip myself as much as I can, to get ready to go home, to go back out into the workplace'. 'When I came to prison', responded Bruce, serving eight years, who was particularly motivated and had completed his Leaving Certificate, 'I set out to programme myself that I was to survive my sentence. I had to keep myself moving'. Vincent had spent just under a year in prison and had left education after primary school. He seemed to encapsulate the variety of reasons behind attending school in prison. 'Because I find that it passes the time and takes the tension off my mind', he suggested. 'I find I'll benefit when I get out. And because I am getting the chance to do them [academic subjects]'. Hugh, serving over 15 years, had left university for personal reasons after two years of a degree programme. He was studying a range of subjects, and working towards an Open University qualification. He admitted that 'while I do come here to learn', it had the added benefit of being 'sometimes a distraction from the prison routine'.

Having only completed primary school and recognising that lack of education may have been one of the factors that led to his offending, Charles, serving life, suggested that he 'missed out on education a lot in my younger days ... I didn't think I needed it'. Taking the opportunity for second chance education, he now believed that the lack of education 'was the biggest problem in my life'. Rory, also a lifer, who had completed his Junior Certificate (intermediate exam in high school), acknowledged that while he began attending school 'just to get out of the workshop', he now believed that 'an education is one of the most priceless gifts anyone could have'.

As prison education is not under the control of the Irish Prison Service, it allows for greater flexibility and possibly even a site for 'quasi-political learning with non-political authority figures' (Fairchild, 1977: 303). Education is not only a way of keeping the mind active, but with subjects such as political education, philosophy and sociology on offer, encourages critical learning. Some prison schools have become places of social and political empowerment (Behan, 2008; Duguid, 2000; Sbarbaro, 1995). As students attend school voluntarily, with a wide choice of subjects, this gave them an opportunity to participate as citizens and assert their autonomy even within the rather restrictive regime of a prison. Interviewees saw the school as a place apart. While some prison schools are physically located in different buildings from the rest of the prison, they are also separate because of the space they offer to express individuality. Early in the prison sentence, education provided an opportunity for survival and adaptation, while for some, as their sentence progressed, it encouraged a sense of agency and possibly even enabled active citizenship.

Volunteering
The most common form of volunteering in prison (perhaps partly because opportunities are so few) is participating in charitable activities. Sporadically, prisoners themselves, and from time to time in collaboration with chaplains, teachers or officers, undertake charitable initiatives. Others volunteer by organising sporting tournaments, or contribute to their community by involvement in the Catholic Church choir and Christian Bible study groups. Co-operation among individuals, especially in the cause of others, builds trust, mutuality and encourages individuals to move beyond narrow self-interest, essential for co-operative citizenship. A majority of interviewees volunteered (n = 26), mainly making furniture in workshops for children's charities, fun-runs for local children's hospitals, collections for Saint Vincent de Paul and making podiums and flags for the Special Olympics (held in Ireland in 2003). (While these interviews were being undertaken, preparations were being made for a sponsored charity run in one of the institutions.) These 'strengths-based practices ... provide opportunities ... to develop pro-social self-concepts and identity' (Burnett and Maruna, 2006: 84) and encourage participation in their immediate or wider community.

People outside prison get involved in and give to charity for a variety of reasons (see Putnam, 2000). While the amounts collected for charitable causes within prison may be considerably lower than outside, one overriding motivation for taking part, which reflects the nature of the population, was the feeling of guilt and a desire to seek atonement for their crime (see Maruna, 2001: Chapter 5 on redemption). 'Guilt. Most people feel guilt while they are in prison and they seek means to make amends, whether it is through charity or doing work for the less fortunate', believed Harry who had participated in various charitable activities during more than five years of his life sentence. Andrew, who was serving 14 years, agreed: 'There is a sense of responsibility that is linked to guilt . . . To try to make amends'. Half way through his nearly 15-year sentence, Peter, who had attended Alcoholics Anonymous, reflected on how to ameliorate the hurt he had caused:

> In my case, I've done quite a bit this time in prison for charity. I have a few friends who are dead. I did bad things to them. I feel guilty. With the Twelve Steps programme, I had to make amends. It puts my time to good use. To make me feel good about myself . . . I do it now because I want to do it. It started because I wanted to make amends.

Victor, who was serving ten years, agreed. 'I felt obligated to do it for my crime . . . I did a charity run [while in prison] . . . for the children's cancer ward . . . I felt I had to make amends for my crime'. Oran, who was serving life, reflected the view of many of the interviewees who participated in charitable activities: 'I think when you lose your liberty, some people believe they owe a debt to society and this is a good way to do it'.

A universal humanity and the desire to give something back to society was a recurring theme. Time in prison offered space for contemplation and opportunity to change. Prisoners undertake charitable activities because 'they are trying to change. They are trying to see things better for themselves, for people worse off than themselves', argued Vincent. 'It's a way of giving something back. People, regardless of sentence, can also have a wanting to help other people', believed Gavin who was serving life. It was a combination of helping others and the possibility of redemption, suggested Hugh, coming towards the end of a sentence of over 15 years: 'I think they get involved to contribute back to society, possibly. It makes them feel better about themselves. There isn't a lot of opportunities to do that in prison'. Samuel, who was serving life, agreed: 'anything that makes you feel good about yourself in prison is good'. 'Truthfully?' asked Fionn, a life-sentenced prisoner, when invited to give his opinion as to why he got involved in charity: 'It is nice to feel good about yourself every once in a while. When you come to prison you realise some of us have led a charmed life and others don't get the chance. If we can help them in some way, that is as good a place to start'. These motivations seem to concur with Crewe's (2012: 160) *Enthusiasts*, who got involved in projects 'that would demonstrate to their loved ones, to themselves, and to the law-abiding world with which they sought to identify that they were fundamentally "good people" with pro-social aspirations'.

Some interviewees felt there might be a more cynical motive; more compliance than growth (see Burnett and Maruna, 2006, for discussion). It was 'guilt, or else they wanted to look good trying for early release. And then there are other people who are genuinely charitable', according to Niall, who had served one third of his nine-year sentence. Reflecting a quasi-religious motive, Enda, serving six years, believed it was 'like finding God. A lot of people seem to be as nice as pie and all that. I think it's a bit of a front'. However, he conceded that there 'are probably dead genuine blokes who do it as well'. There were 'different reasons', according to Jake, who was serving life. 'Some people for reviews, a target for release. It is something that they can do to help other people and it helps themselves'. Sean, serving 12 years, was quite frank. Involvement in charitable activities was simply 'something to do. Something positive to improve self-esteem. Because everything is negative in prison. They may also feel guilt for what they have done and they would get brownie points for Heaven. That might be simplifying it a little. [It is] a way of assuaging their conscience for committing a crime'. Ben, serving five years, agreed that there were different reasons. 'I suppose they want to help the charities, to help the less fortunate. Plus it's great to be involved in something as your sentence goes quicker if you are not sitting around idle. You are keeping your mind occupied'.

Volunteering for Cathal, who was serving life, had another incentive. He was keen to move beyond the stereotype of the prisoner: 'there are not bad people in here. They have hearts'. Prisoners are 'different to what the media make them out to be', argued Daniel, a life-sentenced interviewee in his sixties. Dylan was coming towards the end of his seven-year sentence and, '[h]aving spoken to several prisoners who have taken part in charitable events for outside organisations', he believed:

> they obviously get satisfaction. They want to be seen to be members of society while they are inside ... part of a community. Prisoners have their own agenda – to show the community that they have humanity, that they are capable of giving back to society with humanity. They feel the issues of the world just as much as they do outside.

In their examination of citizen activities in British prisons, Levenson and Farrant (2002: 200) found that 'prisoners ... would prefer to volunteer to help the community than work on behalf of the prison service or private companies'. Working for prison enterprises amounted to supporting the prison service. Organising charitable activities themselves seemed not only to be an opportunity to engage in a non-prison activity but also to help others and a chance for positive autonomous activity. Shane, serving four years, felt it was an opportunity to do some good as 'I think initiative is stifled in prison'.

Many interviewees recognised that, as the perception of prisoners in society was very negative, participation in charitable activities was a means of affirming their self-worth and dignity, firstly to themselves and also of demonstrating this to the outside world. They wished to move beyond identification with their crime. Burnett and Maruna (2006: 85) pointed out that charitable activities undertaken by prisoners often 'are developed with no clear rationale, except that doing good deeds is good'. At times there seemed a reluctance on behalf of the prison service and even the charity benefiting from the contribution in time or money to publicise it for fear of negative repercussions. With no determined policy by prison authorities to publicise these activities, Cathal, who had served over ten years of a life sentence, saw this as a missed opportunity: 'I don't think prisoners are considered part of society. I think the Prison Service could do a lot more to portray a more positive image of prisoners. There is an awful lot of good that prisoners could do, even in jail. And that opportunity is not being exploited'.

Other forms of volunteering include participation in the Listener Scheme (Samaritans peer-support scheme operating in prisons). This is somewhat unique because it is one of the few available opportunities to provide peer-support to fellow prisoners. The Listener Scheme was in its infancy in the Republic of Ireland in 2007. (For examples of established Listener schemes in the UK, see Levenson and Farrant, 2002.) Nevertheless, a number of more mature prisoners had trained to be Listeners and two had been on the Steering Committee of the Listener Scheme.

Levenson and Farrant (2002: 196) found that volunteering in the community can provide a way for prisoners to support each other 'as well as establishing a connection between prisoners and the outside world'. While temporary release for community volunteering occurs in some Irish prisons, this option was not available to most prisoners. If they wished to participate, it was from confinement. While there was no direct personal contact with the people being helped, sometimes representatives from organisations visited the prison to accept the proceeds of charitable events.

Volunteering opportunities in prison are few, but for this study volunteering was taken as one of the indicators of active citizenship. As with the outside world, there are other possible motives, rather than mere altruism, especially when, as a number of interviewees pointed out, a parole board hearing is looming. While a number suggested that guilt motivated their participation, volunteering involved stand-alone activities unrelated to their crime or crime in general. Nobody suggested they had organised charitable activities for organisations such as Victim

Support, or specifically for their victim. For a number of respondents there was a deep yearning to be seen as more than just their crime. There was an overwhelming desire to allay guilt, to make amends, to help others and, significantly, to portray a more positive image of prisoners to the outside world.

Political contact
The results from the survey outlined in Chapter 4 found low levels of trust across a broad range of political and civic institutions, from the media to politicians. Chapter 5 revealed that lack of political engagement from political parties and individual politicians, especially during election time, was a cause of concern, even anger, which some suggested had put them off voting. Nevertheless, if prisoners have political concerns (and rather like the public outside, concerns unrelated to politics), they can contact public representatives. The Inspector of Prisons pointed this out to prisoners he met during his visit to Arbour Hill in 2007 (Inspector of Prisons, 2007a: 32–3).

Politicians in Ireland regularly make representations to the Minister for Justice on behalf of prisoners from their constituencies. These are primarily about sentence management, including requests for early release. Periodically, this practice causes difficulties for politicians. Following the resignation of a junior minister in 2002 after he made representation to a judge concerning a case the latter was scheduled to hear, a newspaper undertook an investigation into political representation on behalf of prisoners. It found that in a 22-month period, 89 TDs (out of 166), ten senators (out of 60) and two MEPs (out of 15) made representations on behalf of those 'charged with or convicted of crimes'. The most prolific was Fine Gael (opposition) spokesman on Justice, Jim Higgins, with 15 representations, and the next was the Taoiseach, Bertie Ahern, with eight (Brennock, 2002: 3).

Six years later, another newspaper report found that in just over a year up to early 2007, there were 55 representations to the Minister for Justice, Equality and Law Reform on behalf of prisoners. Among the petitioners were the Taoiseach, Bertie Ahern, and other members of his cabinet. During this period, the Minister for Justice, Equality and Law Reform 'turned down 27 representations for the early release or prison transfers, granted 17, and responded to 11 other general inquiries from TDs' (Brennan, 2008).

Despite the distrust, even disdain, for politicians, 26 per cent (n = 13) of the interviewees had made representations to a TD or directly to a minister while incarcerated. Politicians (other than the Minister for Justice) are not among those who can be written to confidentially under

Prison Rules. Perhaps mindful of this, there was some hesitancy about personally contacting politicians; in six of the 13 cases, family or friends made representations on their behalf. These contacts were primarily in connection with their incarceration.

Charles, serving life, had contacted a politician during a previous sentence. The latter 'wrote a letter to the governor, [telling him] that I came from a respectable family. He asked would he let me out for TR [Temporary Release]'. On that occasion, he believed his communication led to his request being granted. Sean, serving over ten years, a politically aware interviewee, contacted a politician, but he recognised that there 'is not a lot they can do for you. It was regards my conviction, so they don't really want to get involved'. Three of the 13 believed they had been moved to Arbour Hill (which pleased them) because of representations being made on their behalf by a politician.

The possibility of increased remission (up to one third) under the new prison rules prompted Ross to contact the Minister for Justice, 'asking what one had to do to qualify for remission and where one should apply'. As he had completed over two thirds of his nine year sentence, he had a particular interest in this communication. However, he received 'a standard letter that didn't deal with my question. I then applied for a third remission through the normal channels and didn't get a response'.

Some interviewees argued that politicians were hesitant about representing prisoners, and therefore there was no point in contacting them. Thomas, who was serving over 15 years, related it to the change in legislation to enfranchise prisoners: 'Whilst I am allowed to vote, there appears to be reluctance on behalf of political representatives to make representations on behalf of prisoners. I have a right to vote. I should be allowed to be represented on my behalf'. Cian, serving 15 years, had not contacted a politician, but 'wanted to'; however, he believed 'you can't'. This was not about a particular issue but rather with a view to voting for a candidate in the general election. 'During the recent election, if I wrote a letter asking for politicians to come in on a visit and explain things to me, that's not going to happen'. While this may be the case during election time, the rather large number of representations made by parliamentarians seems to somewhat challenge the assertion that politicians will not represent prisoners, even those convicted of the most serious offences. Some may have wanted to contact politicians but were cautious about any action that could attract unwarranted attention and have them labelled a troublemaker. However, even with this possibility, over one quarter of the interviewees pursued an activity traditionally associated with free citizens. This was in light of the fact that many were happy in Arbour Hill (the prison they wished to be in) and had no desire to complain to politicians or anyone else. They accepted their sentence and the prison as legitimate.

The issue of politicians lobbying on behalf of prisoners entered the public domain again in January 2009, when it was reported that a number of years previously, the then Minster for Justice had communicated with a former Minister for Justice about the conditions under which a high profile constituent was being held. Michael McKevitt was serving 20 years for directing terrorism as leader of the Real IRA. When the contact became public, it created some media controversy with calls for the resignation of the minister, who denied any wrongdoing in the case. One particularly outraged newspaper editorial suggested that this is 'a reminder that the practice of politicians seeking favours for prisoners should stop'. However, even though they were incensed by the practice, the leader writer stopped short of suggesting that prisoners be denied access to ministers. 'If there is a fair case to be made, prisoners or their relations can make it themselves. Involving TDs in the process brings the entire system into disrepute, even when the case is comparatively trivial' (*Irish Daily Mail*, 2009).

As interviewees claimed that letters can be read and censored, and phone calls can be listened to, they may be reluctant to engage in what could be seen as overtly political acts. Despite this, the number of prisoners contacting politicians, at over 25 per cent, is greater than among the general population. In the year up to 2006, just over 15 per cent of the general public contacted a public representative (Taskforce on Active Citizenship, 2007b: 7). Gallagher and Komito (2005: 244) reported that results from the 2002 Irish National Election Study showed that in the previous five years, 21 per cent of the general public contacted a TD. They concluded: 'Most of those who contact a TD seem to be satisfied with the experience, as 88 per cent of them say they would do the same in future in similar circumstances'. Six out of thirteen prisoners had received favourable responses and were positive about the contact.

Engagement is a two-way process and while prisoners asserted their right to contact politicians, the number of political communications made on behalf of prisoners also indicated a willingness on the part of politicians to represent their confined constituents. However, from the respondents in this survey and the general tone towards politicians, it seems that the latter are used, rather than appreciated. Politicians were contacted about individual complaints rather than the general conditions of the institution or the wider penal system. If they wish to complain about their conditions, they must do so elsewhere.

Oversight and monitoring bodies

Few avenues are open to prisoners to participate in the governance of prisons, to alter or influence their community, an essential element of citizenship. Even doing this legitimately can be difficult; some interviewees believe that to be labelled a 'troublemaker' can have consequences. There are, however, a number of avenues open to prisoners who wish to make complaints about their conditions or treatment, or feel their rights have been violated. In a democracy, this is essential, because 'citizens should have accessible procedures for appeal or redress if they believe they have been unjustly treated' (Faulkner, 2003: 288). This can be done through various oversight and monitoring bodies, including the UN Committee against Torture (CAT), European Committee for the Prevention of Torture and Inhuman or Degrading Treatment or Punishment (CPT), the Inspector of Prisons and the Prison Visiting Committee. NGOs such as the Irish Penal Reform Trust, the Irish Council for Civil Liberties and the Conference of Prison Chaplains also observe and report on conditions within prisons.

Nearly half of those interviewed (n = 24) had been in contact with either the CPT, Prison Inspector or visiting committee. One third (n = 8) of these had received what they characterised as a positive response, mainly a transfer to another prison. Some who had not contacted these bodies stated that they had nothing to complain about and were very positive about the prison. Others, however, claimed that if they communicated by letter this would be censored or stopped by the prison authorities and, possibly, repercussions would follow.

Prior to this study, the CPT had visited Ireland on four occasions; in 1993, 1998, 2002 and 2006. It had never visited Arbour Hill. During each of its four visits, the CPT visited Mountjoy Prison. Limerick Prison was visited on three occasions, Cork Prison, Cloverhill Remand Prison and St Patrick's Institution for Young Offenders on two occasions each (CPT, 1995; 1999; 2003; 2007a). This supports the view that it is a well-ordered place; if there were concerns about Arbour Hill, it would most likely have been visited, given the small number of prisons in the state and the repeat visits to some of them. Therefore, while it is not surprising that very few interviewees had dealings with the CPT, it was possible for long-term prisoners who had been in other institutions to have met them.

In 2002, the Republic of Ireland's first Inspector of Prisons since independence was appointed. The position was put on a statutory basis five years later in the Prisons Act 2007. The Inspector issues an annual report on each prison inspected to cover its general management, level of its effectiveness and efficiency, conditions, general health and welfare of prisoners, staff conduct, compliance with prison rules and international standards, prison programmes, facilities, security and discipline.

Between 2002 and 2008 the Inspector visited Arbour Hill on a number of occasions, including in January 2007 to examine how registration for the upcoming election was proceeding (Inspector of Prisons, 2007a: 36). During a further visit that year, among the issues prisoners raised were the low level of temporary release, unavailability of places for sex offenders in open centres, uncertainty about the length of time life-sentenced prisoners must serve, lack of a sentence plan, access to their children, prices in the tuck shop, lack of psychological services, accommodation on release for those convicted of sex offences, problems living in the community, including press exposure, and transfer to another jurisdiction (Inspector of Prisons, 2007b: 33–6).

Many of these issues were raised in the course of the interviews. Gavin, a lifer, spoke to the Inspector of Prisons on two occasions but remained unconvinced about the utility of the office. 'It had already been said to me that regardless of the report, it carried no weight. It was sadly just a paper exercise again'. Cathal had already spent over ten years of his life sentence in prison, during which time he met both the visiting committee and the Inspector of Prisons. The outcome was unsatisfactory, he believed, because of the limitations of these bodies. 'Both were unable to effect change. Both responded that they hadn't got the power to act. They are there as oversight. That's all'. Some of these limitations were set out in the legislation: 'It is not the function of the Inspector to investigate or adjudicate on a complaint from an individual prisoner, but he or she may examine the circumstance relating to the complaint where necessary for the performing of his or her functions' (Prisons Act 2007, Section 31 (6)).

Access to the Inspector was an important issue. Despite 'notices placed on notice boards' of the Inspector of Prisons upcoming visit and 'in all 14 prisoners' being seen on a 'one-to-one basis' during that inspection (Inspector of Prisons, 2007b: 32), some who were keen to speak to him felt they were not in a position to do so. Only a 'certain amount of people were picked to talk to him, hand-picked', suggested Evan, also a lifer. 'I didn't get to speak to him. Only the good boys get to talk to him. I will put it this way – the people who get to talk to him will not ask too much awkward questions'. Louis, another life-sentenced prisoner, was equally critical: 'I don't see the point to them'.

> In all my years, I have never experienced anything that they have done to change or help, so I haven't a positive experience with them ... It was the same when the judge [Kinlen, former Inspector of Prisons] came in. You

didn't get to put your name forward ... It wasn't like an open floor or anything like that. A handful of prisoners were picked out, went off and had a discussion with him.

Jake, who had been in a number of institutions, and was serving life, echoed what he felt was restricted access to the Inspector:

> When the Inspector of Prisons visited, they picked who goes to see them. Only a small group represents the prison body as such. When a previous Inspector visited ... only six to eight people were picked and spoke to him. You could put your name forward. But not everybody who put their name forward was picked. I don't know what criteria they used to pick the individuals they picked at the time.

The first Inspector of Prisons was conscious of the limitations of his office and he made prisoners aware of these. On a visit to Arbour Hill, prisoners raised legal issues, and were advised by the Inspector to speak to their legal representatives (Inspector of Prisons, 2007b: 33–6). During his visit, he informed the 14 prisoners he met of the statutory limitations and they 'were advised of the route they could take if they had a personal complaint such as to the Governor, the Visiting Committee, the C.P.T. the Minister, the Courts or their politician'. He believed that they 'all recognised and acknowledged the restraints' (Inspector of Prisons, 2007b: 32–3).

Visiting committees oversee conditions in each of the 14 prisons throughout Ireland. Their role is 'from time to time and at frequent intervals to visit the prison in respect of which they are appointed and there to hear any complaints which may be made to them by any prisoner' (Prisons (Visiting Committee) Act, 1925, Section 3.1 (a)). The visiting committee 'shall at all times have free access either collectively or individually to every part' of the prison (Section 3.2). The Minister for Justice appoints members on 'foot of representations, usually either by individuals nominating themselves or from local representatives nominating a constituent' (Department of Justice and Equality, 2008. For a legal interpretation of the powers, duties and functions of the visiting committee, see McDermott, 2000: 23–9). As these are political appointees, they are usually aligned with the parties in government. They visit prisons on a regular, usually monthly basis and each visiting committee issues an annual report to the Minister for Justice, which is later published.

Shane, a young interviewee, serving a four-year sentence, had a positive experience with the visiting committee. 'I was in Cork Prison. I wanted to get off the landing. I asked to go to the pad [padded cell]. I was speaking to them in Cork and I was telling them how I was feeling.

I think it could be with their help that I got here'. Harry, who had served over five years of his life sentence, had not contacted any of the monitoring bodies simply because he had 'nothing to complain about'. Only beginning his sentence, and having spent short periods in other prisons, Jason, serving life, saw no need to contact the visiting committee. He saw 'no inhumane treatment whatsoever, except for in other places. This place [Arbour Hill] is fabulous'. Oisin, also serving life, believed while there was little they could do in the event of a grievance, there was little to complain about. 'It's prison – it's not perfect ... Management and staff are very humane, understanding and compassionate'. Rory, serving life, with over ten years completed, had spoken to the CPT, the visiting committee and the Inspector of Prisons. 'Personally I spoke of my own experiences. I felt that in this prison nobody could make a complaint about the routine or regime. Whereas in Wheatfield, Midlands, Mountjoy [prisons] it is different. I think I was just being honest'.

Despite most respondents speaking positively about the environment in Arbour Hill they were sceptical of the efficacy of the visiting committee. Having spoken to the visiting committee, Hugh, who had served over ten years, found them 'very helpful' but he was resigned to his somewhat powerless position; they could do little for him. 'I just accepted my lot. Let's put it that way'. Dylan, serving seven years, spoke to visiting committees on several occasions. It was a very positive outcome, 'eventually'. However, 'the [prison authorities] said to me, "At the end of the day, they don't run this prison, we do. We have the final decision. And you can speak to whoever you like." I know that the authorities resent outside bodies coming to the prison'.

There was a sense of resignation at the lack of response from the visiting committee. Oran had served over ten years of his life sentence, and had asked for an area for visits with his daughter. That had been three years previously and he was still awaiting a reply. 'I would only go to them [visiting committee] if I had a burning issue', remarked Killian, who was coming towards the end of his four-year sentence. 'And the only burning issue I have is to get out of here and they are not going to help me in that direction'. Geoff, a life-sentenced interviewee, wanted to contact the visiting committee and the CPT but was hesitant to do so. However, he felt more informal avenues were open to him, as there was a positive prisoner–staff relationship. 'If you have a problem', he suggested 'you can talk to the governor about it and what he says goes. I find him very fair anyway. Their hands are tied in lots of ways'.

Not all the experiences with the visiting committee were positive. Tadhg, who was beginning a two-year sentence, had experience of the visiting committee during a previous sentence. They were 'useless. I had no faith in the visiting committee. I had no faith at all'. Sean, who was coming towards the end of his sentence of just over ten years, was scathing in his criticism. 'Absolute shower of useless bastards. Feathering their nest, like Bertie's [Ahern, former Taoiseach] crowd. Some of them seem to be political appointees. They didn't do anything'. Oliver was starting his four year sentence, but had been in prison before. His view was that:

> You say what you need to say. They say it to the [prison authorities] and they just push it under the carpet. They mean nothing to me. If they are for prisoners' rights, they are not doing their job. They are not staying to see the whole thing carried out. They are even worse than the government – the VC – more empty promises.

Visiting committee Annual Reports detail a list of complaints received in the course of the year. In 2004, four prisoners met the Arbour Hill Visiting Committee. Two complaints concerned medical treatment, another was about the lack of reply from a minister and another sought a transfer to an open centre or temporary release (AHVC, 2005: 4). In 2005, three prisoners met the committee to raise similar issues (AHVC, 2006: 3). In 2006, seven prisoners met the committee to discuss issues, including travel to and from court, temporary release, medical concerns, bullying and one 'complained that an officer pushed him during a fire evacuation exercise' (AHVC, 2007: 2–3). In the course of 2007, the Arbour Hill Visiting Committee received no formal complaints. However, it stated that 'in this context it should be borne in mind that the Committee maintained a high profile on the prison floor and were always available to listen and respond to any prisoners' concerns: this would obviously impact on prisoners' need to formally seek a meeting with the Committee' (AHVC, 2008: 3). These accounts concur with O'Donnell's (2008) description of visiting committee reports as generally brief and uncritical.

In an institution that houses a wide variety of people who are held against their will, the low level of complaints (whether justified or not, upheld or rejected) could be because of the well-ordered and just running of an institution. It could also be related to a perception that the visiting committee mechanism is partial, as many respondents suggested, and of little assistance in upholding their rights. O'Donnell (2008: 123) has pointed out that the brevity of visiting committee reports leaves us with a lack of understanding of life in Irish prisons. However, he observed that the 'report of the Castlerea Prison Visiting Committee, which stretched onto a third page, interpreted the fact that few prisoners wished to communicate with it as "an indication of how well the prison is been [sic] run"'. He concluded: 'Other less benign, and more plausible, explanations for prisoners' apathy are not considered'. The evidence from the interviews reveals similarities with prisoners' experience in England and Wales, with their Boards of Visitors (since replaced with Independent Monitoring Boards), where concern was expressed by both prisoners and commentators that they seemed 'content to pursue a low profile and somewhat cosy relationship with the prison authorities' (Livingstone *et al.*, 2008: 12–13).

There was also a concern that making a complaint that was not upheld by the visiting committee could lead to a formal sanction. Under the 2007 Prison Rules, a prisoner can be punished if he or she makes 'false allegations against the Governor, any prison officer, any prisoner, any visitor to the prison or any other person' (Schedule 1 (12)). It could also lead to an informal sanction. 'I suggested that I was going to contact one of them', said Rian, serving life. 'I was told that if I made threats like that I would be transferred to another prison'. Luke, who was coming towards the end of his three-year sentence, summed up the reason for being careful about involving outside monitoring bodies.

> Firstly, I haven't had any need, thankfully. Secondly, if there is a chance you can get something done, it could be outweighed by possible repercussions. Prison is seen as self-regulating. If you fuck up, you are moved on. Very simple, that's what you are told when you get here first. People don't want to be moved on. It is one of the better prisons to keep your dignity. They fear being moved on. And that's one of the threats they have over you. Even if it is within your rights, generally people will not complain for fear of being moved on.

Some interviewees had taken the opportunity to speak with monitoring and oversight bodies and on minor issues they were happy. Despite the 1947 Rules for the Government of Prisons and the 2007 Prison Rules stating explicitly that certain categories of correspondence could not be opened, including with the monitoring bodies, some interviewees had concerns about writing to them. There was much confusion among prisoners and concern from the CPT. Bernard, who was one third of the way through his nine-year sentence, and had been in a number of institutions, made a complaint to the Inspector of Prisons and was happy with the response. 'We got the prices in the shop reduced'. However, there was a much more serious issue on his mind. '[W]e were unable to resolve the issue of legal privilege regarding letters. I have an ongoing battle regarding letters to and from solicitors. I am trying to get letters from solicitors unopened'. Communicating by letter with these bodies could have consequences, believed some of the respondents. Ben, serving five years, was one of those who had not contacted any of the monitoring bodies, not because he had no issues, but he believed his letter would not be sent. 'Because if you wrote to the Inspector of Prisons, all your letters are censored. So if they thought that you were writing to the Inspector of Prisons about the prison, they wouldn't let it go out, so there's no point'. Jake, serving life, had already spent over ten years in various prisons and was similarly dismissive of the visiting committee. 'Nobody gives much credence to the visiting committee. Writing to them, no, because it's going to go through a censor. Even though they might declare it is not, it is still going through a censor'.

During their 2006 visit to Ireland, the CPT reported that it was 'concerned to note that correspondence between prisoners and lawyers may be inspected and read by prison staff'. The European Court of Human Rights 'in relation to this matter would suggest that, save in exceptional situations, such an interference is contrary to Article 8 of the European Convention on Human Rights' (CPT, 2007a: 42). The Irish government responded that 'prisoners are entitled to send a letter to their legal advisors and that the letter is sent without delay and without it being opened'. They continued: 'Likewise letters to prisoners from their legal advisors are given to prisoners without delay and are only opened to the extent necessary to determine that they are indeed letters from legal advisors. Any examination is in the presence of the prisoner to whom the letter is addressed' (CPT, 2007b: 45).

Under the 1947 Rules, all communication by letter, including correspondence with legal advisors, save in the case of remand prisoners, could be opened and censored. The 2007 Prison Rules allow confidential communication with, among others, the Minister for Justice, the Prison Visiting Committee, the European Court of Human Rights, the CPT, the Inspector of Prisons and the Irish Human Rights Commission. The CPT reported after its 2006 visit that it 'trusts that appropriate instructions will be given to prison establishments to ensure that the inviolability of correspondence between the CPT and prisoners is assured' (CPT, 2007b: 5). The Irish Government responded that it is 'committed to giving its fullest co-operation to the CPT ... It is the policy of the Irish Prison Service not to open correspondence between prisoners and the CPT. Any breaches of policy that might occur from time to time are failures of implementation and are regretted' (CPT, 2007b: 5; underline in original). Despite these assurances from the government and the new Prison Rules, there was a lack of trust from prisoners when it came to personal correspondence with the monitoring bodies. Without the unrestricted access allowed for in the Prison Rules, prisoners are unlikely to engage with the oversight and accountability structures and these bodies might get a rather rosy view of Irish prisons.

Many interviewees were critical of the method of appointment to visiting committees and had suggestions for reform. Conor, serving life, suggested that it was 'jobs for the boys. Make it voluntary and not being paid and not being appointed by the Minister for Justice'. (Members of visiting committees are not paid for their work. They receive expenses for their visits. This is regularly confused with payment and criticised, especially because members are usually political associates of the party in government, have little or no experience of penal or criminal justice issues, travel long distances and accrue large expenses.) He believed the Saint Vincent de Paul and the prison chaplains did a lot more positive work for prisoners than the visiting committee. While considering the visiting committee as 'a waste of time', Andrew, who was serving 14 years, believed that with prisoner representation they had potential. 'If they really wanted to help prisoners [there had to be an] acknowledgement and acceptance of having ex-prisoners on them'. Because of the political patronage of the visiting committee, it was almost universally seen as toothless. Rory, serving life, agreed with Andrew about the lack of a voice and argued that it was essential to listen to prisoners, not have others speaking on their behalf.

> I don't see it ever happening but I think it would be a very good thing if the Department of Justice decided to have some ex long-term prisoners involved in discussion of prison running, how better it should be managed, because I think people who have been in the system a long time learn a lot on how things could be done better.

Until 2002, despite criticism and shortcomings, the visiting committee was the only Irish monitoring body with regular contact available to prisoners. The criticism of the visiting committee is neither new nor the preserve of prisoners. Eighty years earlier, during the debates to establish the visiting committees in the 1920s, opposition politicians expressed similar concerns about the method of appointment. Tom Johnson TD, leader of the Labour Party, argued that the Minister for Justice appointing people to safeguard prisoners' interests 'seems to me it is a wrong principle'. He believed that 'there ought to be embodied in some way the idea that the persons who are to be appointed as visitors should represent or be nominated by some authority, not a Government authority' (Dáil Debates, 1925, vol. 10, col. 263–4). However, former prisoner and then Minister for Justice, Kevin O'Higgins, rejected the criticism because he refused to accept that members of the visiting committee were 'emanations of the Minister' and therefore do 'not adequately represent the general public'. He was, however, clear about the role of the visiting committee: 'It is not so much a question of representation for the prisoners or their relatives as representation for the general public, to see that the prison system is conducted humanely and as they would wish it' (Dáil Debates, 1925, vol. 10, col. 264). Commenting on the visiting committees 60 years later, the Whitaker Report echoed some of these criticisms and recommended changes in 'their method of appointment, their procedures and their duties' (Whitaker, 1985: 16).

There was little faith that engagement with the bodies established to monitor prison conditions would make a difference, other than in a negative way. Many interviewees who had spent time in other prisons suggested that while Arbour Hill was, relative to other institutions, a very progressive place, violence-free, with a healthy officer–prisoner relationship and a good education department, they believed that there was always the threat of being moved hanging over any action that one may consider undertaking. However, without access to an effective visiting committee to allow individual prisoners to question their conditions of detention (and without access to the Ombudsman or a dedicated Prisoner Ombudsman: see Chapter 7), they must rely on other bodies and institutions, in which they have little faith. Of all the monitoring bodies, most cynicism, indeed near universal disdain, was reserved for the visiting committee, even from those who had communicated with them. This is rather paradoxical; the organisation that had most contact with prisoners through regular prison visits had the least respect among those they were intended to protect. Even with all the positive comments, concern that access to the various bodies was restricted or circumscribed eroded their legitimacy. If there is little trust in these bodies, this reduced the likelihood that prisoners would approach them and undermined their legitimacy if prisoners failed to engage with them.

Compliant citizens

Each of the activities examined offered an opportunity for active citizenship. However, despite this potential, it seems that it is an individual experience for those who take part. Prisoners attending school saw it as an opportunity to acquire skills, normalise the regime and break the routine. Contacting politicians was not for improvement of general conditions within the prison, penal reform or political progress. It was to achieve (perhaps, understandably) personal improvement in their circumstances. A general complaint to any of the monitoring bodies, it was felt, would be frowned upon, leading to possible negative consequences. Even participating in charitable activities did not directly connect with community life outside. There was no sense of group solidarity in any of the activities, and little feeling of mutuality or co-operation, indeed quite the opposite. Prisoners remained relatively powerless. They were collectively unorganised and atomised. There seemed little accumulation of social capital. Those involved in these activities were busy rather than active citizens.

Prison seemed to create short-term compliant rather than active citizens. Compliant citizens are not necessarily active citizens because 'adopting a broader sense of responsibility is not the same as requiring people to be more obedient to authority or to conform to existing norms or patterns of behaviour' (Honohan, 2005: 173). Prisoners wished to keep their head down and were wary of being identified as troublemakers, even those politically aware and active on the outside. Prison seemed to engender compliance, where individuals do not act or do as they felt, and 'choices suppressed or pacified lead only to organisationally determined identities; one becomes what the environment dictates' (Milanovic and Thomas, 1989: 49). There was a pervading sense that time in prison is to be endured and this should be done without attracting any attention to oneself. Do your time, keep your head down, do not complain and do not cause, or be seen to cause any trouble. It was a similar sentiment expressed to Carrabine (2005: 905) by a British prisoner: ' "you're in gaol, you don't want to be there, but most prisoners they want to get in, do their time and get out" '.

Approaching monitoring bodies, according to some interviewees, may even make doing that time more difficult with a potential move to another prison, further away from loved ones, where the regime and quality of life are inferior. The desire for a quiet life seems to be a universal theme among many prisoners. In the United Kingdom, Pryor (2002: 2) reported that one prisoner summed it up as follows: 'keeping your head down is what is rewarded, not challenging or stretching yourself'. Many just want to quietly complete their sentence and to do so, they 'minimise their individuality and obscure their personality in order to blend in and avoid drawing attention to themselves' (Burnett and Maruna, 2006: 93). The interviewees seemed cautious about any actions that may be misconstrued by the prison authorities and this led them to silence themselves rather than either seeking redress for their grievances or attempting to influence change in their environment. Passivity, prisoners believed, was seen as a virtue in the eyes of the authorities. It echoes Fairchild's (1977: 315) finding that: 'Any drive to empowerment of the individual, to make him less dependent, has to take individualistic forms rather than collective forms, in order to seem desirable to prison authorities'. From the evidence of these interviews, prison tends to create compliant prisoners rather than facilitating active citizens.

Conclusion

This chapter examined the opportunities for, and level of, active citizenship among a group of prisoners. The context in which individuals find themselves impacts on their actions. This is especially the case in a prison environment. The institution dominates daily life and invariably impinges on the perspectives of the individual. However, these men did not enter the prison environment as blank slates. They brought with them levels of education, political and civic engagement, age, attitudes, class background and much more. All of these have an impact on their engagement, whether inside or outside prison.

Many of those who participated in the different citizenship activities did not see themselves as building up social capital. They had much more prosaic and utilitarian purposes. They were restrained in raising issues for fear, not of violence or disciplinary sanctions, but of more informal measures, which could upset their quality of life. Prisoners lacked the opportunity to contribute to the running of their community and were invisible in public dialogue about prison conditions and penal policy. The oversight and monitoring bodies, from the point of view of the interviewees, need transformation because citizens 'can and will participate if they see their efforts make a real and positive difference' (Taskforce on Active Citizenship, 2007a: 12). However, active citizenship 'requires the creation of institutional frameworks that make it possible' (Honohan, 2005: 176). Otherwise citizens are likely to disengage. While there are opportunities for prisoners to engage in civic activities and participate in their community, their activities were individualised. Many prisoners were active in a number of ways, but these lacked the co-operative mutuality necessary for deliberative engagement. Prison, if it has not created passive citizens, has created compliant citizens, the antithesis of active citizenship. In terms of political and civic activity, it was a case of isolated, compliant and ultimately disconnected citizens.

7

Imprisonment and citizenship

This chapter brings the book to a close by making the case that enfranchisement is one element, albeit an important one, within wider fields of prisoners' rights and opportunities for participative citizenship. It outlines the challenges for prisoners in embracing the franchise and makes some suggestions about how to re-engage a section of the population disconnected from society and disillusioned with political and civic institutions. If the goal of enfranchisement is inclusion and allowing prisoners to participate as citizens, more needs to be done to achieve this, both within and without the prison. Encouraging prisoners to participate as citizens, with opportunities and meaningful spaces in their community on a daily basis rather than just on election day, offers the potential for lived citizenship. However, this necessitates reframing penal policy, reimagining the role of imprisonment and re-conceptualising enfranchisement, regarding it as not merely enabling prisoners to vote, but rather as part of a process of engaging and empowering citizens.

The first part of this book outlined the political, philosophical and legal debates and motivations behind, and implications of, disenfranchisement. These deliberations usually reveal something deeper about the objective of incarceration; those who wish to disenfranchise argue that this should be only one of many restrictions on the rights of the imprisoned. Prison is to be used *for* rather than *as* punishment. Conversely, advocates of enfranchisement believe it conveys inclusion, treats convicts as citizens and encourages them to live that citizenship by voting and participation, leading, it is hoped, to a more pro-social outlook, moving away from a life of crime.

Prisoner enfranchisement remains one of the few contested electoral issues in twenty-first century democracies. The survey of international jurisprudence, examined in Chapter 2, considered the encounter between judicial authority and executive and parliamentary power, highlighting different judicial cultures. In some jurisdictions, the judiciary were keen to allow legislators to determine the limits of citizenship. In others, the courts were unwilling to allow the elected to determine the electorate and sought to push out the frontiers of the franchise within legal and constitutional boundaries. These debates raise issues around the use of prison as punishment and what limits, if any, there should be on the franchise.

In the US and UK, prisoner enfranchisement has led to political debate and legal challenge and engaged public opinion more widely than in any other jurisdiction. However, there is a distinction between the discourse in the UK and the US: debates in the former concentrate more on prisoners and the franchise, while the focus in latter tends to be on ex-prisoners. This reflects a perspective more prevalent among many US legislators that a conviction should deny citizenship rights, even post-imprisonment. In jurisdictions with severe post-release restrictions, disenfranchisement and other diminutions on citizenship are both a real and symbolic obstacle to participation in civic society even after a sentence is served. These limits on citizenship disproportionately disadvantage minority and marginalised communities, and undermine the building up of social capital and the fostering of co-operative mutuality encouraged in modern civic society.

While the second part of the book examined the case of the Republic of Ireland, the findings have more general relevance. Enfranchisement went against the trend in the early twenty-first century as 'much prison policy strengthens the 'criminal' as an identity rather than an incarcerated "citizen"' (Stern, 2002: 137). When the Minister for the Environment, Dick Roche, introduced legislation to enfranchise prisoners, he proudly proclaimed to the Oireachtas that 'Ireland is one of the most progressive nations in the world. This would be the exception rather than the rule' (Oireachtas Select Committee on Local Government, 2 November 2006). While legislation alone is not enough to make Ireland one of the most progressive nations in the world, nevertheless, the Irish case was indeed exceptional because it was politicians who were proactive in the introduction of legislation after the Supreme Court decided that ambiguity – the legal right to register without the facility to vote – was constitutional. In contrast to other jurisdictions, there was no major civic society or prisoner campaign for enfranchisement. The lack of political and media interest in the passage of the legislation was significant, considering how the media reports on crime and tends to demonise and 'other' prisoners. Irish parliamentarians, some of whom proclaimed to be open to the winds of influence from Anglo-American penal policies, adopted a more European human rights based approach. They did not resort to the language of punitiveness or engage in the discourse on punishment that has dominated discussions in the US and UK. The quiet passing of this legislation stands in contrast to the experience in most other jurisdictions, not only because politicians enfranchised all confined citizens, regardless of crime or sentence, but due to the absence of political, media or public opposition. However, a change in the law is not the end of the story. The following section examines the unfinished business of enfranchisement, because as Lijphart (1997: 10) pointed out: 'After universal suffrage, the next aim for democracy must be universal or near-universal *use* of the right to vote' (emphasis in original).

Embracing the franchise: re-engaging citizens

Enfranchisement of prisoners has the potential to achieve universal suffrage. Nevertheless, there is clearly some distance to be travelled if prisoners are to use the right to vote and reconnect with the electoral and political process. This study indicates that, despite enfranchisement, challenges remain for politicians, policymakers, prison administrations, educationalists, civic society and prisoners. If these are not overcome, then enfranchisement of prisoners becomes more symbolic than real and will not achieve the objective of inclusion in civic society. Legislation alone will not overcome the marginalisation, social exclusion and structural challenges inherent in trying to engage citizen convicts. Even on enfranchisement, there are clearly some initiatives needed to overcome the obstacles (both real and perceived) that put prisoners off utilising the vote. The following are some suggestions to overcome the lack of engagement among prisoners, which may also have application to other marginalised groups in society.

Registration and voting

During the debates on prisoner enfranchisement, Minister Dick Roche suggested that there would be ongoing analysis by his department of voting in prisons. 'It will not be an enormous undertaking but it will be very interesting to monitor it, because if people do not use the facility we will know something is wrong' (Oireachtas Select Committee on Environment and Local Government, 2 November 2006). The low levels of registration and voting in the first polls among prisoners indicate that something is wrong. Some reasons for the low participation are unique to the location. However, with low levels of registration and only a minority of the prison population voting, even in institutions with older, better educated and more long-term prisoners (those most likely to vote), there remain both structural and political impediments to widespread political participation among prisoners.

There are a number of reasons for low levels of registration. These reflect the age, education levels, voting traditions and social backgrounds of those incarcerated. Individuals do not enter prison with a clean slate, but bring in characteristics from the outside. Issues such as marginalisation, low educational attainment, urban degeneration, homelessness, family break-up impact on the levels of civic engagement outside and it would be naïve to think that they would not have an impact on the level of civic engagement inside. The educational level of citizens has an impact on interest in politics, registration for elections and turn-out at the polls. As outlined in Chapters 4 and 5, the low level of conventional educational attainment and literacy difficulties among the prison population effectively exclude many from the public sphere.

Traditionally, there are low levels of civic engagement in the communities where the majority of prisoners lived before their incarceration, with high levels of social and economic disadvantage (see Breen, 2010; O'Donnell *et al.*, 2007). Citizens from these communities have traditionally been less inclined to vote. If a citizen did not vote outside, they were unlikely to do so in prison. The reasons behind the low levels of political participation and civic engagement in some communities are outside the scope of this book, but they undoubtedly impact on citizens behind bars. Lijphart (1997: 1) found that representation is 'systematically biased in favour of more privileged citizens – those with higher incomes, greater wealth, and better education – and against less advantaged citizens ... over time, the level of voting participation and class inequality are strongly and negatively linked'.

A number of prisoners did not vote because of the difficulties of registration at a home address. For some, it was lack of a home prior to incarceration and for others, they were no longer welcome at that address or their household had moved on. A more flexible approach to prisoner registration would be beneficial, with registration either at their home address or their home or prison constituency. The latter is especially relevant for long-term prisoners, as the institution has become their home. For those with no home prior to incarceration, constituency registration would also increase the potential for participation. While this would necessitate a review of the legislation, constituency registration was advocated by the Irish Penal Reform Trust and suggested by Labour TD, Eamon Gilmore, during the debates on prisoner enfranchisement. As to the concern about a voting bloc skewing the result in a constituency, not all prisoners would want to register in the prison.

And as this study has shown, there is no evidence that prisoners vote as a bloc, either for the same party or candidate. Constituency rather than residency registration would have the added benefit of allowing those who are homeless and not incarcerated the opportunity to register in the constituency with which they are most associated.

The confusion surrounding the registration procedure, especially in 2008, was also partly responsible for the low levels of registration. It became apparent that many eligible citizens were unaware that they had to register for the postal vote *annually* and therefore missed out on exercising their franchise. The requirement for annual registration for postal voters adds another layer of bureaucracy beyond that necessary to vote outside. All postal voters have to register for a postal ballot if they have not already registered, within two days of the calling of an election or referendum. A crucial time for the election process is the registration period, which can be long before an election or referendum occurs. If they register, prisoners are likely to follow this up by voting, as indicated with high turnout in prisons among predominantly long-term prisoners (in Arbour Hill and Portlaoise prisons) compared to institutions with a high turnover of prisoners with short-term, transitory populations (Cloverhill remand prison and Shelton Abbey open prison). During the registration period, election officials or, if this is not feasible, NGOs such as the Vincentian Partnership for Social Justice which already conducts citizenship courses in the community, could visit prisons to conduct a registration campaign.

There is a legal obligation, in the absence of legislation stating otherwise, on publicly funded and statutory bodies to ensure they carry out their responsibilities to all citizens, regardless of location. Local authorities annually compile the Register of Electors and while officials have been employed to verify the voting register by calling door to door, the responsibility to ensure that their name is on the electoral register is up to each individual elector. Citizens can make sure their name is on the register at their local authority head office, library, garda station or online (Whelan, 2000: 9). Prisoners do not have ready access to the electoral register, either online or in person. But as one interviewee suggested, this could be simply overcome; the Register of Electors could be provided on a CD ROM and accessed through the prison library. While there was communication between local authority officials and prison authorities during the registration periods, there was no interaction between election officials and individual prisoners. With a population distrustful of all bureaucracy, especially prison authorities, it is important to maintain a direct link between citizens and registration officials.

Ultimately, the responsibility to inform the public about registration and voting procedures, including prisoners, lies with the Department of the Environment who have statutory responsibility for the organisation of elections. They use a variety of media to encourage citizens to register to vote. Prisoners could be included among the 'hard to reach' groups, who need extra effort to effectively include them in the franchise. Groups such as the National Adult Literacy Association (NALA) have been active in promoting wider participation among those with literacy difficulties. Recognising that citizens who are marginalised educationally can be effectively excluded from civic participation, NALA published a *Plain English Guide to Political Terms* (2006) and co-operated with the Houses of the Oireachtas to produce *A Brief Guide to How Your Parliament Works* (2011). In the 1990s, in an attempt to increase levels of voting and widen political participation among those with literacy difficulties, photographs were introduced on ballot papers. During the 2008–9 registration campaign, a greater effort was made to include new voters to Ireland in preparation for the forthcoming local and European elections (EU citizens are eligible to vote in European and local elections and all registered residents are eligible to vote in local elections). Billboard posters and advertising literature was published online in a number of different languages, including Polish, Romanian and Mandarin (www.environ.ie; accessed 29 October 2008).

If prisoners are given the right to vote, they should also have the opportunity to participate in elections on an equal (if not the same) basis as citizens outside. While this may not be an easy task for prison administrators, under European Prison Rules (Council of Europe, 2006: Rule 24.11), prison authorities in jurisdictions that allow them to vote are obliged to 'ensure that prisoners are able to participate in elections, referenda and in other aspects of public life'. Undoubtedly, some restrictions would still apply; new approaches would have to be considered to engage captive citizens, through the distribution of literature, debates, even campaigns (with some modifications due to their location). As outlined in Chapter 5, in some countries, candidates, with the agreement of prison governors, enter prisons for electioneering.

A template exists for civic engagement in closed institutions. During the 2009 by-elections, patients at the Central Mental Hospital, Dublin (a national forensic facility), who were included in the 2006 enfranchisement legislation, were the first to vote. Prior to the poll, three by-election candidates in the constituency where the Central Mental Hospital is located – George Lee (Fine Gael), Alex White (Labour) and Shay Brennan (Fianna Fáil) – attended a question and answer session for patients. While most of the discussion was on mental health and ethical issues, other topics concerning both their confinement and more general matters were debated. By the close of polling, one newspaper report suggested that the participation rate was expected to exceed 60 per cent in all three polls, i.e. local, European and by-elections (Houston, 2009). This seems quite high, on the basis of the findings set out in Chapter 4 but it is possible that the event increased participation in the elections. However, the panel discussion during the 2009 elections was an imaginative response to political and security concerns.

Low turnout raises wider issues about the responsibility to encourage people (whether inside or outside prison) to register and vote. Parkes (2003: 102) pointed out that when prisoners are allowed to vote, there is an obligation on government and prison officials to make this a reality, because 'in many jurisdictions, neither prison, nor election officials take any action to facilitate prisoner voting'. She concluded, that 'without the involvement and co-operation of public officials, the right to vote will remain illusory for many prisoners'. It is significant that even though only 14 per cent registered for the 2007 poll and just under 8 per cent for the 2011 general election, the vast majority of prisoners who took the time to register, 71 per cent in 2007 and 76 per cent in 2011, subsequently voted.

Ispahani (2009: 51) concluded that prisoner voting is 'relatively cheap and easy to administer because the inmate population is constantly supervised and is subject to inexpensive administrative control'. Asked if prisoner voting compromised prison security, 'none of the dozens of countries' surveyed by her 'had ever experienced a single instance in which prison discipline was disrupted by the electoral process'. Mirroring the experience internationally, the inclusion of prisoners as another category of postal voters in Ireland was neither costly nor impractical. Nevertheless, Livingstone and Owen (1999: 470) recognised that 'perhaps the most difficult rights to accommodate in the prison context are what may be described as public participation rights ... to what extent prisoners remain citizens eligible to participate in public debate'. However, as access to confined citizens is restricted for electoral authorities there is a greater responsibility on those who come into contact regularly with prisoners to promote and facilitate participation.

Enhanced efforts by prison administrators and electoral officials could overcome or at least reduce some of the impediments to participation. A study of voting rights of prisoners in 2003 noted that: 'Even though several nations do allow prisoners to vote by law, practical issues of registration are often problematic and obscure these rights' (Rottinghaus, 2005: 14). It argued for clarity during the registration process because being 'eligible to vote and being allowed to vote are two very different items here ... Clearly identifying when and where prisoners are allowed to register to vote is an important part of the citizen education process for election administrators' (Rottinghaus, 2005: 41).

In the limited data available elsewhere (Ewald and Rottinghaus, 2009), Ireland is not alone in facing challenges in the area of prisoner registration and turnout. Due to the age, educational attainment and social background of prisoners internationally, all things being equal, prisoners are unlikely voters. In the 2000 Canadian Federal elections, only 5,194 (22.5 per cent) of eligible prisoners cast their ballots. In 1992, 29 per cent of eligible prisoners in the Canadian province of Ontario voted in a constitutional referendum. In a 1996 election in Utah (prior to a change in the state constitution) only 95 prisoners registered to vote in Salt Lake County and voter turnout by eligible prisoners was estimated at 5 per cent (Parkes, 2003: 101). In a survey of Danish prisons, Storgaard (2009: 254) estimated varying levels of turnout in different prisons, between 20 and 80 per cent at parliamentary elections, between 5 and 70 per cent at local elections and between 10 and 50 per cent at European referenda. Mauer (2011: 564) found that in Italy and the Netherlands, turnout was between 20 and 60 per cent. Manza and Uggen (2006: 180) suggest that while there is generally lower turnout among ex-felons than the rest of the electorate, if all ex-felons were eligible to vote in the 2000 and 2004 presidential elections, up to one third, or 1.5 million extra citizens would have voted.

In contrast to the low turnout elsewhere, in the Canadian province of Quebec, voting by prisoners in three elections in the early 1990s reached 74 per cent (Parkes, 2003: 101). In the 2006 Israeli general election, turnout was 63.5 per cent of registered voters (Diskin and Hazan, 2007: 710) compared to 53 per cent turnout among captive citizens (Ispahani, 2009: 49). In a 2011 vote among the San Francisco county jail population (who are entitled to vote), 79 per cent of eligible voters cast their ballots in elections that included ballots for district attorney and sheriff (Roberts, 2011). In Belgium, Lithuania and Romania, Mauer (2011: 564) reported that more than 60 per cent of prisoners vote. The reasons behind the higher turnout in these jurisdictions could be examined to determine what lessons may be learnt for jurisdictions with low levels of political engagement among the prison population.

Disillusion and disconnection
This study found that prisoners were disillusioned with civil society and profoundly disconnected from government, politicians and the political system in general. While this study examined the case of Ireland, con-

sidering the similarities in the demographics of the prison population internationally, similar attitudes are likely among the prison population in other jurisdictions. The lack of personalised candidate engagement, which is particularly important among the Irish electorate, discouraged greater participation within prison. Significantly, it seemed to reinforce the alienation felt by many prisoners. It added credence to the responses elaborated in the interviews that there was a cynical reason behind their enfranchisement and lack of engagement discouraged prisoners from the original objective of enfranchisement – political inclusion. Citizenship is not just about voting; it is about participation in the electoral process in an educated, engaged and informed manner.

Even those interviewees who voted in the general election and were self-identified as political were generally critical about how, as a group, prisoners are treated by politicians. They believed politicians refused to engage with them, either personally or politically. There was no evidence that during the 2007 general election or subsequent polls that any politician sought to enter prisons to canvass. If politicians visited prisons, it would send a powerful message to prisoners that they are not only legally enfranchised, but that their participation matters. There is also an obligation on political parties to engage with all citizens, as they are funded by the state. If any group (in this case, prisoners) are not engaged and only have the opportunity to participate 'in public debates far from the locus of decision making they may begin to think that participation as citizens is little more than a placebo, an activity the main purpose of which is to facilitate the sense that one is participating, but has little or no possibility of affecting outcomes' (Riordan, 2003: 61).

Prisoners as agents in the political process also need to take responsibility for their right to vote and make an informed decision on participation. Lijphart (1997: 1) found that 'unequal turnout spells unequal influence'. Without prisoner participation, quite simply, their perspectives will not be heard and they will have no influence. While prisoners felt both government and society had little interest in their concerns, the right to vote challenges them to seize the opportunity to participate. Easton has argued that enfranchisement has 'real value' by giving prisoners some influence in the political process, with politicians more likely to take notice of their views. She concluded: 'So it may strengthen prisoners' position in terms of influencing policies which may affect them while in prison, and when they return to the community' (Easton, 2011: 230). Richards and Jones (2004: 224) argue that the restoration of voting rights to prisoners may have 'interesting repercussions for prison conditions and correctional budget demands'. They believe that if prisoners are allowed to vote, politicians may become more interested in providing increased budgets for prison programmes. 'At the very least, restoring voting rights to prisoners would encourage state politicians to visit prisons', leading to improved prison conditions.

While there is little evidence that enfranchisement of prisoners' influenced political decisions or penal priorities, prisoners as citizens have a legitimate contribution to make to society. By voting, participating in civic society and engaging in public discourse, prisoners may generate a more holistic understanding of the prison system. Their insights might inform discussions about prison conditions, prisoners' rights and penal reform. Prisoner experiences could contribute to deliberations on the place of prison in the matrix of punishment and an understanding of the wider criminal justice system.

When Irish prisoners were enfranchised, it was a significant but small piece of electoral legislation. However, it was not part of a wider reframing of the criminal justice system or integral to a penal reform agenda. This approach was partly responsible for both its success and its failure. As an electoral reform, it passed the Oireachtas without the controversy that similar initiatives have caused in other jurisdictions. However, it has failed to encourage widespread participation, possibly because it was not part of a wider penal reform agenda to improve the conditions under which Irish prisoners are housed or recognise their rights as confined citizens. Taken alone, perhaps it was always destined to fail to live up to expectations of those who passed the legislation.

Other movements for the right to vote have 'been secured through struggle as weak groups have fought to improve their conditions' (Easton, 2011: 229). In the case of African Americans in the US, it was after civil rights struggles and mass campaigns of disobedience (Keyssar, 2000). Women's suffrage was achieved in the UK after a concerted campaign by women's groups for the franchise (Foot, 2005: 171–237). Working-class suffrage was only achieved after mass political campaigns of the nineteenth and twentieth centuries (Foot, 2005). However, just as the widening of the franchise to include women, the working classes and minority communities did not lead to their equality and empowerment, nor indeed did it have the revolutionary outcome feared by those who opposed wider enfranchisement. More transformative measures were, indeed are, needed, than change in legislation if the goals of inclusion, participation and equality are to be achieved. While modifications in the law can be a harbinger of social change, nothing replaces political activity to engage citizens in the process of political change and to empower them in their transformation.

Enfranchisement has rarely caught prisoners' imagination in the same way as campaigns for the vote by other disenfranchised groups. It has been won, not after collective action by prisoner groups, but usually after court cases by individual prisoners – 'jailhouse lawyers'. Without an active and wider campaign among prisoners, it is perhaps understandable there were not high levels of registration and voting. Rather ironically, if there had been wide scale political or media opposition to enfranchisement, it may have created a greater sense of 'victory' over the authorities and subsequently greater numbers voting, as an act of defiance over 'officialdom'.

Prisoners did not respond in large numbers, perhaps, because they did not feel ownership of the campaign for enfranchisement. Many were initially unaware of the significance of the *Hirst* judgment or even the passing of the Electoral (Amendment) Act in 2006. It did not have the same immediacy as the conditions under which they are housed or issues such as visitation rights, access to programmes and remission. More mundane day-to-day matters, understandably, seem to concern prisoners – adapting to surroundings, coping with their sentence, observing (or in some cases, overcoming) prison rules, maintaining relationships and quality of life issues.

In the course of the interviews, there emerged a widely held view that the community outside perceived prisoners as somehow detached from civic society. Some who refused to be surveyed or interviewed were so disengaged that they believed this study was a waste of time. Nobody was interested in their views, so what was the point. Even those who were interviewed believed that their voices and opinions were silenced in the 'hierarchy of credibility' (Becker, 1967: 242), by politicians who used them as political fodder, the media who demonised them and consequently the general public, who believed they were treated too well. Prisoners did not feel they had an opportunity to participate equally in public discourse. They felt no sense of belonging and therefore disconnected from the polity. And politicians, interviewees believed, demonised rather than defended prisoners. Without recognition of their rights in other areas, prisoners seemed to view the motivation behind enfranchisement somewhat cynically, at odds with the reasons politicians expressed during the enfranchisement debates. Despite achieving the right to vote, they remained disillusioned and disconnected.

Citizenship post imprisonment
Even after enfranchisement, prisoners felt they were not treated equal to other citizens. Many believed their exclusion did not end on release. In the twenty-first century, some elements of 'civil death' still exist, with legal disabilities post-imprisonment. These 'invisible punishments' are 'collateral consequences' of imprisonment (Travis, 2002: 16) that

undermine and limit citizenship, even after completion of the sentence, with laws which suggest to prisoners that they are not equal to others in the polity. This is especially the case when rhetoric from those who support permanent criminal status alienates prisoners while incarcerated, and undermines the potential to rebuild their lives outside.

Internationally, many countries impose restrictions on former prisoners, reminding them that their punishment has not finished. In various American states, there are restrictions on the right to serve on a jury, fulfil functions as a parent, access public employment and vote (LaFollette, 2005; Olivares *et al.*, 1996). In England and Wales, among those disqualified from jury service are individuals who are currently on bail, have ever been sentenced to imprisonment for life or to imprisonment for five years or more, those who have in the previous ten years served any part of a sentence of imprisonment or detention, or received a suspended sentence (Criminal Justice Act 2003: Schedule 33). In Ireland, many ex-prisoners are not allowed to serve on juries, including anyone who has ever been sentenced to a term of imprisonment of five years or more, and those who within the last ten years have been sentenced to a term of imprisonment of at least three months (Juries Act 1976: Section 8). Excluding prisoners makes jury deliberations less representative and sends a message to prisoners that even after their sentence is served they are 'less than the average citizen'. Serving on a jury is not only deciding on the guilt or innocence of an accused; it is an essential part of civic participation.

For much of its history, Ireland was unusual among developed nations in that there was no facility to allow for the expunction of adult convictions (Law Reform Commission, 2007). Those with a criminal record were effectively excluded from employment in the civil and public service (NESF, 2002: 12). This not only cuts off an avenue for employment but also sends a very negative message to the private sector. These are real and symbolic impediments to prisoner and ex-prisoner engagement. The continuation of civil death statutes and restrictions post release indicate to ex-prisoners that they are not fit to serve on juries because they have in the past shown contempt for the law and are unlikely to have been changed by the experience of, or during, their time in prison. The time in prison follows them even after their sentence has been served. It institutionalises a pessimistic view of prisoners – they are not capable of transformation. It reinforces the negativity towards the incarcerated and increases the sense of rejection many prisoners and ex-prisoners already feel.

Maruna *et al.* (2004: 21) pointed out that living a law-abiding life and desisting from crime are difficult processes. Civic engagement is two-way route. There was a feeling from prisoners that their perspective mattered little to the world outside. In their study of re-entry in the US, Uggen *et al.* (2004: 288) concluded that 'communities are ill-prepared to accept felons as fellow citizens'. Civic engagement is wider than a change in the law because attempts to 'encourage citizens to accept some sense of responsibility or ownership of prisons would move into uncertain territory' (Faulkner, 2003: 305). No matter how good the programmes and strategies put in place in prison, some issues are outside the control of the institution, prisoners and staff. Prisoners' connection with the wider community adds a societal dimension to their participation after release. It also challenges communities to face up to their responsibilities towards released prisoners. Roberts and Hough (2005: 300) observed that, if the general public are unaware of daily life in its penal institutions, 'it seems likely that they know little about the many problems confronting ex-prisoners as they make the transition from custody to community'.

Communities can be hesitant to embrace former prisoners. The stigma of imprisonment is possibly the greatest barrier to inclusion in civic society and being part of a law-abiding community. Even though the right to vote is central to participation as a citizen in democratic society, access to housing, education and employment may at times be more important and immediate. Civil disqualifications make re-connection with civic society more difficult for ex-prisoners. There are still barriers to participation and '[t]o best fulfil the duties of responsible citizenship in a democratic society, former felons require the basic rights and capacities enjoyed by other citizens in good standing' (Uggen *et al.*, 2006: 305).

Even when prisoners are legally included, as ex-prisoners in many ways they are still excluded from the opportunities of participative citizenship because of, among other impediments, the stigma of incarceration. The collateral consequences of imprisonment can also be more enduring than the actual experience of incarceration, because 'civil disqualifications are potentially more damaging in their impact than formal penal sanctions' (Easton, 2006: 444). Denying the 'full *rights* of citizenship' makes performing 'the *duties* of citizenship' difficult (Uggen *et al.*, 2006: 281; emphasis in original). Examined from a wider perspective of citizenship, rather than voting rights, even when enfranchised, prisoners remain at a distance from civic society. As many of the interviewees suggested, voting gave them a sense of belonging and ownership in society but while it was now open to them to vote, they felt there were still impediments to embracing enfranchisement.

Reforming penal systems and engaging convicts

If prisoner enfranchisement is to be more than just a change in the law, wider reform of the penal system must be considered. The solution to the low level of participation in elections lies beyond legislative change, but necessitates both a wider examination of the treatment of prisoners in other social arenas and interrogating the meaning of enfranchisement. This section considers some examples of when prisoners acted and were treated as active citizens. Enfranchisement has given prisoners the opportunity to maintain one of the core rights as a citizen, the right to vote. However, enfranchisement should be about more than just the right to vote, but examined in the context of citizens playing a role in the civic life of the community. At its core, citizenship is about inclusion and participation. Ignatieff (1989: 72) has argued that 'the practice of citizenship is about ensuring that everyone has the entitlements necessary to exercise their liberty'. However, entitlement alone will not encourage voting and other citizenship activities.

Prisoners and citizenship

Voting must be examined in the wider context of citizenship. Even when prisoners have the legal right to vote, opportunities to participate remain circumscribed. Low levels of turnout indicate that the objectives of enfranchisement – voting and inclusion – have not been achieved. While voting is 'by a substantial margin the most common form of political activity' (Putnam, 2000: 35), it is not the only method of participating in political and civic society. However, it is indicative of further engagement (or disengagement). Lijphart (1997: 10) found a 'spillover effect' from voting to participation in the workplace, churches and voluntary organisations and *vice versa*. Civic participation led to higher levels of voting which, according to Putnam (2000: 35) is 'an instructive proxy measure of broader social change'. He continued:

> Compared to demographically matched non-voters, voters are more likely to be interested in politics, to give to charity, to volunteer, to serve on juries, to attend community school board meetings, to participate in public demonstrations, and to co-operate with their fellow citizens on community affairs. It is sometimes hard to tell whether voting causes community engagement or vice versa, although some recent evidence suggests that the act of voting itself encourages volunteering and other forms of good citizenship.

Cardinale (2004: 5) in his survey of disenfranchised ex-felons found that losing 'the right to vote does not prevent persons with a felony conviction from participating in other forms of civic engagement ...

but it appears to have this effect anyway, presumably through the political alienation and distrust that it fosters in disenfranchised individuals'. The NAACP (2011: 26) pointed to the indeterminate and inter-generational consequences: 'Voting, like many forms of civic participation, is often a learned behaviour; a child whose parent is unable to vote can herself develop an alienation from the culture of voting'.

Rottinghaus (2005: 42): has suggested that voting in prisons is highly susceptible to a 'democratic disconnect' between the 'promise of rights granted to citizens and the practice of extending these rights'. He concluded that this gap must 'be closed and full citizenship rights extended to those to whom the rights are granted'. If prisoners, similar to other citizens, are to be encouraged to use the vote, rights and opportunities in other areas of the polity need to be considered. A healthy democracy has citizens who are well-informed, engaged, with confidence that they can make a difference by participating. Low levels of turnout in elections undermine active citizenship and there is a need:

> to consider barriers in terms of interest, information, opportunity and capacity for civic engagement. Lack of interest may not be the barrier to greater civic engagement so much as a lack of confidence on the part of citizens that their efforts and time will have an impact, as well as practical difficulties in terms of registration and access. (Taskforce on Active Citizenship, 2007c: 16)

Some of the barriers to civic engagement and political participation are unique to incarceration and others may have resonance with other marginalised groups. While low levels of political engagement undoubtedly indicate a lack of interest in politics among some prisoners, there is something deeper and wider that needs corrective action to encourage them to give their time and effort to embracing the rights, responsibilities, opportunities and power of citizenship. Enfranchising convicts alone does not create citizens. Participation makes citizens. That includes the opportunity to participate (but also the right to refuse) in wider citizenship activities – from voting to prison governance to public discourse, because citizens engage or disengage long before election day.

Making citizens
Rousseau remarked that 'citizens are not made in a day'. To 'make' citizens behind bars comes from not just a legal change, however welcome, but consideration of a new concept of imprisonment, and its place in society. While the modern prison 'and associated regimes' emerged in the 'search for new forms of discipline in the wake of social and political upheavals of the eighteenth and nineteenth centuries' (Tomlinson, 1995:

196), Bosworth (2007: 68) argues that the modern criminal justice system is more than just a way of dealing with lawbreakers. 'It is also a primary means of creating accountable and thus governable and obedient citizens'.

Perhaps the essence of imprisonment and its 'associated regimes' are inimical to ideas of agency, critical reflection and judicious deliberation essential for engaged citizenship. In its modern manifestation, the prison creates an institutionalised bureaucracy that takes little account of the agency of individuals and seeks to create compliant and obedient citizens. The bureaucracy relies on a regime that is influenced by the conditions of confinement, penal policy, prison rules, control mechanisms and sanctions, both formal and informal. It begins with a view of the prisoner as irresponsible, lacking agency and proceeds with policies and practices from that perspective. Despite the best intentions of the most well-meaning staff, the individual needs, desires and wants of the incarcerated are subsumed in an attempt to regularise the deprivation of liberty and deny autonomy.

Routine and regime can reduce autonomy and engender compliance. It is characteristic of the total institution that 'all phases of the day's activities are tightly scheduled, with one activity leading at a prearranged time into the next' (Goffman, 1961: 17). Robert McCleery (1961: 154) pointed out that 'the heart of custodial controls in traditional prisons lies in the daily regimentation, routine and rituals of domination which bend the subjects into a customary posture of silent awe and unthinking acceptance'. While the extent to which prisoners are bent into compliance may be exaggerated, the general point about the corrosive effect of routine is well made. Routine is used to create order, maintain control and attempt to produce compliant prisoners, which undermines the concept of enfranchised and engaged citizens.

Many prisoners find themselves steeped in an authoritarian structure that allows little individual responsibility and yet tries to instil it. In an institution that diminishes individual choice and independent action, it is difficult to encourage an individual to become a responsible actor. No matter how well intentioned governments and policymakers are, 'it is hard to train for freedom in a cage' because 'the rhetoric of imprisonment and the reality of the cage are often in stark contrast' (Morris and Rothman, 1998: x–xi). Without prisoners being allowed the space and opportunity to exercise agency, autonomy is reduced and independent thought and action discouraged.

Crewe (2012: 144) in his study of one late-modern prison found 'little room for trust, for prisoners meaningfully to contest how their best interests were defined or to challenge the relative weight given to public interests over personal rights'. He concluded: 'From the prisoner's vantage point, autonomy was offered with a smile, but backed by threat'.

Incarceration excludes prisoners physically from society and takes away their 'duties and responsibilities', and removes the 'prisoner's status and dignity as citizen' (Faulkner, 2002: 2). The implications from this study are clear. If prisoners are not afforded rights and opportunities and treated as citizens in other areas, it is perhaps not surprising that they do not fulfil that role in large numbers on election day. As Pateman (1970: 24–5) pointed out: 'Rousseau's ideal system is designed to develop responsible, individual social and political action through the effort of the participatory process'. If citizenship is not facilitated every day, the lack of opportunities for participative engagement will not be made up for on election day.

Participative citizens
While enfranchisement has given prisoners the right to vote, this has not been embraced through their turnout at elections. Chapter 6 found that prison created atomised and compliant rather than connected citizens. One way greater engagement might be achieved is to enable prisoners to participate in their immediate communities by reform of the governance structures. Suggestions from prisoners included the creation of meaningful accountability and oversight bodies. International best practice for independent oversight of prisons includes a local visiting/monitoring committee, prison inspector and ideally a prisoner ombudsman, or at least access to the general ombudsman (Owers, 2004 and 2006). The CPT has argued that it was of 'the view that an independent complaints system should to be established' to deal with prisoner complaints. 'Such a system', they contend, 'would reinforce prisoners' confidence in the complaints mechanism and also assist prison management to deal appropriately with that minority of prison officers who overstep the mark' (CPT, 2007a: 21).

While this might challenge the more traditional form of prison governance, prisoner criticism of the accountability and oversight mechanisms reiterates what has been suggested in various reports (Council for Social Welfare and Irish Commission for Justice and Peace 1986; CSW, 1983; Whitaker, 1985). Visiting committees should be transformed, including opportunities for prisoner and ex-prisoner participation. Consideration should be given to prisoners' suggestions on the prison rules that govern their daily routine. Prisoners should be allowed, at a minimum, to engage with the ombudsman, or have a designated prisoner ombudsman as suggested in numerous prison reports. The government-appointed Inspector of Prisons pointed out that: 'Ireland does not have an ombudsman for prisoners to investigate individual complaints. This seems to suggest a *lacuna* in the system' (Inspector of Prisons, 2009b: 37). While there have been some developments in prison oversight since this study, the new framework falls short of international best practice of access to an ombudsman. With so little confidence in the oversight and accountability mechanisms, to be seen as a trouble-maker, with the only real option of instigating litigation, can have adverse consequences. Furthermore, courts are ill-equipped to deal with prisoners' rights and Irish courts have 'largely taken a "hands-off" approach to the issue' (Hamilton and Kilkelly, 2008: 69).

Engaging citizens entails listening to the voice of the prisoner, encouraging their sense of autonomy and reducing the isolation of incarceration. This might allow them as individuals to co-operate in their common good, and to act as citizens every day. Encouraging a citizen identity more often might yield a more authentic form of change in prisoners, facing up to their responsibilities and engaging in active citizenship. This would entail individuals not just obeying the law, but locating that law in a wider social and political context. Such an approach challenges the imprisoned to become reflective agents for change rather than passive law-abiding citizens.

Those who commit crimes can be viewed as breaking the bonds of community. Imprisonment deepens that disconnection. Reconnecting and positively identifying with community and civil society is essential to the process of embracing citizenship, and voting can be an important part of that process. Individuals cannot be separated from the context in which they are located. They bring into custody with them varying (but usually low) levels of civic participation and these are generally further deflated by incarceration. Prisons as institutions do not seek to promote co-operative activity among prisoners. Quite the contrary — the individualised experience of imprisonment discourages it, and the emphasis on compliance inside and recidivism outside as the key measures of 'success' draws the parameters of the debate too narrowly. Taking 'success' in the penal sphere beyond compliance, towards personal autonomy, is more difficult because 'complexity . . . is more likely the order of the day in considering how individuals respond to imprisonment, while simplicity is more likely the explanation of how prisons respond to individuals' (Duguid, 2000: 89).

Prisoners are rarely encouraged by prison authorities to engage in political activity and collective action or to participate in communicative dialogue with the outside world. To create a participative citizenship within a prison environment entails challenges on multiple levels, from reducing the political emphasis on 'tough' incarceration to empowering men and women who feel distanced from their fellow citizens. Prisons, like all social institutions, contain an 'extraordinary complex set of social relations' (Cressey, 1961: 1). When an individual enters prison, it is into a 'complex social system with its own norms, values, and methods of control' (Sykes, 1958: 134). In this context, encouraging co-operation and building social capital, an integral part of active citizenship, is a difficult process. It is intangible, 'for it exists in the *relations* among persons' (Coleman, 1988: 100–1). Not only do prisons physically break the connection with outside, they frustrate attempts at forming positive social relations to campaign for the collective good on the inside.

During the Oireachtas debates on prisoner enfranchisement, politicians were keen to make the point that they were not only giving prisoners the right to vote; this was another way of encouraging prisoners to act responsibly. However, individual responsibility impacts on more than just the prisoner. The concept of responsibility can be used to exonerate management from the consequences of its actions and government from its treatment of prisoners. Most importantly it individualises the experience, over-emphasizes individual agency and fails to locate prison and prisoner in a wider social, economic and political context. Rarely are reformed, rehabilitated or responsible prisoners mentioned in the context of rehabilitated prisons, reformed prison governance or responsible penal policy. Rehabilitation is usually defined by whether an individual re-offends, and rarely in terms of whether the individual becomes a re-connected member of civil society. When what constitutes individual responsibility is defined by prison authorities and government ministers in narrow and often legalistic terms, especially when equated with the recidivism rate, it becomes easier to measure 'success'.

Yet the concept of responsibility reveals a deeper meaning. The onus has shifted from government and prison authorities to the prisoner. It is now part of his or her responsibility to transform him or herself by engaging in the electoral process. Voting 'embodies the most fundamental democratic principle of equality. Not to vote is to withdraw from the political community' (Putnam, 2000: 35). Non-engagement by prisoners may be interpreted as a further example of their neglect of personal responsibility. If an individual does not take the opportunity to exercise their franchise, they are yet again refusing to face up to their responsibilities. However, if the ultimate goal of enfranchisement is to create law-abiding and responsible citizens, a change in the law alone will not achieve this because reintegration and desistance from crime (essentially what governments and prison authorities term rehabilitation) is 'both an event and a process' (Maruna *et al.*, 2004: 5). By enfranchising prisoners, governments may be seen to have reduced the process to a simplified formula with a legal change supposedly acting as a catalyst for shifts in attitude and behaviour. If prisoners are allowed to participate more widely as citizens, it may have surprising results in other aspects of their lives. Richardson (1983: 55) suggested that participation 'not only enhances the individual's ability to cope intelligently with a new range of issues' but also increases 'self-confidence to tackle problems in other spheres. Through discussion and consideration of various types of issues, people are given a chance to learn about new problems and solutions to them; if they make mistakes they will learn from them'. 'Participation is', she concludes, 'about making more fully developed human beings'.

Prisoner representation
Sykes (1958: 76) suggested that one of the pains of imprisonment was the 'helpless or dependent status of the prisoner' which 'clearly represents a serious threat to the prisoner's self-image as a fully accredited member of adult society'. In the process of re-imagining imprisonment, traditional prison governance, which effectively excludes the prisoner, could be examined. Prison administrations could consider more widespread co-operation and participation with prisoner representation, through prisoner unions or councils as exist in some European countries. That would mean the institutional authorities ceding some power. It would enter new territory. But if this happened, and prisoners saw that they could realise improvements, this would likely strengthen participation and democracy and encourage greater involvement by prisoners in other civic spheres. The act of co-operation builds up social capital, develops mutuality and creates participative citizens.

At times prisoner unions have sought representation and used collective bargaining, which historically developed as a 'natural extension of civil rights' (Marshall, 1950: 44). Internationally, there has been a tradition of prisoners organising inside to improve conditions and outside to pursue penal reform. In the late 1960s and early 1970s, prisoner unions were formed in the US (Davis, 2012; Fairchild, 1977; Huff, 1974), Scandinavia (Ward, 1972) and the United Kingdom (Ryan, 2003). The early 1970s saw the rise of various prisoner organisations in the United Kingdom, a period when 'prisoners attempted to find a collective voice' (Ryan, 2003: 49). During the disturbances around the Attica rebellion in the early 1970s, one of the demands included a union for prisoners. The United Prisoners' Union also devised a Bill of Rights for the Convicted Class (Davis, 2012: 31).

In 1972, in the wake of prison disturbances in the United Kingdom, the Union for the Preservation of the Rights of Prisoners (PROP) was established to 'democratize and prise open the prison system' (Ryan, 1978: 113) and represent prisoners with prison officers and governors. PROP was to operate as a trade union for prisoners. It welcomed sympathisers, but full membership was only open to prisoners and ex-prisoners: 'it was their experience that was to count' (Ryan, 2003: 50). In 1983, Women in Prison (WIP), founded by a former prisoner, sought active membership of ex-prisoners. Women in Prison was concerned that women's imprisonment was largely ignored by prison campaigners and advocated on issues of concern for all prisoners as well, but especially women's imprisonment. With the establishment of WIP, 'women prisoners got their voice and made their own demands' (Ryan, 2003: 64).

It was also in this period that prisoner movements sprang up in Scandinavia, notably KROM, KRUM and KRIM. The KROM, the Norwegian Association for Penal Reform, was led by, among others, penal abolitionist Thomas Mathiesen who was chair from its inception in 1968 until 1973. Challenging the hegemony of the prison system, it organised conferences on penal reform to confront the dominant discourse, and to create 'an alternative public space ... which in the end may compete with the superficial public space of mass media' (Mathiesen, 2005: 461). Forty years later, these conferences were still being held annually in the mountains and what makes them particularly remarkable is the attendance of politicians, prison officials, interested individuals, members of the media and serving prisoners. 'An important effect of these meetings is to include prisoners in the joint moral community of the decision-makers' (Christie, 2000: 42).

Established in Sweden, KRUM was an organisation of prisoners, ex-prisoners and sympathisers. They ascertained the right to a grievance council to discuss matters with the prison authorities, the only exception being security issues. This led to more liberal visiting conditions, more home visits and an end to censorship of prisoner newspapers. KRUM even confidentially called for the construction of new prisons to be stopped. They were so successful that prison service management accepted the need for 'prison democracy'. The language was more optimistic than realistic, but it created a new discourse (Ward, 1972). In Denmark, the KRIM represented the interests of prisoners with demands for improved conditions for visits and more home visits (Ward, 1972). In Finland, a prisoners association, Toverikunta, dates back to the 1960s. Elections are held for prisoner representatives and in one prison, Kerava, issues discussed included extended family visits at weekends, longer time on the telephone and more materials for the prison library (Warner, 2009: 208). However, these movements in Scandinavia were more successful in achieving political engagement because they emerged in different social, political and economic environments (see Pratt, 2008a and 2008b).

In various European countries, legislation exists to permit participation through prisoner councils (Bishop, 2006; Solomon and Edgar, 2004). These give a voice to prisoners and offer opportunities for active citizenship. Under the 2006 European Prison Rules (EPR), prisoners are now encouraged to take an integral part in their own sentence management. Rule 56.2 allows that, whenever possible, prison authorities should use mechanisms of restoration and mediation to resolve disputes with and among prisoners. 'Subject to the needs of good order, safety and security' according to an innovation included in the 2006 EPR, 'prisoners shall be allowed to discuss matters relating to the general conditions of imprisonment and shall be encouraged to communicate with the prison authorities about these matters' (Rule 50). This was a significant advance in prison governance because suggestions for improvement in prison conditions 'should not be the sole prerogative of national inspection bodies or the CPT. Prisoners, too, have a legitimate reason to convey their views on this matter' (Bishop, 2006: 3).

In the wake of the Woolf Report, which recommended that prisoners 'should be able to contribute to and be informed of the way things are run' (Woolf, cited in Solomon and Edgar, 2004: 3), prisoner councils were introduced in the UK. At a time when British prisoners are still prevented from voting, the 'councils provide the only opportunity for them to get involved in a democratic process' (Solomon and Edgar, 2004: 11). While a 2002 Prison Service Order states that they should not compromise good order or discipline, they have functioned with mixed results, depending usually on the attitude of local prison management. While personal and security issues are outside the remit of prisoner councils, they offer prisoners an opportunity to engage in conflict resolution, management of their community and participation in the democratic process. Advocating the more widespread adoption of prisoner councils, Solomon and Edgar (2004: 35) concluded that they are more than just representative opportunities for prisoners but challenge society to see prisoners:

> in a new light, as citizens and individuals who have a right to make choices. Having a say about the conditions in which they are held and the politics that regulate their lives is a vital process of fostering personal

responsibility. It is a recognition that prisoners are not powerless, but are members of a community which requires their consent if it is to exercise its authority legitimately.

Both prisoner unions and prisoner councils offer the opportunity for prisoners to contribute to their community and participate in public discourse on the penal system. It also encourages the community outside prison to see them differently, as citizens. Ryan (2003: 71) concluded that while prisoner representative groups (and other organisations from this period such as the NAPO Members' Action Group (NMAG) and the abolitionist Radical Alternatives to Prison) in the UK may have been small and unrepresentative 'through their arguments and their practice, backed up and supported by a less deferential political culture, they helped to disturb the complacency that had surrounded the operation of the criminal justice system in Britain and to undermine the self-confidence of those who ran it'. Significantly, convicts brought their 'own knowledges from below to challenge those of the experts who had previously claimed to speak for them in the corridors of power' (Ryan, 2003: 69). These groups were important because they gave a voice to the prisoner and possibly even more importantly to prisoners collectively.

Despite some very vocal interviewees expressing strong opinions, Irish prisoners do not have a strong tradition of collective representation. While prisoners' organisations and support groups were springing up throughout Europe in the 1960s and 1970s, Rogan (2011: 143) has argued that 'one of the striking features in any assessment of Irish prison policy ... is the paucity of organisations, committees or unions established by prisoners themselves'. In the 1970s, a group of republican prisoners in Portlaoise established a committee to 'work for basic human rights for all prisoners' which eventually led to the creation of the Prisoners Union. Over a four year period, it published a regular periodical. The *Jail Journal* had articles written by prisoners smuggled out of the prison and copies of the periodical were smuggled in (Rogan, 2011: 143–4). In 1973, the Prisoners' Rights Organisation was established. It held regular meetings and demanded that prisons be 'rehabilitative rather than punitive' (Kilcommins *et al.*, 2004: 71). However, by the late 1980s, the Prisoners' Rights Organisation was moribund.

At the beginning of the second decade of the twenty-first century, Irish prisoners did not have a representative body inside or outside prison. Unlike the UK or the US, there is no prisoner newspaper and few avenues are available to voice their concerns. Whatever grievances prisoners have, individually or collectively, they rarely permeate the prison walls. Objections to prison governance or penal policy tend to be strictly within the parameters set out in the prison rules, regulations and individualised governance in prison. Prisoners' voices have been largely absent from public discourse about prison conditions, penal policy or the wider criminal justice system. There is little sense of collective identity. Interviewees in this study believed their opinions mattered little. They had not been consulted about the enfranchisement legislation; they had not been canvassed during election, they had no role in prison governance, little faith in the monitoring bodies and felt their voice was ignored in public discourse.

Reimagining imprisonment
If prisons are to allow for citizenship, they must be re-imagined. Sparks (1994: 15) pointed out that the irony of the modern prison is that it operates as an autocracy in a democratic polity. It was not always this way. Historically there have been examples of prisons run with a democratic ethos which provide models of prisoner–officer negotiation and co-operation. Prisoners were viewed differently and not reduced to irresponsible individuals. These included US prison reformer Thomas Mott Osborne's Auburn Prison and Alexander Maconochie's Norfolk Island Prison (Eggleston and Gehring, 2000). Ireland, pre-independence, pioneered a distinctive type of imprisonment with a different view of prisoners in Walter Crofton's Intermediate System (Dooley, 2003).

Pratt (2008a and 2008b) has considered an alternative approach to imprisonment in Scandinavia in more recent times. It reflects a different view of the prisoner, treating them as citizens first (see also Warner, 2009). In Norway, the Enforcement of Sentences Act 2002 stated: 'prisoners have the same rights to services and activities, and the same obligations and responsibilities as the population at large' (cited in Nordic Council of Ministers, 2009: 92). Duguid (2000: 146) examined a number of innovative prison programmes in the US, Canada and UK which put prisoner participation at the core of their development, 'a focus on the prisoner first and foremost as an individual'. These included the Barlinnie Special Unit in Scotland, the Santa Cruz Women's Prison Programme and the NewGate programmes in the US, and concluded that these heralded 'a genuine renaissance in the objective of the prison becoming an agent of individual transformation'. The experience of the Santa Cruz Women's Prison Programme 'clearly led to political awareness, self esteem, and interest in personal change' (Duguid, 2000: 109).

The Barlinnie Special Unit in the United Kingdom offered an alternative form of imprisonment, albeit in a therapeutic setting. It was an institution 'where prisoners were given a significant role in decision-making; they were held responsible for their own behaviour and that of their peers' (Cooke, 1989: 129). Grendon Prison in the United Kingdom has a 'regime which places a high value on consultation, openness and democratic decision making process' (Bennett, 2006: 130). Each unit in Grendon is relatively small and autonomous, with 40 to 46 prisoners in each, organised along democratic lines and prisoner responsibility is encouraged by participation. A prisoner security committee reports to the main prison security committee (Bennett, 2006: 138). It is regularly pointed out by its critics that Grendon is a unique therapeutic form of confinement and not suitable for all prisoners. But that is as it should be. As prisoners differ, so should prisons. The ethos in Grendon, Barlinnie and the other examples suggests that individuals respond positively to being treated differently. While it is argued that these institutions may not be appropriate for all prisoners, neither are the security, regime and routine associated with the more traditional modern prison.

In Irish prisons, some types of active citizenship are encouraged, with volunteering and charitable activities organised independently by prisoners or in prison workshops. Areas such as education departments encourage active citizenship. Many offer art, drama and creative writing which encourage personal deliberation and positive engagement as innovative ways to encourage participative citizenship. Subjects such as civic and political education, sociology and philosophy encourage critical reflection and active citizenship. While it may seem somewhat utopian to argue for the allocation of resources for prisoners to engage in such learning, rather than more utilitarian subjects and skills-based training, 'social awareness, attitudes and practical capacities need time and practice to develop. Thus, education is central to active citizenship' (Honohan, 2005: 177–8). These subjects encourage students to participate, take responsibility and engage in self-directed learning (Behan, 2008). These activities create a positive learning environment outside of subject-based teaching and offer opportunities to embrace a citizen role and encourage prisoners to act as agents in their process of change.

Prisoners are stakeholders in the penal system. In the modern management jargon pervading wider society and influencing penal discourse, they may even be considered consumers of punishment within the criminal justice system. In the professionalised discourse of modern management, the prisoner's agency tends to be undervalued, sometimes negated, while experts determine how to 'rehabilitate' him or her. Prisoners, many interviewees argued, have an important contribution to determine what might be the best way of not just managing their sentence, but contributing to their immediate community (the prison) and preparing for participation in society after release. Indeed they, it could be argued, have the most important contribution. As individuals and as a group, they could be involved in examining prison rules, conditions, regimes and quality of life issues, essentially developing frameworks for participating as citizens in their community.

For enfranchisement to be more than just a change in the law, however welcome, necessitates a transformation in the way prisoners are treated; it challenges how prisons are organised and prisoners governed. To encourage civic engagement, citizens must be given the opportunity to participate, contribute and live citizenship. Active participation by citizens, including prisoners, will guarantee rights, not privileges dispensed from above or guaranteed by courts. It is imperative that the right to vote is safeguarded, not by courts, legislation or even politicians, but by engaged and empowered citizens. Otherwise, should a future government decide to disenfranchise, legislation allowing prisoners to vote could be repealed.

Conclusion

'Citizenship by proxy', argued Putnam (2000: 160), 'is an oxymoron'. Citizens cannot engage through others. In the course of this study, prisoners lamented that they had no voice; others spoke at them, to them, about them, for them. Gavin began this book with a plea for prisoners' voices to be listened to. To avoid representing their voice by proxy, it is perhaps appropriate that a prisoner provides a synthesis of the place of voting in wider citizenship. Thomas welcomed, but remained critical of, the limits of enfranchisement. He suggested some ways to make it more meaningful. His comments are worth reproducing to remind us of the contribution prisoners can make to the debate about political participation and civic engagement.

> I believe that while it is a positive development that prisoners are now allowed to vote, it is in reality little more than a cosmetic exercise. It is recognition by the state of the entitlement of every citizen to participate in the electoral system. So yes, it is a good idea but it raises more questions than it answers.
>
> In terms of whether it will make better citizens I would be doubtful. It does raise a number of questions as to how prisoners could be made to be 'better citizens'. It is interesting that the state considers it important to maintain the link between the prisoner and participation in the political system and yet it does not appear to treat prisoners' involvement in other systems as important . . .
>
> It is also the case that prisoners are denied all involvement in the community while they are incarcerated. Clearly this could cause the prisoner to become alienated from the community. While it may be difficult in

practice to allow prisoners temporary release to engage in community activities it could easily be arranged to bring the community into prisons.

For example, if prisoners can vote, why are the political parties not establishing branches within the prisons? Such branches could be organised by a couple of members of the local branch in the community coming into the prisons on even a monthly basis. The same is true for other community sports or musical organisations such as the GAA, Comhaltas Ceoltóirí Éireann or local drama groups for example. Such interactions would not only be beneficial to the prison community but would also benefit the outside community by giving them an insight into prison life.

The making of prisoners into 'better citizens' will only occur when the state begins to implement a prison policy which has meaningful and lasting benefits for both the 'citizen prisoner' and the society he/she is part of. Granting voting rights, while a welcome development, is not providing a structural change in the system, and until structural change begins, then voting rights will be seen as an irrelevancy by prisoners, much as they are by a large proportion of the citizens within the communities from which the majority of the prison population is drawn. The statistics in the number of prisoners who actually even registered to vote, never mind voted, would appear to bear that position out.

As Thomas pointed out, obstacles remain to prisoners' embracing enfranchisement fully. While it has been very significant symbolically, prisoners' rights and opportunities for participative and lived citizenship need to be dealt with more comprehensively. The right to vote is one part of the mosaic of citizenship. For convicts to be encouraged to participate as citizens necessitates a fundamental re-imagining of imprisonment and its place in the matrix of punishment. It is also time to reconceptualise enfranchisement, transforming it from a legal concept to a wider notion of civic engagement and community participation. This necessitates consideration of enfranchisement as more than just a change in the law to enable prisoners to vote, but rather as part of a process to engage and empower citizens.

At the time of writing (June 2013), legislators in a number of jurisdictions are considering the issue of prisoners and the franchise. The reflections articulated by Thomas and others in this study could provide some guidance to policymakers and politicians in these deliberations, enhancing their understanding of the challenges associated with prisoner enfranchisement. They may even offer insights into how to encourage a more engaged and participative citizenry, outside of the penal sphere. Given the opportunity, citizen convicts have much to contribute to the debate on prisoners, politics and the vote.

Bibliography

Abramsky, S. (2006), *Conned: How Millions Went to Prison, Lost the Vote, and Helped Send George Bush to the White House*. New York: The New Press.
Alexander, M. (2010), *The New Jim Crow: Mass Incarceration in the Age of Colorblindness*. New York: The New Press.
Altman, A. (2005), 'Democratic Self-Determination and the Disenfranchisement of Felons', *Journal of Applied Philosophy*, 22 (3): 263–73.
Arbour Hill Visiting Committee (AHVC) (2005), *Annual Report 2004*. Available at: www.justice.ie (accessed 15 August 2007).
Arbour Hill Visiting Committee (AHVC) (2006), *Annual Report 2005*. Available at: www.justice.ie (accessed 1 September 2007).
Arbour Hill Visiting Committee (AHVC) (2007), *Annual Report 2006*. Available at: www.justice.ie (accessed 30 January 2008).
Arbour Hill Visiting Committee (AHVC) (2008), *Annual Report 2007*. Available at: www.justice.ie (accessed 27 May 2009).
Bailey, V. (1997), 'English Prisons, Penal Culture, and the Abatement of Imprisonment, 1895–1922', *Journal of British Studies*, 36: 285–324.
Barak, G., Leighton, P. and Flavin, J. (2007), *Class, Race, Gender & Crime: Social Realities of Justice in America* (2nd edn). Plymouth: Rowman & Littlefield.
BBC (2005), *UK Prisoners Right to Vote*. Available at: www.news.bbc.co.uk/2/hi/uk_news/4316148.stm, 6 October (accessed 23 October 2008).
BBC (2007), *Court Rules on Prison Voting Ban*. Available at: www.news.bbc.co.uk/2/hi/uk_news/scotland/6294973.stm, 24 January (accessed 29 October 2008).
Becker, H. (1967), 'Whose Side Are We On?', *Social Problems*, 14 (3): 239–49.
Behan, C. (2008), 'From Outside to Inside: Pedagogy Behind Prison Walls', in R. Wright (ed.), *In the Borderlands: Learning to Teach in Prisons and Alternative Settings* (2nd edn). San Bernardino: California State University.
Behan, C. (2011), '"The Benefit of Personal Experience and Personal Study": Prisoners and the Politics of Enfranchisement', *The Prison Journal*, 91 (1): 7–31.

Behan, C. (2012), ' "Still Entitled to our Say": Prisoners' Perspectives on Politics'. *The Howard Journal*, 51 (1): 16–36.
Behan, C. and O'Donnell, I. (2008), 'Prisoners, Politics and the Polls: Enfranchisement and the Burden of Responsibility', *British Journal of Criminology*, 48 (3): 319–36.
Bennett, P. (2006), 'Governing a Humane Prison', in D. Jones (ed.), *Humane Prisons*. Oxford: Radcliffe Publishing, pp. 129–39.
Beresford, D. (1987), *Ten Men Dead: The Story of the 1981 Hunger Strike*. London: Grafton Books.
Bishop, N. (2006), 'Prisoner Participation in Prisoner Management', *Penal Field*, 3: 1–12.
Blais, A., Massicotte, L. and Yoshinaka, A. (2001), 'Deciding Who Has the Right to Vote: A Comparative Analysis of Election Laws', *Electoral Studies*, 20: 41–62.
Boston Globe (1997), 'Cellucci's Crackdown', *The Boston Globe*, 16 August.
Bosworth, M. (2007), 'Creating the Responsible Prisoner: Federal Admission and Orientation Packs', *Punishment and Society*, 9 (1): 67–85.
Bottomley, P. (2004), 'Don't Deny the Vote', *The Guardian*, 2 March.
Breen, J. (2010), 'Secondary Effects of Imprisonment: The New Direction of Prison Research', *Irish Probation Journal*, 7: 46–64.
Brennan, M. (2008), 'Low-profile TD for Kerry North Sent More Letters on Behalf of Prisoners than any other Dáil Deputy', *Irish Independent*, 7 July.
Brennan Center for Justice (2009), *My First Vote*. New York: Brennan Center for Justice.
Brennock, M. (2002), 'Minister Flooded with TDs' Queries on Legal Matters', *Irish Times*, 23 October.
Brown, D. (2007), 'The Disenfranchisement of Prisoners: *Roach* v. *Electoral Commission & Anor.* – Modernity v. Feudalism', *Alternative Law Review*, 323 (2): 132–7.
Burnett, R. and Maruna, S. (2006), 'The Kindness of Strangers: Strengths-based Resettlement in Theory and Action', *Criminology and Criminal Justice*, 6 (1): 83–106.
Byrne, E. (2012), *Political Corruption in Ireland: A Crooked Harp?* Manchester: Manchester University Press.
Byrne, R., Hogan, G. and McDermott, P. (1981), *Prisoners' Rights: A Study of Irish Prison Law*. Dublin: Co-op Books.
Campbell, B., McKeown, L. and O'Hagan, F. (1994), *Nor Meekly Serve My Time: The H-Block Struggle 1976–1981*. Belfast: Beyond the Pale Publications.
Campbell, M. (2007), 'Criminal Disenfranchisement Reform in California: A Deviant Case Study', *Punishment and Society*, 9 (2): 177–200.
Cardinale, M. (2004), *Triple-Decker Disenfranchisement: First-Person Accounts of Losing the Right to Vote among Poor, Homeless Americans with a Felony Conviction*. Washington: The Sentencing Project.
Carey, T. (2000), *Mountjoy: The Story of a Prison*. Cork: Collins Press.

Carrabine, E. (2005), 'Prison Riots, Social Order and the Problem of Legitimacy', *British Journal of Criminology*, 45 (6): 896–913.

Cassidy, T. (1998), 'Lawmakers Act to Rescind Voting Rights of Prisoners', *The Boston Globe*, 30 July.

Cavadino, M. and Dignan, J. (2006), *Penal Systems: A Comparative Approach*. London: Sage.

Central Elections Commission (CEC) Palestine (2005), *Report on Second Presidential Elections, January 9, 2005*. Ramallah: Central Elections Commission.

Chapman, J. (2005), 'Kennedy: Let Prisoners Vote'. *Mail Online*, Available at: www.dailymail.co.uk/news/article-339908/ Kennedy-Let-killers-vote.html, 3 March (accessed 29 September 2011).

Cheney, D. (2008), 'Prisoners as Citizens in a Democracy', *Howard Journal*, 47 (2): 134–45.

Christie, N. (2000), *Crime Control as Industry: Towards Gulags Western Style*. London: Routledge.

Clegg, R. (1999), *Testimony to House Sub-Committee on the Constitution*. Available at: www.judiciary.house.gov.Legacy/cleg1021.htm (accessed 20 September 2008).

Clegg, R. (2001), 'Who Should Vote?', *Texas Review of Law and Politics*, 6: 159–77.

Clegg, R., Conway, G. and Lee, K. (2006), 'The Bullet and the Ballot? The Case for Felon Disenfranchisement Statutes', *Journal of Gender, Social Policy and the Law*, 14 (1): 1–26.

Coleman, J. S. (1988), 'Social Capital in the Creation of Human Capital', *American Journal of Sociology*, 94 (Supplement): S95–S120.

Committee for the Prevention of Torture (CPT) (2007a), *Report to the Government of Ireland on the Visit to Ireland Carried Out by the European Committee for the Prevention of Torture and Inhuman or Degrading Treatment or Punishment (CPT) from 2 to 13 October 2006*. Available at: www.cpt.coe.int/documents/irl/2007-40-inf-eng.pdf (accessed 21 January 2011).

Committee for the Prevention of Torture (CPT) (2007b), *Response of the Government of Ireland to the report of the European Committee for the Prevention of Torture and Inhuman or Degrading Treatment or Punishment (CPT) on its Visit to Ireland from 2 to 13 October 2006*. Available at: www.cpt.coe.int/documents/irl/2007-41-inf-eng.pdf (accessed 21 January 2011).

Connolly, S. (1999), *The Oxford Companion to Irish History*. Oxford: Oxford University Press.

Cooke, D. (1989), 'Containing Violent Prisoners: An Analysis of the Barlinnie Special Unit', *British Journal of Criminology*, 29 (2): 129–43.

Correctional Service of Canada (2008), *Aboriginal Initiatives*. Available at: www.csc-scc.gc.ca/text/prgrm/abinit/who-eng.shtml (accessed 1 February 2012).

Costelloe, A. and Warner, K. (2008), 'Beyond "Offending Behaviour": The Wider Perspectives of Adult Education and the European Prison Rules', in

R. Wright (ed.), *In the Borderlands: Learning to Teach in Prisons and Alternative Settings* (2nd edn). San Bernardino: California State University.
Costello, J. (1985), 'Votes for Prisoners', *Irish Times*, 3 January.
Council of Europe (1950), *European Convention on Human Rights*. Strasbourg: Council of Europe.
Council of Europe (1990), *Education in Prison: Recommendation No. R (89) 12*. Strasbourg: Council of Europe.
Council of Europe (2006), *European Prison Rules*. Strasbourg: Council of Europe.
Council for Social Welfare (CSW) (1983), *The Prison System*. Dublin: Council for Social Welfare.
Council for Social Welfare and Irish Commission for Justice and Peace (1986), *Response to the Report of the Committee of Inquiry into the Penal System*. Dublin: Irish Commission for Justice and Peace.
Courtney, M. and Gallagher, M. (2011), 'The Parliamentary Election in Ireland, February 2011', *Electoral Studies*, 31 (1): 231–4.
Coyle, A. (2005), 'Prison Works? International Comparisons', *Journal of the Scottish Association for the Study of Offending*, 11: 7–17.
Coyle, A. (2008), 'The Treatment of Prisoners: International Standards and Case Law', *Legal and Criminological Psychology*, 13 (2): 219–30.
Cressey, D. R. (ed.) (1961), *The Prison: Studies in Organization and Change*. New York: Holt, Rinehart and Winston.
Crewe, B. (2012), *The Prisoner Society: Power, Adaptation, and Social Life in an English Prison*. Oxford: Oxford University Press.
Crutchfield, R. (2007), 'Abandon Criminal Disenfranchisement Policies', *Journal of Criminology and Public Policy*, 6 (4): 707–16.
Dáil Debates, 1922, vol. 1, col. 2321–2.
Dáil Debates, 1923, vol. 4, col. 1379–83.
Dáil Debates, 1923, vol. 5, col. 31–2.
Dáil Debates, 1925, vol. 10, col. 263–4.
Dáil Debates, 1947, vol. 105, col. 594.
Dáil Debates, 1970, vol. 247, col. 121–2.
Dáil Debates, 1981, vol. 326, col. 65.
Dáil Debates, 1981, vol. 328, col. 1072–3.
Dáil Debates, 1991, vol. 404, col. 1824.
Dáil Debates, 1998, vol. 495, col. 806.
Dáil Debates, 2000, vol. 523, col. 1145–6.
Dáil Debates, 2004, vol. 586, col. 1345.
Dáil Debates, 2005, vol. 612, col. 1115.
Dáil Debates, 2006, vol. 624, col. 1978–2004.
Dáil Debates, 2006, vol. 628, col. 846–9.
Davidson, H. (1995), 'Possibilities for Critical Pedagogy in a "Total Institution": An Introduction to Critical Perspective on Prison Education', in H. Davidson (ed.), *Schooling in a 'Total Institution'*. Westport, Connecticut: Bergen and Garvey, pp. 1–21.

Davis, A. (2003), *Are Prisons Obsolete?* New York: Seven Stories Press.

Davis, A. (2012), 'Attica Futures: 21st Century Strategies for Prison Abolition', in M. Mauer and K. Epstein (eds), *To Build a Better Criminal Justice System*. Washington: Sentencing Project, pp. 30–1.

Department for Constitutional Affairs (DCA) (2006), *Voting Rights of Convicted Prisoners Detained within the United Kingdom – The UK Government's Response to the Grand Chamber of the European Court of Human Rights in the Case of* Hirst *v.* United Kingdom. Consultation Paper CP29/06. Available at: www.dca.gov.uk/publications.htm (accessed 30 March 2007).

Department of Justice and Equality (2008) 'Prison Visiting Committees'. Available at: www.justice.ie/en/JELR/Pages/Prison_visiting_committees (accessed 14 October 2012).

Department of Social, Community and Family Affairs (2000), *Supporting Voluntary Activity: Government White Paper*. Dublin: Government Publications.

Dhami, M. (2005), 'Prisoner Disenfranchisement Policy: A Threat to Democracy?', *Analyses of Social Issues and Public Policy*, 5 (1): 235–47.

Diskin, A. and Hazan, R. (2007), 'The Knesset Election in Israel, March 2006', *Electoral Studies*, 26 (3): 707–11.

Dooley, E. (2003), 'Sir Walter Crofton and the Irish or Intermediate System of Prison Discipline', in I. O'Donnell and F. McAuley (eds), *Criminal Justice History: Themes and Controversies from Pre-Independence Ireland*. Dublin: Four Courts Press.

Duff, A. (2005), 'Introduction: Crime and Community', *Journal of Applied Philosophy*, 22 (3): 211–16.

Duguid, S. (2000), *Can Prisons Work? The Prisoner as Object and Subject in Modern Corrections*. Toronto: University of Toronto Press.

Easton, S. (2006), 'Electing the Electorate: The Problem of Prisoner Disenfranchisement', *Modern Law Review*, 69: 443–52.

Easton, S. (2011), *Prisoners' Rights: Principles and Practice*. Oxford: Routledge.

Economic and Social Research Institute (2002), *Election Survey 2002*. Available at: www.issda.ucd.ie/ines/2002/ines2002-questionnaire.pdf (accessed 1 October 2007).

Economic and Social Research Institute (2007), *Election Survey 2007*. Available at: www.issda.ucd.ie/ines/2007/ines2007-questionnaire.pdf (accessed 1 October 2007).

Edgar, K., Jacobson, J. and Biggar, K. (2011), *Time Well Spent: A Practical Guide to Active Citizenship and Volunteering in Prison*. London: Prison Reform Trust.

Eggleston, C. and Gehring, T. (2000), 'Democracy in Prison and Prison Education', *Journal of Correctional Education*, 51 (3): 306–10.

European Commission (2007), *Eurobarometer Poll 68: Public Opinion in the European Union National Report: Ireland*. Available at: www.ec.europa.eu/public_opinion/archives/eb/eb68/eb68_ie_nat.pdf (accessed 28 July 2008).

European Commission (2008), *Eurobarometer Poll 69: Public Opinion in the European Union National Report: Ireland*. Available at: www.ec.europa.eu/public_opinion/archives/eb/eb69/eb69_ie_nat.pdf (accessed 28 July 2008).

Ewald, A. (2002), ' "Civil Death": The Ideological Paradox of Criminal Disenfranchisement Law in the United States', *Wisconsin Law Review*, 1045–137.

Ewald, A. (2004), 'An "Agenda for Demolition": The Fallacy and the Danger of the "Subversive Voting" Argument for Felony Disenfranchisement', *Columbia Human Rights Law Review*, 36: 109–44.

Ewald, A. and Rottinghaus, B. (eds) (2009), *Criminal Disenfranchisement in an International Perspective*. Cambridge: Cambridge University Press.

Fairchild, E. (1977), 'Politicisation of the Criminal Offender', *Criminology*, 15 (3): 287–317.

Farrall, S., Sharpe, G., Hunter, B. and Calverley, C. (2011), 'Theorising Structural and Individual-Level Processes in Desistance and Persistence: Outlining an Integrated Perspective', *Australian and New Zealand Journal of Criminology*, 44 (2): 218–34.

Faulkner, D. (2002), 'Turning Prisons Inside-out', *Relational Justice*, 16: 1–3.

Faulkner, D. (2003), 'Taking Citizenship Seriously: Social Capital and Criminal Justice in a Changing World', *Criminal Justice* 3 (3): 287–315.

Fineout, G. (2007), 'Crist Ready to Restore Ex-Convicts' Rights', www.MiamiHerlad.com (accessed 13 April 2008).

Flynn, B. (2011), *Pawns in the Game: Irish Hunger Strikes 1912–1981*. Dublin: Collins Press.

Foot, P. (2005), *The Vote: How it Was Won and How it Was Undermined*. London: Viking.

Ford, R. (2005), 'Prisoners Granted the Right to Vote', 7 October. Available at: www.timesonline.co.uk/tol/news/uk/article575790.ece (accessed 1 June 2009).

Foxe, K. (2009), 'Hundreds of Prisoners Apply for New Remission Scheme: Just One Is Approved', *Sunday Tribune*, 25 January.

Gallagher, C. (2001), 'The Captive Vote: Prisoners' Suffrage in Ireland', *University College Dublin Law Review*, 1: 1–31.

Gallagher, M. and Komito, L. (2005), 'Dáil Deputies and their Constituency Work', in Coakley, J. and Gallagher, M. (eds), *Politics in the Republic of Ireland*. Limerick: PSAI Press.

Gallagher, M. and Marsh, M. (2008), *How Ireland Voted: The Full Story of Ireland's General Election*. London: Palgrave Macmillan.

Garland, D. (2001), *The Culture of Control: Crime and Social Order in Contemporary Society*. Oxford: Oxford University Press.

Gaziano, T. (1999), 'Testimony to House Sub-Committee on the Constitution', October 1999. Available at: http://judiciary.house. gov.gazianoLegacy/1021.htm (accessed 10 January 2008).

Goffman, E. (1961), *Asylums: Essays on the Social Situation of Mental Patients and Other Inmates*. London: Penguin Books.

Goffman, E. (1997), *The Goffman Reader*, ed. C. Lambert and A. Branaman. Oxford: Blackwell Publishers.
Grayeff, Y. (2006a), 'Yigal Amir Among 9,000 Jailed Voters', *Jerusalem Post Online*, 27 May.
Grayeff, Y. (2006b), '14 Prisoners in Israeli Jails Elected', *Jerusalem Post*, 26 January.
Greenberg, G. and Rosenheck, R. (2008), 'Homelessness in the State and Federal Prison Population', *Criminal Behaviour and Mental Health*, 18: 88–103.
Griffin, D. and O'Donnell, I. (2012), 'The Life Sentence and Parole', *British Journal of Criminology*, 52(3): 611–29.
Halpern, D. (2005), *Social Capital*. Cambridge: Polity Press.
Hamilton, C. and Kilkelly, U. (2008), 'Human Rights in Irish Prisons', *Judicial Studies Institute Journal*, 2: 59–85.
Hamilton, C. and Lines, R. (2009), 'The Campaign for Prisoner Voting Rights in Ireland', in A. Ewald and B. Rottinghaus (eds), *Criminal Disenfranchisement in an International Perspective*. Cambridge: Cambridge University Press.
Hansard, HC Debates, 18 May 1849, vol. 105, col. 668–9.
Hansard, HC Debates, 10 February 1870, vol. 119, col. 126.
Hansard, HC Debates, 10 February 1870, vol. 199, col. 151.
Hansard, HC Debates, 18 February 1875, vol. 222, col. 539.
Hansard, HC Debates, 28 February 1882, vol. 266, col. 1869.
Hansard, HC Debates, 15 December 1999, vol. 341, col. 300.
Hansard, HC Debates, 2 November 2010, vol. 517, col. 772.
Hansard, HC Debates, 3 November 2010, vol. 517, col. 921.
Hansard, HC Debates, 10 February 2011, vol. 523, col. 494.
Hansard, HC Debates, 10 February 2011, vol. 523, col. 502.
Hansard, HC Debates, 10 February 2011, vol. 523, col. 586.
Hansard, HC Debates, 23 May 2012, vol. 545, col. 1127.
Hansard, HC Debates, 22 November 2012, vol. 553, col. 745–7.
Hansard, HC Debates, 22 November 2012, vol. 553, col. 750–5.
Hansard, HL Debates, 20 October 2003, vol. 653, col. 143.
Hansard, HL Debates, 20 April 2009, vol. 709, col. 1248.
Hansard, HL Debates, 7 April 2010, vol. 718, col. 1643.
Harris, C. (ed.) (2005), *Engaging Citizens: The Case for Democratic Renewal in Ireland. Report of the Democracy Commission*. Dublin: New Island Books.
Harvard Law Review (HLR) (1989), 'Note: The Disenfranchisement of Ex-Felons: Citizenship, Criminality, and "the Purity of the Ballot Box"', *Harvard Law Review*, 1102: 1300–17.
Healy, D. (2009), 'Ethics and Criminological Research: Charting a Way Forward', *Irish Probation Journal*, 6: 171–81.
Hegarty, P. (1999), *Peadar O'Donnell*. Dublin: Mercier Books.
Hennessy, M. (2004), 'Government to Examine Ruling on Prisoners' Right to Vote', *Irish Times*, 5 April.

Hennessy, M. (2008), 'Short Deadline to Register Criticised', *Irish Times*, 20 May.
Holland, K. (2007), 'More than 400 Inmates to Vote from Prison', *Irish Times*, 19 May.
Hong Kong Correctional Services (2009), 'CSD Strives to Build a Safer and More Inclusive Society'. Available at: www.csd.gov.hk/textonly/english/news/news_pr/news_pr_20100128_1.html (accessed 8 November 2011).
Hong Kong Special Administrative Region (HKSAR) (2009a), *Consultation Document on Prisoners' Voting Rights*. Hong Kong: Special Administrative Region Constitutional and Mainland Affairs Bureau.
Hong Kong Special Administrative Region (HKSAR) (2009b), *Report on Public Consultation on Prisoners' Voting Rights*. Hong Kong: Special Administrative Region Constitutional and Mainland Affairs Bureau.
Honohan, I. (2005), 'Active Citizenship in Contemporary Democracy', in C. Harris (ed.), *Report of the Democracy Commission. Engaging Citizens: The Case for Democratic Renewal in Ireland*. Dublin: New Island Books.
Houses of the Oireachtas (2011), *A Brief Guide to How Your Parliament Works*. Dublin: Houses of the Oireachtas.
Houston, M. (2009), '60% Per Cent Turnout at Hospital Poll', *Irish Times*, 30 May.
Huff, C. (1974), 'Unionization Behind the Walls', *Criminology*, 12 (2): 175–93.
Ignatieff, M. (1989), 'Citizenship and Moral Narcissism', *The Political Quarterly*, 60 (1): 63–74.
Inspector of Prisons (2006), *Portlaoise Prison Inspection: 6th–10th November 2006*. Available at: www.justice.ie (accessed 25 November 2008).
Inspector of Prisons (2007a), *Fifth Annual Report of the Inspector of Prisons and Places of Detention for the Year 2006–2007*. Available at: www.justice.ie (accessed 21 November 2008).
Inspector of Prisons (2007b), *Arbour Hill Prison Revisit Inspection: 12th–14th February 2007*. Available at: www.justice.ie (accessed 22 November 2008).
Inspector of Prisons (2009a), *Annual Report 2008*. Available at: www.inspectorofprisons.gov.ie (accessed 1 February 2013).
Inspector of Prisons (2009b), *Report on an Inspection of Mountjoy Prison by the Inspector of Prisons*. Available at: www.inspectorofprisons.gov.ie (accessed 12 May 2013).
International Centre for Prison Studies (2013), *World Prison Brief*. Available at: www.prisonstudies.org/info/worldbrief/wpb_country.php?country=145 (accessed 14 May 2013).
Irish Daily Mail (2009), 'Stop these Tawdry Letters for Criminals' (editorial), *Irish Daily Mail*, 19 January.
Irish Prison Education Service (2003), *Strategy Statement on Prison Education for 2003 to 2007*. Dublin: Irish Prison Education Service.

Irish Prison Education Service (2007), *Directory of Irish Prison Education, 2007*, Available at: www.pesireland.org (accessed 1 July 2008).
Irish Prison Service (IPS) (2001), *Strategy Statement 2001–2003*. Dublin: Irish Prison Service.
Irish Prison Service (IPS) (2004), *Annual Report 2003*. Dublin: Irish Prison Service.
Irish Prison Service (IPS) (2007), *Annual Report 2006*. Longford: Irish Prison Service.
Irish Prison Service (IPS) (2008), *Annual Report 2007*. Longford: Irish Prison Service.
Irish Prison Service (IPS) (2009), *Annual Report 2008*. Longford: Irish Prison Service.
Irish Prison Service (IPS) (2010), *Annual Report 2009*. Longford: Irish Prison Service.
Irish Prison Service (IPS) (2013), *Annual Report 2012*. Longford: Irish Prison Service.
Irish Times (2007a), 'Elections 2007 Supplement', *Irish Times*, 28 May.
Irish Times (2007b), 'Jailed Councillor Allowed to Vote', *Irish Times*, 5 July.
Ispahani, L. (2009), 'Voting Rights and Human Rights: A Comparative Analysis of Criminal Disenfranchisement Laws', in A. Ewald and B. Rottinghaus (eds), *Criminal Disenfranchisement in an International Perspective*. Cambridge: Cambridge University Press.
Itzkowitz, H. and Oldak, L. (1973), 'Restoring the Ex-Offenders Right to Vote: Backgrounds and Developments', *American Criminal Law Review*, 11: 721–70.
Jacobs, J. (1980), 'The Prisoners' Rights Movement and Its Impacts, 1960–1980', *Crime and Justice*, 2: 429–70.
Jenkins, S. (2012), 'Give Prisoners the Vote. But Not Because Europe Says So', *Guardian*, 23 November.
Jerusalem Post (1996), 'Voters Visit Rabin's Grave on Way to Polls', *Jerusalem Post*, 30 May.
Jesuit Centre for Faith and Justice (JCFJ) (2012), *The Irish Prison System: Vision, Values, Reality*. Dublin: Jesuit Centre for Faith and Justice.
Jewkes, Y. (2002), *Captive Audiences: Media, Masculinity and Power in Prisons*. Cullompton: Willan.
Johnson-Parris, A. S. (2003), 'Felon Disenfranchisement: The Un-conscionable Social Contract Breached', *Virginia Law Review*, 89: 109–38.
Joint Committee on Electoral Law (1961), *Interim, Second, Third Interim and Final Reports*. Dublin: Stationery Office.
Keogh, D. (1994), *Twentieth Century Ireland: Nation and State*. Dublin: Gill and Macmillan.
Keyssar, A. (2000), *The Right to Vote: The Contested History of Democracy in the United States*. New York: Basic Books.
Kilcommins, S., O'Donnell, I., O'Sullivan, E. and Vaughan, B. (2004), *Crime, Punishment and the Search for Order in Ireland*. Dublin: Institute of Public Administration.

King, R. (2006), *A Decade of Reform: Felony Disenfranchisement Policy in the United States*. Washington, DC: The Sentencing Project.

Kirby, M. (2007), 'Let Australia Never Be a Prisoner to Exclusion', *Sydney Morning Herald*, 1 October.

Kissane, K. (2007), 'Court Reverses Prisoner Vote Ban', *The Age* (Australia), 31 August.

Kleinig, K. and Murtagh, K. (2005), 'Disenfranchising Felons', *Journal of Applied Philosophy*, 22 (3): 217–39.

Korr, C. and Close, M. (2008), *More than Just a Game: Football v Apartheid*. London: Collins.

LaFollette, H. (2005), 'Collateral Consequences of Punishment: Civil Disabilities Accompanying Formal Punishment', *Journal of Applied Philosophy*, 22 (3): 241–61.

Law Reform Commission (2007), *Report on Spent Convictions*. Dublin: Law Reform Commission.

Lee, J. (1989), *Modern Ireland: 1912–1985*. Cambridge: Cambridge University Press.

Levenson, J. and Farrant, F. (2002), 'Unlocking Potential: Active Citizenship and Volunteering by Prisoners', *Probation Journal*, 49: 195– 204.

Lijphart, A. (1997), 'Unequal Participation: Democracy's Unresolved Dilemma', *American Political Science Review*, 91 (1): 1–14.

Livingstone, S. and Owen, T. (1999), *Prison Law* (2nd edn). Oxford: Oxford University Press.

Livingstone, S., Owen, T. and McDonald, A. (2008), *Prison Law* (4th edn). Oxford: Oxford University Press.

Lyons, F. S. L. (1973), *Ireland Since the Famine*. London: Collins/Fontana.

MacBride, S. (1982), *Report of the Commission of Enquiry into the Penal System*. Dublin: Ward River Press.

Manfredi, C. (1998), 'Judicial Review and Criminal Disenfranchisement in the United States', *The Review of Politics*, 60 (2): 277–305.

Manfredi, C. (2009), 'In Defense of Prisoner Disenfranchisement', in A. Ewald and B. Rottinghaus (eds), *Criminal Disenfranchisement in an International Perspective*. Cambridge: Cambridge University Press.

Manza, J. (2009), 'Foreword: Waves of Democracy and Criminal Disenfranchisement', in A. Ewald and B. Rottinghaus (eds), *Criminal Disenfranchisement in an International Perspective*. Cambridge: Cambridge University Press.

Manza, J., Brooks, C. and Uggen, C. (2004), 'Public Attitudes toward Felon Disenfranchisement in the United States', *Public Opinion Quarterly*, 68 (2): 275–86.

Manza, J. and Uggen, C. (2006), *Locked Out: Felon Disenfranchisement and American Democracy*. New York: Oxford University Press.

Marley, L. (2010), *Michael Davitt: Freelance Radical and Frondeur*. Dublin: Four Courts Press.

Marsh, M., Sinnott, R., Garry, J. and Kennedy, F. (2001), 'The Irish National Election Study: Puzzles and Priorities', *Irish Political Studies*, 16 (1): 161–78.

Marshall, T. H. (1950), *Citizenship and Social Class and Other Essays*. Cambridge: Cambridge University Press.
Maruna, S. (2001), *Making Good: How Ex-Convicts Reform and Rebuild their Lives*. Washington: American Psychological Association.
Maruna, S., Immarigeon, R. and LeBel, T. (2004), 'Ex-Offender Re-Integration: Theory and Practice', in S. Maruna and R. Immarigeon (eds), *After Crime and Punishment: Pathways to Offender Re-integration*. Willan Publishing: Cullompton.
Mathiesen, T. (2005), 'Contemporary Penal Policy – A Study in Moral Panics', in A. Bondenson (ed.), *Crime and Justice in Scandinavia*. Copenhagen: Forlaget Thomson.
Mauer, M. (2011), 'Voting Behind Bars: An Argument for Voting by Prisoners', *Howard Law Journal*, 54 (3): 549–66.
Mbodla, N. (2002), 'Should Prisoners Have a Right to Vote', *Journal of African Law*, 46 (1): 92–102.
McCleery, R. (1961), 'The Governmental Process and Informal Social Control', in D. Cressy (ed.), *The Prison: Studies in Institutional Organisation and Change*. New York: Holt, Rinehart and Winston.
McConville, S. (2003), *Irish Political Prisoners, 1848–1922: Theatres of War*. London: Routledge.
McConville, S. (2013), *Irish Political Prisoners, 1920–1962*. London: Routledge.
McDermott, P. A. (2000), *Prison Law*. Dublin: Round Hall.
McEvoy, K. (2001), *Paramilitary Imprisonment in Northern Ireland: Resistance, Management and Release*. Oxford: Oxford University Press.
McEvoy, K. and Shirlow, P. (2009), 'Re-imagining DDR: Ex-combatants, Leadership and Moral Agency in Conflict Transformation', *Theoretical Criminology*, 13 (1): 31–59.
McKenna, G. (2003), 'Mitchell Calls for Prisoners to be Given Vote', *Irish Independent*, 29 July.
Milanovic, D. and Thomas, J. (1989), 'Overcoming the Absurd: Prisoner Litigation as Primitive Rebellion', *Social Problems*, 36 (1): 48–60.
Milland, G. (2009), 'Europe Says: Give Votes to Convicts', *Daily Express*, 9 April.
Ministry of Justice (2009), *Voting Rights of Convicted Prisoners Detained in the United Kingdom: Second Stage Consultation*. London: Department of Justice. Available at: www.justice.gov.uk/consultations/docs/prisoner-voting-rights.pdf (accessed 25 April 2009).
Mitchel, J. (1854), *The Jail Journal*. Dublin: Browne and Nolan.
Morgan, M. and Kett, M. (2003), *The Prison Adult Literacy Survey: Results and Implications*. Dublin: Irish Prison Service.
Morris, N. and Rothman, D. (1998), *The Oxford History of the Prison*. New York: Oxford University Press.
Morton, F. L. (2002), 'Once Again: Court-made Law', *National Post* (Canada), 2 November.

Muntingh, L. (2004), 'South African Constitutional Court Rules on Inmates Right to Vote', *Corrections Today* (December): 74–9.

Murray, C. (2013), 'A Perfect Storm: Parliament and Prisoner Disenfranchisement', *Parliamentary Affairs*, 66: 511–39.

National Adult Literacy Agency (2006), *Plain English Guide to Political Terms*. Dublin: NALA.

National Association for the Advancement of Colored People (NAACP) (2011), *Defending Democracy: Confronting Modern Barriers to Voting Rights in America*. Baltimore: NAACP.

National Economic and Social Forum (NESF) (2002), *Re-integration of Offenders*. Dublin: NESF.

Nelson, J. and Kerr, D. (2006), *Active Citizenship in INCA Countries: Definitions, Policies, Practices and Outcomes*. Available at: www.inca.org.uk/pdf/Active_Citizenship_Report.pdf (accessed 10 January 2009).

New York Times (2008), 'Prison Nation' (editorial), *New York Times*, 10 March.

Nordic Council of Ministers (2009), *Nordic Prison Education: A Lifelong Perspective*. Copenhagen: Norden.

O'Donnell, I. (2005), 'Crime and Justice in the Republic of Ireland', *European Journal of Criminology*, (2) 1: 99–131.

O'Donnell, I. (2008), 'Stagnation and Change in Irish Penal Policy', *Howard Journal of Criminal Justice*, 47 (2): 121–32.

O'Donnell, I. (2011), 'Crime and Punishment in the Republic of Ireland: A Country Profile', *International Journal of Comparative and Applied Criminal Justice*, 35 (1): 73–88.

O'Donnell, I. and O'Sullivan, E. (2003), 'The Politics of Intolerance – Irish Style', *British Journal of Criminology*, 43: 41–62.

O'Donnell, I., Teljeur, C., Hughes, N., Baumer, E. and Kelly, A. (2007), 'When Prisoners Go Home: Punishment, Social Deprivation and the Geography of Reintegration', *Irish Criminal Law Journal*, 17 (4): 3–9.

Office of Public Works (2007), *Iris Oifigiuil – Seanad Electoral Roll*, 29 June. Dublin: Government Publications.

Olivares, K., Velmer, B. and Cullen, F. (1996), 'The Collateral Consequences of a Felony Conviction: A National Study of State Legal Codes 10 Years Later', *Federal Probation*, 60: 10–17.

O'Malley, E. (1978), *On Another Man's Wound*. London: Roberts Rheinhart.

Ó Muineacháin, S. and Gallagher, M. (2008), 'The Parliamentary Election in Ireland, May 207', *Electoral Studies*, 27: 151–4.

O'Regan, M. (2006), 'Prisoners to Get Postal Votes Under New Roche Legislation', *Irish Times*, 6 October.

O'Sullivan, E. and O'Donnell, I. (2007), 'Coercive Confinement in the Republic of Ireland: The Waning of a Culture of Control', *Punishment and Society*, 9: 27–48.

O'Sullivan, E. and O'Donnell, I. (2012), *Coercive Confinement in Ireland: Patients, Prisoners and Penitents*. Manchester: Manchester University Press.

Owers, A. (2004), 'Prison Inspection and the Protection of Human Rights', *European Human Rights Law Review*, 2: 107–16.
Owers, A. (2006), 'The Protection of Prisoners' Rights in England and Wales', *European Journal of Criminal Policy*, 12: 85–91.
Palestine Media Centre (2005), 'Israeli Supreme Court Rejects PNA Appeal on Prisoners'. Available at: www.palestine-pmc.com/details.asp?cat=1& id=772&search=1&key1=Palestinian%20Prisoners (accessed 12 November 2008).
Parkes, D. (2003), 'Ballot Boxes Behind Bars: Towards the Repeal of Prisoner Disenfranchisement Laws', *Temple Political and Civil Rights Law Review*, 74: 71–111.
Pateman, C. (1970), *Participation and Democratic Theory*. New York: Cambridge University Press.
Pew Center on the States (2008), *One in 100: Behind Bars in America 2008*. Washington, DC: Pew Charitable Trusts.
Plannic, Z. (1987), 'Should Imprisoned Criminals Have a Constitutional Right to Vote?', *Canadian Journal of Law and Society*, 2: 153–64.
Porter, N. (2010), *Expanding the Vote: State Felony Disenfranchisement Reform, 1997–2010*. Washington DC: The Sentencing Project.
Pratt, J. (2008a), 'Scandinavian Exceptionalism in an Era of Penal Excess. Part I: The Nature and Roots of Scandinavian Exceptionalism', *British Journal of Criminology*, 48: 119–37.
Pratt, J. (2008b), 'Scandinavian Exceptionalism in an Era of Penal Excess. Part II: Does Scandinavian Exceptionalism Have a Future?', *British Journal of Criminology*, 48: 275–92.
Prison Reform Trust /Unlock (2007), *Response of the Prison Reform Trust/ Unlock to the Consultation Document Produced by the Department for Constitutional Affairs*. Available at: http://unlock.org.uk/userfiles/file/ Votes/UNLOCK_Response_to_DCA_Consultation.pdf (accessed 16 July 2009).
Prison Reform Trust (PRT)(2013), *Bromley Briefings*. London: Prison Reform Trust.
Pryor, S. (2002), 'The Responsible Prisoner', *Relational Justice*, 15: 1–3.
Putnam, R. (1995), 'Bowling Alone: America's Declining Social Capital', *Journal of Democracy*, 6: 65–78.
Putnam, R. (2000), *Bowling Alone: The Collapse and Revival of American Community*. New York: Simon and Shuster.
Rabb, D. (2011), *Strasbourg in the Dock: Prisoner Voting, Human Rights and the Case for Democracy*. London: Civitas.
Radzinowicz, L. and Hood, R. (1979), 'The Status of Political Prisoner in England: The Struggle for Recognition', *Virginia Law Review*, 65 (8): 1421–81.
Ramsay, P. (2013), 'Faking Democracy with Prisoners' Voting Rights', London School of Economics Legal Working Paper 7/2013. Available at: http://papers .ssrn.com/sol3/papers.cfm?abstract_id=2214813 (accessed 25 May 2013).

Redman, R., Brown, D. and Mercurio, B. (2009), 'The Politics and Legality of Prisoner Disenfranchisement in Australian Federal Elections', in A. Ewald and B. Rottinghaus (eds), *Criminal Disenfranchisement in an International Perspective*. Cambridge: Cambridge University Press.

Reiman, J. (2005), 'Liberal and Republican Arguments Against the Disenfranchisement of Felons', *Criminal Justice Ethics*, 24: 3–18.

Richards, S. and Jones, R. (2004), 'Beating the Perpetual Incarceration Machine: Overcoming Structural Impediments to Re-entry', in S. Maruna and R. Immarigeon (eds), *After Crime and Punishment: Pathways to Offender Reintegration*. Cullompton: Willan Publishing.

Richardson, A. (1983), *Participation*. London: Routledge, Keegan and Paul.

Riordan, P. (2003), 'Citizenship: Burden or Challenge', *Administration*, 51 (3): 58–72.

Riordan, P. (2004), 'New Prospects for Citizenship: Civil Society and Civic Republicanism', *Administration*, 51 (4): 47–61.

Roberts, C. (2011), 'SF's Best Voter Turnout – 79 Percent – at County Jail', *SF Appeal Online Newspaper*. Available at: http://sfappeal.com/2011/12/too-many-mayoral-candidates-boring (accessed 28 September 2012).

Roberts, J. and Hough, M. (2005), 'The state of prisons: exploring public knowledge and opinion', *Howard Journal of Criminal Justice* 44(3): 286–306.

Roche, D. (2007), Interview with Author. Tape-recorded, 13 November.

Rogan, M. (2009), 'Prison Policy in Ireland: A Historical Overview', *Prison Service Journal*, 186: 3–12.

Rogan, M. (2011), *Prison Policy in Ireland: Politics, Penal-welfarism and Political Imprisonment*. Oxford: Routledge.

Rozenberg, J. (2012), 'Prisoner Votes: Government Is Playing for More Time', 22 November. Available at: www.guardian.co.uk /law/2012/nov/22/prisoner-votes-government-more-time (accessed 23 November 2012).

Rottinghaus, B. (2005), 'Incarceration and Enfranchisement: International Practices, Impact and Recommendations for Reform'. Available at: www.ifes.org/publication/4bbcc7feabf9b17c41be87346f57c1c4/08_18_03_Manatt_Brandon_Rottinghaus.pdf (accessed 28 September 2012).

Rottinghaus, B. and Baldwin, G. (2007), 'Voting Behind Bars: Explaining Variations in International Enfranchisement Practices', *Electoral Studies*, 26 (3): 688–98.

Rousseau, J. J. ([1762] 1973), *The Social Contract and Discourses*. London: Everyman.

Ryan, M. (1978), *The Acceptable Pressure Group*. Farnborough: Saxon House.

Ryan, M. (2003), *Penal Policy and Political Culture in England and Wales*. Winchester: Waterside Press.

Ryan, M. and Sim, J. (2007), 'Campaigning For and Campaigning Against Prisons: Excavating and Reaffirming the Case for Prison Abolition', in Y. Jewkes (ed.), *Handbook on Prisons*. Cullompton: Willan.

Ryle Dwyer, T. (1980), *Eamon de Valera*. Dublin: Gill and Macmillan.

Sbarbaro, E. (1995), 'Teaching "Criminology" to "Criminals"', in H. Davidson (ed.), *Schooling in a 'Total Institution'*. Connecticut: Bergen and Garvey.
Scraton, P., Sim, J. and Skidmore, P. (1991), *Prisons Under Protest*. Milton Keynes: Open University.
Seanad Debates, 1992, vol. 132, col. 1732–6.
Seymour, M. and Costello, M. (2005), *A Study of the Number, Profile and Progression Routes of Homeless Persons Before the Courts and in Custody*. Dublin: Department of Justice, Equality and Law Reform.
Sentencing Project (2013), 'Total Corrections Population'. Available at: www.sentencingproject.org/map/map.cfm (accessed 23 May 2013).
Sheridan, K. (2007), 'A Stroke Too Far for Fahy', *Irish Times*, 24 March.
Sinnott, R. (2008), 'Deeper Look at Poll Illuminates Complex Reasons for Result', *Irish Times*, 14 June.
Solomon, E. and Edgar, K. (2004), *Having Their Say: The Work of Prisoner Councils*. London: Prison Reform Trust.
Sparks, R. (1994), 'Can Prisons Be Legitimate? Penal Politics, Privatization, and the Timelessness of an Old Idea', *British Journal of Criminology* (Special Issue), 34: 14–28.
Sparks, R., Bottoms, A. and Hay, W. (1996), *Prisons and the Problem of Order*. Oxford: Oxford University Press.
Standards in Public Office Commission (2008), *Expenditure by Qualified Political Parties of Exchequer Funding Received by Them in 2007*. Available at: www.sipo.gov.ie (accessed 20 December 2008).
Staunton, D. (2008), 'Spotlight Turns to Republicans', *Irish Times*, 30 August.
Stern, V. (2002), 'Prisoners as Citizens: A Comparative View', *Probation Journal*, 49: 130–9.
Stewart, A. (1995), 'Two Conceptions of Citizenship', *British Journal of Sociology*, 46 (1): 63–78.
Storgaard, A. (2009), 'The Right to Vote in Danish Prisons', in A. Ewald and B. Rottinghaus (eds), *Criminal Disenfranchisement in an International Perspective*. Cambridge: Cambridge University Press.
Sykes, G. (1958), *The Society of Captives*. Princeton: Princeton University Press.
Taskforce on Active Citizenship (2007a), *The Concept of Active Citizenship*. Dublin: Taskforce on Active Citizenship.
Taskforce on Active Citizenship (2007b), *Statistical Evidence on Active Citizenship in Ireland*. Dublin: Taskforce on Active Citizenship.
Taskforce on Active Citizenship (2007c), *Report of the Taskforce on Active Citizenship*. Dublin: Taskforce on Active Citizenship.
Thompson, J. (1996), 'Really Useful Knowledge: Linking Theory and Practice', in B. Connolly, T. Fleming, D. McCormack and A. Ryan (eds), *Radical Learning for Liberation*. Maynooth Adult and Community Education Occasional Series, No. 1.
Thompson, K. (2008), 'For Those Once Behind Bars, A Nudge to the Voting Booth', www.washingtonpost.com (accessed 1 December 2008).

Tomlinson, M. (1995), 'Imprisoned Ireland', in V. Ruggiero, M. Ryan and J. Sim (eds), *Western European Penal Systems*. London: Sage.
Travis, J. (2002), 'Invisible Punishment: An Instrument of Social Exclusion', in M. Mauer and M. Chesney-Lind (eds), *Invisible Punishment: The Collateral Consequences of Mass Imprisonment*. New York: The New Press.
Uggen, C. and Manza, J. (2002), 'Democratic Contraction? Political Consequences of Felon Disenfranchisement in the United States', *American Sociological Review*, 67: 777–803.
Uggen, C. and Manza, J. (2004), 'Voting and Subsequent Crime and Arrest: Evidence from a Community Sample', *Columbia Human Rights Law Review*, 193–215.
Uggen, C., Manza, J. and Behrens, A. (2004), ' "Less Than the Average Citizen": Stigma, Role Transition and the Civic Re-integration of Convicted Felons', in S. Maruna and R. Immarigeon (eds), *After Crime and Punishment: Pathways to Offender Re-Integration*. Cullompton: Willan Publishing.
Uggen, C., Manza, J. and Thompson, M. (2006), 'Citizenship, Democracy, and the Civic Re-integration of Criminal Offenders', *Annals of the American Academy of Political and Social Science*, 605: 281–310.
Uggen, C., Van Brakle, M. and McLaughlin, H. (2009), 'Punishment and Social Exclusion: National Differences in Prisoner Disenfranchisement', in A. Ewald and B. Rottinghaus (eds), *Criminal Disenfranchisement in an International Perspective*. Cambridge: Cambridge University Press.
Uggen, C., Shannon, S. and Manza, J. (2012), *State-Level Estimates of Felon Disenfranchisement in the United States, 2010*. Washington: The Sentencing Project.
United Nations (1955), *Standard Minimum Rules for the Treatment of Prisoners*. Available at: www.unhchr.ch/html/menu3/b/h_comp 34.thm (accessed 13 August 2011).
United Nations (1966), *International Covenant on Civil and Political Rights*. Available at: www.hrweb.org/legal/cpr.html (accessed 15 August 2011).
Van Zyl Smit, D. and Snacken, S. (2009), *Principles of European Prison Law and Policy: Penology and Human Rights*. Oxford: Oxford University Press.
Wall Street Journal (1999), 'Jailhouse Vote', *Wall Street Journal*, 7 December.
Ward, D. (1972), 'Inmates Rights and Prison Reform in Sweden and Denmark', *Journal of Criminal Law, Criminology and Police Science*, 63 (2): 240–55.
Warner, K. (2009), 'Resisting the New Punitiveness? Penal Policy in Denmark, Finland and Norway'. Unpublished PhD Thesis, University College Dublin.
Washington Post (1996), 'Peres Criticizes Ruling that Allows Rabin's Assassin to Vote in Election', *Washington Post*, 29 May.
Whelan, N. (2000), *Politics, Elections and the Law*. Dublin: Blackhall.
Whitaker, T. K. (1985), *Report of the Committee of Inquiry into the Penal System*. Dublin: The Stationery Office.
White, I. (2008), *Convicted Prisoners and the Franchise. Standard Note SN/PC/10764*. London: House of Commons Library.

White, I. (2013), *Prisoners' Voting Rights. Standard Note SN/PC/01764*. London: House of Commons Library.
Whitehead, T. (2012), 'Cameron Vows to Defy Europe on Prisoner Voting', *Telegraph Online*, 23 May.
White House (2010), 'Open for Questions: More Questions from YouTube'. Available at: http://whitehouse.gov/photos-and-video/video/open-questions-more-questions-you-tube (accessed 10 June 2012).
Wilson, R. (2009), 'The Right to Universal, Equal, and Nondiscriminatory Suffrage as a Norm of Customary International Law: Protecting the Prisoner's Right to Vote', in A. Ewald and B. Rottinghaus (eds), *Criminal Disenfranchisement in an International Perspective*. Cambridge: Cambridge University Press.
Wood, E. and Bloom, R. (2008), *De Facto Disenfranchisement*. New York: American Civil Liberties Union and Brennan Center for Justice.
Wright, R. and Gehring, T. (2008), 'From Spheres of Civility to Critical Public Spheres: Democracy and Citizenship in the Big House, Part II', *Journal of Correctional Education*, 59 (3): 322–38.
YouGov/*The Sun* (2010), *Survey Results: Prisoners and Voting*. Available at: http://d25d2506sfb94s.cloudfront.net/today_uk_import/YG-Archives-Pol-Sun-PrisonersVoting-021110.pdf (accessed 1 November 2012).

Index

Agnew, Paddy 75
Ahern, Bertie 1, 106, 161, 168
Aiken, Frank 71
Alexander, Michelle 5, 20, 43
American Civil Liberties Union 41
August and Another v. Electoral Commission and Others 30–1
Australia 4, 18, 28, 34–5, 136–7, 141

Balls, Ed 54
Blythe, Ernest 69
Boland, Gerald 67, 73
Breathnach v. Ireland and the Attorney General 81–3, 88
Browne, Noel 73
Byrne, Alfred 68–9

Cameron, David 3, 52, 54
Canada 4, 18, 28, 32–4, 136, 141, 198
Cerutti, Paul 40
Chaskalson, Arthur 31–2
civic engagement 4, 6, 16, 20, 70, 101, 104, 113, 115, 123–5, 131, 133, 142–74, 178, 180, 186–9, 200–1
civil death 8–9, 23, 47, 128, 185–6
Civil War (Ireland) 68–9, 72
Clegg, Roger 7, 9, 11–15, 38–41
Collins, Gerard 74, 78
Committee for the Prevention of Torture and Inhuman or Degrading Treatment or Punishment (CPT) 92, 164, 167–70, 191, 196
Conservative Party (United Kingdom) 5, 47, 49–53, 58
Constitution (Ireland)
  Bunreacht na hÉireann 72
  Free State 67

Council of Europe 5, 16, 43, 51, 53, 58, 87, 155, 180
Council for Social Welfare 74
Cosgrave, W.T. 65
Costello, Joe 77–9, 105
Costelloe, Anne 153, 155
Crewe, Ben 86–7, 149, 153, 158, 190

Dáil Éireann 1, 66–87, 98, 100, 105, 113, 135–6, 141, 146, 171–2
Daily Express 51
Davis, Angela 155, 194
Davis, David 53
Davitt, Michael 64
Denham, Susan 82
De Valera, Eamon 1, 65–6, 70, 72
Dhami, Mandeep 14, 19, 39, 49, 88
Disraeli, Benjamin 64
Doherty, Kieran 75
Doyle, Avril 83
Doyle, Michael 68
Draper v. Attorney General 76–7, 82
Duggan, Eamon 67
Duguid, Stephen 155, 157, 192, 198

Easton, Susan 7, 9, 14, 17, 19–20, 42, 145, 183–4, 187
Edgar, Kimmett 101, 150, 196
Eggleston, Carolyn 155, 198
education (prison) 72, 93–4, 150, 151, 154–7, 199
elections (Ireland)
  general (2007) 1–2, 5, 87, 95, 101–3, 105–7, 114–16, 120
  general (2011) 121
  local (2009) 118
  European (2009) 118

Electoral Act (Ireland)
  (1923) 68
  (1963) 76
  (1992) 78–9, 80–1, 134
  (1997) 140–1
Electoral (Amendment) Act (2006) 61–2, 84–7, 96, 107, 135–6, 140, 176–7, 185
Electoral (Amendment) (No.2) Act (1986) 77
European Commission of Human Rights (ECmHR) 80
European Convention on Human Rights (ECHR) 16, 45–6, 50, 52–7, 80–1, 84, 88
European Court of Human Rights (ECtHR) 4, 9, 16–17, 21, 43–4, 46–55, 57–9, 108
Ewald, Alec 3, 7–9, 28, 38, 182

Falconer, (Lord) Charles 48
Fianna Fáil 72, 84, 101–3, 106, 108
Fine Gael 74, 78–9, 83–4, 87, 100, 102, 105, 118, 139, 161, 180
Flynn, Paul 58
Foot, Paul 44, 184
Forfeiture Act (1870) 44, 67
Frodl v. Austria 21, 55

Gardai (Garda Síochána) 67, 76–7, 98, 112–13, 179
Garland, David 18, 59, 86–7
Gaziano, Todd 10, 39
Gilmore, Eamon 106, 136, 178
Gehring, Thom 155, 198
Gladstone, William 63
Goffman, Erving 149, 190
Grayling, Chris 57–8
Green Party 1, 102–3, 119
Green v. Board of Elections of City of New York 13
Greens and MT v. United Kingdom 52–3
Griffith, Arthur 67

Harney, Mary 84, 104, 106
Harper, Mark 52
Higgins, Jim 161
Higgins, Joe 1, 84, 105
Higgins, Michael D. 74
Hirst v. United Kingdom 9–10, 14–17, 21, 43–59, 83–4, 88, 185

Hobbes, Thomas 9
Holland v. Ireland 80–1
Hood, Roger 64
Hong Kong 28, 35–7
Howard League for Penal Reform (UK) 59
Human Rights Act (1998) (UK) 45

Inspector of Prisons (Ireland) 92–3, 97–9, 161, 164–70, 192
International Covenant on Civil and Political Rights 27, 46
Irish Commission for Justice and Peace 88, 191
Irish Daily Mail 163
Irish Examiner 86
Irish Independent 86
Irish Penal Reform Trust (IPRT) 86, 89, 93, 136, 164, 178
Irish Prison Service 87, 97, 107, 117–22, 135, 156, 170
Irish Times 86, 95, 100–1
Israel 4, 28–30, 182

Jail Journal [book] *see* Mitchel, John
Jail Journal [periodical] 197
Jenkins, Bernard 53–4
Johnson, Tom 69, 171

Kant, Immanuel 9
Kavanagh, Sean 67
Keane, Ronan 82
Kennedy, Charles 47
Kenny, Enda 105
Keyssar, Alexander 38, 41, 43–4
Khan, Sadiq 58

Labour Party (Ireland) 69, 73, 102–3, 105–6, 136, 171, 178, 180
Labour Party (United Kingdom) 48, 50, 52–4, 58
Lemass, Sean 71
Lisbon Treaty 116–18, 122
Livingstone, Stephen 145, 169, 181
Locke, John 9
Lynch, Patrick 65

McAleese, Mary 74
MacAskill, Kenny 50
MacBride, Seán 72, 74, 78
MacBride Commission 74, 78
McCaughey, Seán 72

McCleery, Richard 190
McDowell, Michael 83, 88, 106
MacEoin, Sean 67
McGuinness, Joe 65
Mandela, Nelson 30
Manfredi, Christopher 7, 11–12, 33
Manning, Maurice 79
Manza, Jeff 7, 14, 19, 38, 40–2, 83, 87, 100–1, 125, 129, 150, 182
Marini, Francis 40
Maruna, Shadd 145, 150, 157–8, 160, 173, 186, 194
Mauer, Marc 7, 17–18, 39–40, 124, 141, 182
Mellows, Liam 69
Milburn, Alan 47
Minister of Home Affairs v. *National Institute for Crime Prevention and Re-Integration* (NICRO) 12, 31–2
Mitchel, John 63–4
Mitchell, Gay 83–5
Morgan, Arthur 84, 135
Mulcahy, Richard 70

National Association for the Advancement of Colored People (NAACP) 39, 42
New York Times 38
Norway 44, 198

Obama, Barack 42
O'Connell, Daniel 62
O'Donnell, Ian 3, 72–4, 80, 84, 88, 92–3, 97, 125, 131, 168, 178
O'Donnell, Peadar 69–71
O'Donoghue, John 81–2
O'Donovan Rossa, Jerimiah 63
O'Dowd, Fergus 84–5, 87
O'Higgins, Kevin 66–7
O'Higgins, Thomas 77
O'Malley, Ernie 70
ombudsman (prison) 75, 92, 172, 191–2
'othering' of prisoners 18–19
oversight and monitoring of prisons 92, 164–72, 174, 191–2
Owers, Anne 92, 191

Palestine 28–30
Parnell, Charles Stewart 62
Pearson and Others v. *Home Office* 45–6

penal reform 5, 7, 17, 59, 61–2, 64, 67, 72–3, 85, 90, 184, 194–5
Plunkett, (Count) George Noble 65
political contact (by prisoners) 161–3
Prison Reform Trust (PRT) (United Kingdom) 46–9, 131, 135
Prison Rules (Ireland)
  (1947) 73, 93, 137, 146, 153, 169–70
  (2007) 92, 153, 162, 169–70
Prison Rules (European) 16, 180, 196
Prison Study Group 73–4
prisoner councils 150, 196–7
prisoner representative groups 194–7
Prisoners' Rights Organisation (PRO) 74, 76–8, 197
Prisons (Ireland)
  Arbour Hill 93, 95–9, 103, 115, 117, 119–21, 151–2, 154, 161–8, 172, 179
  Castlerea 117, 121, 168
  Cloverhill 98–9, 117, 119–21, 164, 179
  Cork 117, 119, 121, 164
  Dóchas Centre 91, 98–9, 117, 119, 121
  Limerick 91–2, 117, 119, 121, 164
  Loughan House 117, 119, 120–1
  Midlands 117, 119, 121, 167
  Mountjoy (Male) 67, 69–71, 79, 92, 94, 117, 119, 121, 140, 164, 167
  Portlaoise 72, 79, 92, 98–9, 117, 119–21, 175, 197
  St Patrick's Institution 74, 91, 98, 117, 119–21, 164
  Shelton Abbey 93–6, 98–9, 103 117, 119, 121, 153–4, 179
  Training Unit 93–4, 96, 98–9, 103, 117, 119, 121, 153–4
  Wheatfield 99, 117, 119, 121
Prisons Act (2007) 92, 164–5
Prisons (Visiting Committee) Act (1925) 93, 166, 171
Progressive Democrats 1, 84, 102, 105–6, 108
public opinion 13–14
punishment as character forming 12–13
purity of the ballot box 10–12

R v. *Secretary of State, ex parte Toner and Walsh* 50
Rabb, Dominic 5
Rabin, Yitzhak 28–9

Radical Alternatives to Prison 197
Radzinowicz, Leon 64
Ramsay, Peter 7, 10
Ramsbotham, (Lord) David 52
Raymond v. Honey 16
re-enfranchisement 14–15
rehabilitation 6, 15, 33, 46, 49, 79, 85, 87, 89, 193–4
re-integration 19–20
Representation of the People Act
  (1918) 44, 65
  (1981) 45
  (1983) 45, 59
  (2000) 45
Richardson v. Ramirez 22–5
Roach v. Electoral Commission 35
Roche, Dick 1, 84, 87–9, 95, 107, 126, 134, 140, 176–7
Rogan, Mary 69, 72–3, 75, 92–3, 197
Rottinghaus, Brandon 3, 7, 26–7, 38, 43, 83, 121, 181–2, 189
Rousseau, JJ 9, 189, 191
Russell, (Lord) John 62–3
Ryan, Mick 153, 194–5, 197

Sands, Bobby 45, 75, 127
Sauvé v. Canada (Chief Electoral Officer) 32–4, 41
Scopolla v. Italy 54, 56–7
Scottish National Party 50
Seanad Éireann 78–9, 100
Sinn Féin 65–6, 84, 102–3, 135
Sparks, Richard 149, 198
Smith O'Brien, William 62–3
Snacken, Sonja 145
social capital 146–7, 151, 173–4, 176, 193–4
social contract 4, 8–10, 14, 16, 18, 20–5, 36, 40, 45–9, 128
Solomon, Enver 101, 196
South Africa 28, 30–2
Straw, Jack 54
Sturgeon, Nicola 59
Supreme Court (Ireland) 2, 77, 80–3, 176

Sweden 27, 43, 195
Sykes, Gresham 12, 149, 193–4

Tebitt, (Lord) Norman 51
Tomlinson, Mike 72, 74–5, 189–90
Traynor, Oscar 71

Uggen, Christopher 6–7, 19, 38, 40–3, 83, 87, 89, 100–1, 125, 127, 150, 182, 187
United Kingdom 3–5, 14, 37, 44–60, 150, 160, 176–7, 184, 195, 198–9
United Nations Declaration of Human Rights 27
United States of America 2–5, 13–14, 19–23, 27, 37–43, 59–60, 127, 176–7, 184, 187, 194, 197–8

Van Zyl Smit, Dirk 145
visiting committees 93, 164–71, 191–2
volunteering (in prison) 150, 151, 157–61, 199
voting (prisoners)
  attitudes towards 124–42
  registration 79–80, 89, 96–9, 101, 116, 118, 120–3, 129–31, 133–7, 142, 165, 177–82, 185, 189
  turnout 19–20, 23, 96–103, 113–23, 129–38, 151, 177–9, 181–2, 188–9
voting bloc 13, 24, 48, 136, 178

Wallace, Dan 78–9
War of Independence 66
Warner, Kevin 91, 153, 155, 196, 198
Washington v. State 10, 18
Whitaker, T.K. 74
Whitaker Report 74–5, 172, 191
Women in Prison (WIP) 195
Wright, Randall 155
W. Smith v. Electoral Registration Officer 50

X, Malcom 155

EU authorised representative for GPSR:
Easy Access System Europe, Mustamäe tee 50,
10621 Tallinn, Estonia
gpsr.requests@easproject.com

www.ingramcontent.com/pod-product-compliance
Ingram Content Group UK Ltd.
Pitfield, Milton Keynes, MK11 3LW, UK
UKHW021848140426
5217IPUK00022B/1655